COMMUNICATION *and* EDUCATION SKILLS: *The Dietitian's Guide*

COMMUNICATION AND EDUCATION SKILLS: THE DIETITIAN'S GUIDE

BETSY B. HOLLI, Ed.D., R.D.

Associate Professor
Department of Nutrition
Rosary College
River Forest, Illinois

RICHARD J. CALABRESE, Ph.D.

Chairperson
Department of Communication Arts and Sciences
Rosary College
River Forest, Illinois

Second Edition

Lea & Febiger   *Philadelphia*
1991   *London*

Lea & Febiger
200 Chester Field Parkway
Malvern, Pennsylvania 19355
U.S.A.
(215) 251-2230
1-800-444-1785

First Edition, 1986
  Reprinted, 1988, 1989
Second Edition, 1991

Library of Congress Cataloging-in-Publication Data

Holli, Betsy B.
    Communication and education skills : a dietitian's guide / Betsy
  B. Holli, Richard J. Calabrese.—2nd ed.
          p.   cm.
    Includes bibliographical references and index.
    ISBN 0-8121-1386-1
      1. Communication in diet therapy.   2. Patient education.
    3. Interpersonal communication.   I. Calabrese, Richard J.
    II. Title.
  RM214.3.H65   1991
  615.8'54—dc20   90-20796
                                                                CIP

Reprints of chapters may be purchased from Lea & Febiger in quantities of 100 or more.

PRINTED IN THE UNITED STATES OF AMERICA

Print number: 5   4   3   2   1

To Melvin, Susan, and Steven Holli

and

To Alice, Leslie, and Christopher Calabrese

PREFACE

Increasingly, the health professions are recognizing the importance of effective communication skills. These skills are essential for competence in dietetic practice in which the aim of treatment is to facilitate change in the clients' and patients' eating behaviors. Communication skills are not ends in themselves, but are the basis for strengthened interpersonal relationships and are needed for more effective outcomes of treatment. Poor communication skills can affect directly patient adherence to recommendations, patient understanding and satisfaction, and for the manager, relationships with employees and staff.

In the past dietetic education emphasized scientific and technical knowledge and skills, but neglected communication skills. The publication of the American Dietetic Association (ADA) role delineation studies in clinical dietetics, community dietetics, and foodservice systems management in 1981 and 1983 focused attention on the dietitian's use of communication skills. The ADA Standards of Education, implemented in 1987 for educational programs, included knowledge and performance skills in effective communication in the required competencies. The contents of the registration examinations are also based on the role delineation studies. Results of the updated role delineation studies completed in 1989 confirm specific job responsibilities of dietetic practitioners involving skills in communication and education.

The purpose of the book remains the same. The book is intended to help both current practitioners and students improve their communication with their patients, clients, employees, and others, and thus improve their professional practice. One does not develop these skills by only reading about them, however. Actual experience and continued practice are needed. Thus you will find suggested activities following each chapter, including some new ones. The appendix includes a new paraphrase exercise and role plays that may be used to develop interviewing and/or counseling skills.

The book is organized so that skills used primarily in one-on-one encounters are discussed first followed by skills for more effective group presentations. All chapters from the first edition have been expanded to include recent and pertinent information. In addition, two new chapters are added. Following the chapter on behavior modification, a new chapter deals with the individual's cognitions or thoughts, which may be strong influences on dietary behaviors, and how they can be modified. Included is a discussion of relapse prevention for clients involved in behavioral change. A second new chapter focuses on giving effective oral presentations to groups.

We appreciated the many comments and suggestions we received on the first edition of the book and have incorporated as many as possible. Some who adopted the book are using it in a separate course, while others use it as a supplement to another course.

We are troubled by the custom of using the masculine pronoun when the meaning involves both men and women. We have reworded extensively to avoid this, but when nothing else seemed possible, in a few cases we resorted to the conventional form. The terms patient and client are used interchangeably as are dietitian, counselor, interviewer, practitioner, and nutritionist.

We would like to express our appreciation to Christian C.F. Spahr Jr. of Lea & Febiger for publishing the first edition of this book, thus enhancing our goal of improving dietetic education and practice. We wish to thank Ann B. Williams, PhD, for updating the chapter on behavior modification, and Mary Ellen Druyan, PhD, RD, for specific suggestions. Our families allowed us time to work and supported us during the long hours of researching, writing, and rewriting, for which we are very grateful.

Betsy B. Holli
Richard J. Calabrese

River Forest, Illinois

CONTENTS

1

Communication and Education Skills for Dietitians

Dietitians need good communication skills.[1] The job responsibilities of clinical and community dietitians involve communicating with patients, clients, and other institutional staff to educate them about nutrition. Administrative dietitians and managers, who communicate with and train subordinate employees, discover that communication skills are an important key to leadership and managerial effectiveness. Communication is considered a supporting field for dietetics, and a strengthening of communication skills for dietitians at all levels is strongly recommended.[2]

In recent years, all health professionals have become more aware of the need to acquire skills in interpersonal relations because their jobs require frequent interaction with others, such as clients, patients, employees, colleagues, and other health professionals. In addition to having the requisite scientific and technical skills, the dietitian must be able to relate effectively to others. It is not enough to demonstrate competency in dietetics: that competence must be put to use in communicating with others. Human relationships are described as "the media through which technical skills are practiced."[3] Thus there is a need to focus on the process of delivering to others such dietetic services as nutrition intervention through interpersonal communication, counseling, and education. In addition, coordination of team efforts for patient care clearly requires communication and cooperation. Communication is a link connecting all health team members, including the patient. In defining the nutrition goals for the nation, the American Dietetic Association (ADA) recommended that "virtually all routine health contacts with health professionals should include some element of nutrition education and nutrition counseling."[4] Concerning nutrition education for the public, it is the position of the American Dietetic Association that "for the public to achieve optimal nutritional health, nutrition education should be incorporated in all appropriate educational systems, health promotion, disease prevention, and health maintenance programs.[5]

The scope of dietetics is broad. Dietitians and nutritionists are employed in a variety of positions and in a number of different settings.

While the majority are employed in health care facilities (acute care hospitals, medical centers, and nursing homes), others work in commercial business and industry, school feeding, community and public health nutrition programs, wellness centers, or are self-employed in private practice. In a survey, dietitians reported engaging in a wide range of professional activities, including food service management (food purchasing and supervision of employees); the nutritional care of clients, patients, and the management of clinical nutrition services; commercial activities (marketing and sales); the education of dietetic students and other health care professionals; nutrition education of the public; and administrative activities (fiscal planning and public relations).[6]

The five most common divisions of dietetic practice include clinical dietitian, administrative/foodservice management dietitian, dietetics or nutrition educator or researcher, community or public health nutritionist, and consultant or private practice dietitian. Each of these areas of practice may be divided further into subspecialty groups. Within the American Dietetic Association (ADA) are a number of special interest groups:

Community Dietetics
   Public health nutrition
   Gerontological nutritionists
   Dietetics in developmental and psychiatric disorders

Clinical Dietetics
   Renal dietitians
   Pediatric nutrition
   Diabetes care and education
   Dietitians in nutrition support
   Dietetics in physical medicine and rehabilitation
   Sports and cardiovascular nutritionists
   Dietitians in general clinical practice

Consultation and Private Practice
   Consulting nutritionists-private practice
   Consultant dietitians in health care facilities

Management Practice
   Dietitians in business and industry
   ADA members with management responsibilities in health care delivery systems
   School food and nutrition services
   Dietitians in college and university food service
   Clinical nutrition management
   Technical practice in dietetics

Education and Research
   Dietetic educators of practitioners
   Nutrition educators of health professionals

Nutrition education for the public
Nutrition research

All of these specialists use communication skills and education skills in daily practice.

In addition to devoting ongoing attention to and development of communication skills to improve their relationship with staff and clients, dietitians need to be professionally active in a communication network, which consists of people talking to one another and sharing ideas, information, and resources. It is essential for dietitians to have ongoing dialogue with other professionals in their area of expertise. One way to participate in such a dialogue is for dietitians to attend professional meetings and to join one of the subspecialty groups in their area of interest and/or practice. Although sharing information is the primary purpose of networking, the contacts that networks provide are invaluable.

The American Dietetic Association has focused on the knowledge base necessary for professional practice and defined the requisite skills and competencies needed by practitioners. Since 1973, the ADA has been assessing and defining, through role delineation studies, the meaning of competence in the field of dietetics at the entry or minimum level.[7] Information from role delineation studies which identify major and specific responsibilities of the practitioner and the knowledge needed to practice dietetics, is helpful in the credentialing process, in the education of practitioners, and in the process of assurance of quality service and practice.

Role delineation studies have identified the major and specific job responsibilities of entry-level dietetic technicians and registered dietitians and beyond-entry-level registered dietitians related to communication and education, and the skills and knowledge needed for practice.[8,9] Clinical dietitians, for example, are expected to plan, organize, implement, and evaluate nutrition education for clients and patients, give classes to groups, counsel individuals concerning nutrition concepts and desired changes in eating habits, and educate health team members on nutrition-related topics. A study of 180 practitioners involved in direct patient care found strong correlations between dietitians' confidence in their counseling skills and their estimates of the likelihood of client compliance. Dietitians' confidence in their counseling skills was correlated with the intensity of their counseling efforts.[10] Communicating plans for nutrition care to individuals or families, as well as health team members, with documentation in the medical record, is a major responsibility. The development of orientation and training programs for subordinate clinical dietetic personnel is another function.[11] A study of clinical dietitians found that the four activities consuming the largest amount of work time were conducting individual diet instructions, conducting nutrition assessments, reviewing and recording in medical records, and supervising support personnel.[12] Clinical dietitians surveyed reported the need for continuing education topics, such as patient counseling and education, behavior modification and change, interpersonal communication, and patient compliance strategies.[13]

In community dietetics, responsibilities include providing nutrition education to groups and to individual clients for health promotion, health maintenance, and rehabilitation, and developing orientation and training programs for support personnel.[14] Public health nutritionists and graduate faculty ranked "communicating clearly" and "performing direct dietary counseling" as the top two abilities necessary for practice.[15]

In foodservice systems management, the dietitian is expected to interview applicants for identified positions, to orient and train personnel, to counsel subordinates, and to provide educational programs (on-the-job training, inservice training, and continuing education) that meet the needs of employees.[16]

The consultant is a dietitian in private practice who confers with nursing homes and other institutions to provide advice, instructions, or recommendations for obtaining organizational objectives.

For interaction with those being advised, effective communication skills are a high priority.[1] Teaching is a function of most dietitians.

Common knowledge and skills needed by all dietitians for interpersonal relations include principles of verbal and nonverbal communication, public speaking, principles and techniques of interviewing and counseling, theories and strategies for behavior modification and motivation, principles of learning, teaching methods and techniques, and knowledge of working with groups. These are skills which are not innate, but they can be learned and improved with practice.

HELPING OTHERS

Dietetics is a "helping" profession concerned primarily with providing services beneficial to individuals and society, and dedicated to improving the nutritional status of people. Helping professions have been described as process professions that "require doing something with knowledge," such as communicating, interpreting, and applying nutritional science to the language and lifestyles of people to benefit their health.[1] The helping approach may also be utilized in managing subordinate staff. The professional seeks to guide others in bringing about change.[17]

Helping is a process involving a conversation or series of conversations with another person. Whether in social work, nursing, or dietetics, the professional seeks to answer the question: "What is helpful?" A great deal of helping involves problem solving. Resolving the problem may entail arriving at a decision; developing knowledge, insights, or mutual understanding; setting goals for change; or venting feelings. The client or patient requires the assistance of the professional in overcoming and solving his problem when he is unable to do so alone. The individual may be incapable of problem resolution owing to lack of information, knowledge, skill, motivation, resources, or due to emotional feelings, such as anxiety.

Helping offers the potential for growth and development, and for achieving the intended result, which is change.[18] Brammer asserts that helping another person is a "process of enabling that person to grow in the direction he chooses, to solve problems, and to face crises."[19] Thus the clients, not the helper, determine whether they want help at all, and if they do, make decisions about their needs and select the goals for their own change or growth. Clients and patients should not be perceived as passive recipients of services. They are active participants in their treatment, working with the professional to restore or optimize their health. Ultimately, clients or patients are responsible for their nutrition and health. According to Fletcher, most medical care "has been—and always will be—self-care," e.g. self-initiated and self-controlled.[20] The acceptance of help is voluntary, and the aim of the professional is to make people self-sufficient so that eventually they can function on their own, solving future problems alone. Doing something for others without their initiative and consent may be counterproductive.

Since helping is future-oriented, counseling of both clients and employees focuses on what can be done to improve performance; it does not dwell on the failures of the past.[18] When they focus on what is acceptable to, and possible for the individual rather than on the individual's failure to comply with previous recommendations, helpers avoid labeling people as "uncooperative," "unmotivated," or "disinterested."

Problem solving involves listening, communicating, and educating, and is fundamentally a learning experience for the individual.[17] The interaction between the helper and the individual is a goal oriented process through which change occurs in the form of learning new information, knowledge, or skills; gaining new insights and perspectives; modifying feelings; changing behaviors; and developing new resources as decisions are made and problems resolved. Helping is more than the provision of information. Books, magazines, newspapers, television, family, and friends can supply information; one does not need a professional to provide it. The resolution of problems, however, and the personal discovery of the meaning of solutions for one's life come from the interaction between the helper and the individual.

The professional and the client should engage in problem solving together, as partners, joining forces and interacting in seeking solutions to ensure an effective learning experience. Providing pat answers and quick solutions that may be obvious to the dietitian does not help the person learn to solve his problems, and this approach should be avoided. Initially, the professional needs to learn about the person and his circumstances in order to assess the problem and plan to provide effective help. Through engaging in the problem solving process and exploring alternatives with the guidance and encouragement of the professional, the client gains insight into the situation, makes decisions, sets goals, learns to manage resources, and brings about the salutary and desired changes that problem resolution entails. Another benefit of involving individuals in solving their own problems is that it greatly increases self-motivation.

The helping process takes place in the relationship developed between the helper and the individual client, which is a key to the effectiveness of helping and problem solving. The professional strives to create an environment of respect and trust by arranging and maintaining conditions in which individuals perceive themselves as accepted, warmly received, valued, and understood. If the individual feels inferior, dependent, unappreciated, misunderstood, or manipulated, distrust can result, and the individual resists assistance. Trust must be earned; without it, vital self-disclosure on the part of the patient may be limited.[17] Trust in this sense means "the expectation that self-disclosure will be treated with respect and that feedback from the other can be relied on."[3] Respect and trust can be conveyed by avoiding labeling the individual's responses "right" or "wrong," by providing privacy, by showing concern and understanding through careful listening, and by providing nonjudgmental verbal and nonverbal responses, including when necessary, accurate paraphrasing of the meaning of the individual's comments and feelings.

Relationships begin and develop through communication, and the quality of communication influences the quality of the relationship. According to Henderson, the single most important element in interpersonal communication is "sender credibility—the attitude the receiver of a message has toward the sender's trustworthiness."[21] Credibility gaps may occur when the helper fails to project warmth, empathy, friendliness, and concern.

The relationship between the professional and client is probably easiest to establish when the client is similar to the professional in educational level and socioeconomic status. There may be a potential problem when the client is very different from the professional. For example, professionals must deal with clients who are aged, illiterate, uneducated, hearing-impaired, alcoholic, or disabled, and clients may be of various religious, cultural, and ethnic groups, or may be people from lower socioeconomic groups than that of the professional. They may be individuals with critical injuries resulting from automobile accidents and burns, or people with life-threatening diseases, such as cancer and AIDS. Professionals may need to examine their own values and personal attitudes toward others in developing effective interpersonal relationships. This self-awareness provides some insurance against prejudice, or judging others by one's personal values, and enables the professional to function out of concern and respect for those who are different.

A number of skills are needed by helping professionals. They include techniques of interviewing and counseling; ability to relate to groups, individuals, and communities; effectiveness in bringing about change; capacity for self-understanding; establishment of professional, interdisciplinary relationships; and knowledge of personality, group, and societal dynamics.[17] With these skills, the helper can assist others to assess all dimensions of a problem, to explore alternative solutions, and to stimulate action toward positive change and problem resolution. The helper's proficiency in specific communication and helping skills directly affects the success or failure of helping transactions. Since considerable responsibility for desired outcomes must be assumed by the health professional, it is imperative that helpers develop and improve their counseling skills.[18]

PROMOTING CHANGE

The solutions discovered through the problem-solving process, whether used with clients or employees, require some kind of change from people. The client who is learning dietary changes, for example, may be expected to know and remember lists of foods which can or cannot be consumed, to read labels, to shop for and prepare different foods, or to use different cooking methods. An employee may need to learn and to follow new work methods and procedures. Two basic questions include (1) what sort of change do we wish to bring about, and (2) how can this be accomplished.[22]

Peck viewed the successful professional as a "change agent" who needed the ability to intervene in human environments to promote change in behavior.[23] Knowledge of the social, cultural, psychological, and other forces affecting motivation for change in individuals or in groups, either positively or negatively, is necessary. The professional may select from a variety of processes to promote desired change. These processes include communication, counseling, behavior modification, consultation, education, group process, supervision, administration, planning, and evaluation. Before applying change strategies, the professional should establish that the individual is an informed, willing partner.

Some people are more resistant than others to making changes in lifestyles, and such resistance to modifying their old patterns of behavior should be considered normal.[24] Change upsets the established ways of doing things, creates uncertainty and anxiety, and forces the need for adjustments. Because attitudes are thought to be the predisposing agents of practice, they should be explored. Every problem has two aspects—what the person thinks about it, and how he feels about it. A client may THINK, for example, that a dietary regimen would be beneficial, but FEEL that it would be too difficult to follow. An employee may THINK that a new work procedure is interesting, but FEEL that the current methods are preferable. Both thoughts and feelings must be considered and dealt with for problem solving and change to occur.

Although helpers may see exactly what needs changing, they should bear in mind that the client is the one who decides which changes to make and who ensures that they continue. Thus, the client's priorities take precedence over those of the professional. Evaluating the meaning of change to individuals and then motivating them to change are necessary. Those being counseled should be given an opportunity to discuss changes and to ask questions, because the more they internalize the new ideas and solutions, the greater is the likelihood of their being committed to them.

When an individual deals with the necessity of change in food patterns and behaviors, knowledge and education are not in themselves sufficient to motivate change. Many people already know what they should eat! But they do not always act on their knowledge. The health professional cannot assume that recommendations will be followed just because the patient or client knows what to do. Why should any person change a lifetime of unrestricted eating that may be pleasurable? Cooperation of the patient or client is voluntary. Wanting to make changes is a key point to consider in adopting changes in dietary practices. The person's motivation for change should be examined since people can be expected to resist change.[25]

Group sessions are often utilized for nutrition education and for employee communication and training. The effect of support groups on change can be either positive or negative. Face-to-face communication with someone who has successfully altered a behavior can be effective in promoting the adoption of changes by others.[26] While increasing knowledge and growing awareness may be developed in such groups, the actual change occurs through an individual's decision making.[24]

Several other factors influence success in planned change. Important characteristics of the regimen influencing adherence include complexity, effect on values and lifestyle, and cost. The more communicable something is (i.e., the easier to describe), the more clearly it is understood. Simplicity is an advantage, as increasing complexity of a regimen is associated with less readily adopted changes. The change must be compatible with the person's existing values and beliefs. If divisible into parts, a change may be tried out on a small scale so that any barriers can be worked out. The change should have a relative advantage, or be perceived as preferable in efficiency, health, pleasure, economics, prestige, and the like. Pleasure or the absence of it may change the rate of acceptance of new practices. One problem is that many of the less nutritious foods, such as rich desserts, snack foods, and alcoholic beverages, have the highest prestige value. The influence of each factor on change is a relative one. Pleasure may be a major factor in some cases, and cost or ease of food preparation an important factor in another.[27]

NUTRITION COUNSELING

One aspect of nutrition care is the application of the science of nutrition to the health care of people through nutrition counseling and education. The dietitian spends a significant amount of time interacting with patients and clients. Counseling and education are essential to the maintenance of normal nutrition and health, as well as to the management of chronic diseases. Dietary practices are linked to a number of health problems, such as obesity, dental caries, cardiovascular disease, diabetes mellitus, and some types of cancer. The degree of skill in interpersonal interaction effects the quality of nutrition care provided, the amount of success or failure of the patient or client in adapting to his dietary and medical problem, and his future state of health. The following model depicts the relationship of nutrition counseling to health:[28,29]

Nutrition Counseling and Education	Changes in food intake (Compliance)	Altered risk factors	Desirable health outcomes	Economic benefits
-->	------>	--->	--->	

Nutrition counseling and education should lead to changes in food intake that alter the risk factors for disease and produce better health. Although conclusive evidence is not available to prove the first link that nutrition counseling always results in changes in food intake, counseling is the most reliable means of bringing about patient compliance or adherence to recommendations.[30] Economic benefits to be derived are the cost savings that result from a reduction in the incidence of or severity of a disease, such as reduced hospitalization expenses or increased job productivity.

The focus of the dietitian's role has shifted from the "diet instruction" of the past to the process of nutrition counseling, in which specific efforts are made to assist patients or clients in changing their eating behaviors. Formerly the hospital dietitian, upon receipt of the physician's order for a diet instruction, taught the patient his modified diet using a printed sheet of instructions. Too often, the request was received at the last minute prior to hospital discharge, and the instruction was a one-shot, hit-or-miss situation.[31] Fifteen or 20 minutes is not sufficient time to effect significant change in an individual's eating patterns, and nutritional care is too important to health to be handled in this fashion.

The ideal situation for nutrition counseling and education consists of a process over a period of time in which the client develops a growing awareness of his food intake and dietary practices, and of how these factors influence his health. The process of assisting people in establishing and maintaining good nutrition habits is a complex task, as it requires people to make permanent changes in their eating habits. Nutrition counseling and education should not be a one-time service. Follow-up counseling is an important part of care.

The amount of time required to perform nutrition services has been reported to range from 45 minutes to 12 hours or more. A consulting nutritionist employed in a corporate health office reported, for example, that initial visits lasted 45 to 60 minutes, with follow-up appointments of 15 to 30 minutes. As a benefit of employment, nutrition counseling was provided on company time.[32] Hatten spent 45 minutes providing initial nutrition counseling in home care services, with follow-up home visits for those who appeared to be confused or failed to understand recommendations.[33] At the Diabetes Education Center in Minneapolis, a minimum of 6 to 12 hours was the estimated time required to evaluate and educate an individual regarding the diabetic diet, tailoring the diet to the client.[34] This time excludes follow-up after discharge. If the clinical dietitian has insufficient time for counseling, patients can be referred to consultant dietitians in private practice, and to community resources for out-patient follow-up.

DIETARY ADHERENCE

Dietitians are expected to promote good dietary adherence or compliance. Compliance may be defined as the extent to which the individual's food and dietary behaviors coincide with the dietary recommendations and prescriptions. In measuring compliance, some health professionals also consider whether or not appointments are kept. Human noncompliance dates back to the Biblical story of the Garden of Eden, where Eve ate the forbidden apple from the tree of knowledge, thus associating temptation and noncompliance with guilt and sin.[35]

The term "compliance" has authoritarian overtones of a counselor deciding what is best for the individual, who is passive and compliant. The word "adherence" may suggest greater participation by the client in problem solving and decision making regarding dietary changes, which are voluntary behaviors. These terms, however, seem to be used interchangeably. The individual must adopt dietary changes and sustain them over a period of time, often a lifetime if the condition is a chronic one, such as diabetes mellitus, cardiovascular or renal disease. The person is expected to make permanent changes to remain in optimum health. Diet may be only one of several changes the individual is expected to effect; additional changes related to smoking, drinking, or exercise habits, together with the need to take medications, may be seen as overwhelming.

Compliance is a problem area, and some responsibility for noncompliance rests with the providers of care.[36] Although noncompliance may be viewed as failure on the patient's part to cooperate with recommendations, counselors are not excused from other variables that are under their control, such as the quality of the client-counselor relationship and the use of appropriate influence strategies.

Noncompliance with medical advice has been well documented. Adherence to long-term medical regimens averages about 50% and to dietary regimens runs about 30%, with a range of 13 to 75%.[30,35] The figures suggest that some individuals abandon prescribed diets totally. In one study of dietary compliance, all patients disclosed some instances of noncompliance when questioned carefully.[37] In another report, only 2% of dietitians thought that most of their patients adhered to a prescribed diet following hospital discharge.[38] Part of the problem was that dietitians did not aggressively pursue dietary counseling while patients were in the hospital, or did not take much initiative in planning for follow-up.

It is probably unrealistic to expect 100% adherence to dietary changes every day of the week. How many people have never been tempted to stray from eating nutritionally balanced meals every day of every month, including holidays and social occasions? The fact is that most have, and thus short-term goals, such as following the diet two out of three meals daily or 4 days a week, may promote better adherence early in the counseling process: later, the regimen can be extended. Dietitians know exactly what should be done and are steeped in the important reasons for dietary changes. Because they want the patient or client to be just as knowledgeable, they run the danger of setting unrealistic goals for change or giving too much information at one time, accomplishing less than they would by parceling out the recommendations over time.

Factors Influencing Adherence. The many factors influencing adherence to a prescribed dietary regimen are often reported and analyzed in terms of four sets of characteristics, those belonging (1) to the patient or client, (2) to the counselor, (3) to the clinic, and (4) to the regimen.[39]

Some studies investigating demographic variables, such as age, sex, socioeconomic status, marital status, and the like, have not found that these variables predict compliance, but that better comprehension of the regimen tends to be associated with higher educational levels. Recall and comprehension by the patient decrease in direct proportion to the amount of information given, probably because of supersaturation of the client with recommendations, or because of excessive anxiety on the client's part, which interferes with cognitive processes. Dispensing information over a period of time in small and manageable amounts, with repetition, should enhance recall. An imaginative combining of educational techniques, such as verbal and written instructions intermixed with visual aids, should also improve results.[39,40]

Satisfaction with the level of care and with the attitude of the counselor have been reported to influence adherence. Problems may result if good rapport is not developed between the counselor and the client, with the counselor taking into consideration the person's concerns and expectations.[41] The individual's interest level may be perfunctory, or appointments may be missed. Adherence may be more satisfactory if the patient sees the same counselor at each visit, and if clear-cut communication occurs so that the individual fully understands what is best and what is expected.

The characteristics of the clinic are also important. People kept waiting for long periods of time often fail to return for future appointments. A warm and caring environment, created not only by the counselor but the entire office staff, puts clients into a frame of mind that enables them to benefit from their counseling.

The characteristics of the regimen are the most important factors in adherence. Of these, complexity is the most significant. Complexity of a regimen has been negatively associated with adherence, perhaps related to the difficulty of fitting the regimen into one's daily routine.[39] Diets encompass many of the factors associated with a higher incidence of noncompliance. According to Glanz, the factors include required changes in lifestyle, which tend to be restrictive, last a long duration or a lifetime, and interfere with family habits.[30] If other barriers exist—such as high cost of the diet, lack of access to the proper foods, or extra effort, time, and skill required in preparing the diet—the likelihood of nonadherence increases.

Often measures of adherence are based on indirect measures. Self-reports, daily records of food intake, interviews such as diet histories and 24-hour recalls, and the dietitian's subjective rating are used to collect data. All of these methods may tend to overestimate adherence. As a result, interviewing techniques that develop good rapport and are not threatening or judgmental to the client must be utilized if the practitioner is to receive honest, accurate information about adherence to dietary regimens.[30,42] No completely reliable method of assessing adherence is available.[39]

The "Health Belief Model," which attempts to explain preventive health behavior, was developed to interpret the decisions of people not currently suffering disease, but wishing to prevent health problems.[43] It postulates that the person's beliefs about health are determinants of his readiness to take action. The three key beliefs are: (1) the extent to which the person believes that he is susceptible to contacting a disease, or resusceptible in the case of an illness from which he has recovered; (2) how serious he thinks the disease is in affecting some of life's components; and (3) what he perceives are the benefits of a regimen in terms of reducing susceptibility to or severity of the disease, as compared to the barriers to taking action. A diabetic woman, for example, should believe that she has diabetes and is susceptible to serious complications; that adherence to the regimen will reduce the likelihood of serious complications; that she has the ability to comply, and that the benefits of adherence outweigh the costs.[44] If the individual views taking action as unpleasant, expensive, inconvenient, or upsetting, avoidance motives may serve as barriers. Best results are obtained when readiness to act is high and when physical, psychological, financial, and other barriers are low. The model has been used to study compliant behavior.

A revised formulation of the Health Belief Model was utilized in assessing mothers' compliance with physicians' recommendations on infant feeding practices. Failure to adhere to physician's advice was reported by almost 30% of the women. The study found that the health-related attitude "nutrition is important" and having a "concern for health" were significantly related to compliance scores.[45] Another study of individuals with diabetes found that dietary adherers were more health oriented, and they believed that diabetes was a threat to their health.[46] Not everyone makes food choices based on health beliefs, however. The pleasure of eating, cost considerations, accessibility, and social and cultural practices are examples of other factors affecting food choices. One needs to ask, "What does the individual value?"

In the Multiple Risk Factor Intervention Trial (MRFIT), groups of middle-aged men received nutrition counseling to alter food behaviors in an attempt to reduce the risk of coronary heart disease. Participants were to adopt the MRFIT eating pattern, and successful dietary intervention was believed to depend upon the transfer of responsibility for proper food selection to participants. In promoting adherence and assessing dietary compliance, two methods utilized were a food score and food diaries.[47,48]

Nutritionists developed a food-scoring system for participant behavioral self-monitoring based on the cholesterogenic composition of foods. Participants became versed in assessing their own food scores and could evaluate their food choices, thus providing a tool for positive reinforcement of proper food behaviors. Effective change in participants' food behaviors depended on the ability to recognize proper foods with low scores and substitute them for foods with higher scores, a process providing awareness and insight. Individual counseling encouraged achievement of a specific guideline score. The scores became an objective means of assessing dietary adherence and understanding.[47]

A second tool for measuring adherence to the MRFIT eating pattern was a 3-day food record. The food-score concept was used with these records also, and aided counseling concerning appropriate food choices and making changes in foods selected.

Strategies Promoting Adherence. A number of intervention strategies, including counseling, behavior modification, and education, promote better adherence with an informed, willing client, and they should provide the individual with insight into himself and his situation.[36,39,49] They are presented briefly in the following paragraphs and are discussed in more detail in the chapters of the book.

1. Establish a good interpersonal, helping relationship.

2. Provide adequate education about the dietary regimen and the rationale for it. A person must know what to do in order to do it correctly. Individualize the regimen for each person, and minimize and simplify the number of changes to be made. Use a variety of techniques, such as verbal and written instructions with visual aids. Counseling should be carried out over a period of time with the same counselor, with repetition of information to ensure retention, and with provision of practice when skills should be developed.

3. Determine and address the individual's anxieties, concerns, and expectations, and try to meet them. Determine what the person thinks and feels about the dietary regimen. Motivation has multiple facets and is affected by the person's attitudes, beliefs, values, and opinions.

4. Set a limited number (one or two) of clear, attainable short-term goals for dietary change with the individual, and gradually increase the number of goals as the client builds new skills and succeeds at new behaviors. Although the professional may want immediate perfection, people change slowly. Compromise is necessary, and short-term goals can lead eventually to long-term results.

5. Positively reinforce and reward, such as by praising, whatever the individual does correctly, no matter how small the change. Teach the person to alter cues to eating and to use self-rewards. Reinforcement has a potent effect on behaviors.

6. Work with families and significant others so that they can be supportive of the dietary changes. Family members, for example, can assist with controlling the environment by purchasing and preparing proper foods.

7. Have the person keep daily records of food intake, exercise, weight, blood pressure, blood sugar, and the like. Self-monitoring has a value of its own in the person's learning and assuming responsibility for self-care, as well as in diagnosing barriers and adherence problems. Make the system easy to use and provide feedback.

8. Negotiate written contracts for change as a tool for motivation. Include specific, positive behaviors and the rewards for accomplishment.

9. Arrange for follow-up visits. One visit is not enough. Identify the factors and events contributing to non-adherence and help the individual solve problems, setting more short-term goals for change.

10. Use support groups in which some individuals model appropriate behaviors to others. Allow for discussion and problem solving, which use higher cognitive processes.

ADMINISTRATIVE/MANAGEMENT DIETETICS

The administrative dietitian and manager need effective communication and education skills for personal relationships with subordinates and others on the management team in the administration of increasingly complex foodservice systems. The manager deals extensively with employees, and is expected to build good human relationships. Communication is described as "the key to every relationship" with each employee, and the quality of the relationships "largely determines the performance level of that employee."[50] Although one may "develop" human relations skills, there is no substitute for sincerity. A fundamental factor in interpersonal relations is the trust between the superior and the subordinate.

There are a number of interrelated management functions in which communication is important. They include staffing; employee orientation and training; leadership, including motivation, morale, and productivity; and managing change in the organization. The administrative dietitian is expected to develop communication networks, and to "utilize and maintain effective horizontal and vertical lines of communication" within the organization and the surrounding community.[51] The manager needs to be skillful in verbal and nonverbal communication, in listening to others, and in recognizing and eliminating barriers to effective communication. In a survey of dietitians with administrative responsibilities who assessed their own level of competence, the greatest mean difference between career entry and the competence required for current professional practice was found in "communication."[52] A study of members of the Dietitians in Business and Industry practice group and prospective and current employers of dietitians found that both employers and dietitians identified communication skills as "the most influential attribute affecting the employment of dietitians in business and industry."[53]

Education skills are important in the planning, implementation, and evaluation of training programs designed to help achieve the employee's personal goals as well as organizational objectives. In staffing the organization, identified positions are filled by the use of structured interviews with applicants. The new employees selected must be oriented and trained. The manager is also responsible for continuous education of current employees and for inservice education.

Increasingly, the autocratic leadership styles of the past have been replaced by more participative approaches. Employee-centered supervisors recognize the importance of allowing more subordinate participation in decision making. One advantage is that people are more likely to accept decisions that they have participated in making. In addition, supportive and participative approaches may produce better results in terms of productivity, morale, motivation, and lessened absenteeism. Management is concerned not only with what employees can do, but with what they will do, which depends on several forces in the work environment that influence motivation.

Effective communication skills are essential in day-to-day dealings with peers and subordinates. This type of communication is utilized, for example, in discussing with employees the goals of the organization, work that needs to be done, policies, procedures, changes, problems that may be resolved through employee counseling, and performance appraisals. Face-to-face communication with employees can have an important effect on employee attitudes and behavior.

The administrative dietitian works not only with individuals, but also with groups. Communication may be facilitated through the use of meetings and conferences. Meetings may be utilized to dispense or collect information, and for problem solving and decision making. Understanding the nature of groups and group process is essential. Knowledge of the social groupings of employees is necessary for creating conditions that will elicit cooperation, thus maximizing the attainment of organizational goals.

All dietitians need to be confident of their abilities in patient/client and employee interaction. In addition to their scientific and technical competence, dietitians are expected to be skilled in interpersonal relations. With patients and clients, interviewing, counseling, and education are used to influence the behavioral outcomes of dietary regimens for the betterment of the individual's health. With subordinate employees, similar skills are used, but in different environments and for different purposes. Education and communication theories, principles, techniques, and strategies are examined in the following chapters.

REFERENCES

1. Lanz, S.J.: Introduction to the Profession of Dietetics. Philadelphia, Lea & Febiger, 1983.
2. A New Look at the Profession of Dietetics. Chicago, The American Dietetic Assoc., 1985.
3. Muldary, T.W.: Interpersonal Relations for Health Professionals. New York, Macmillan, 1983.
4. ADA is proactive on mid-course review of Promoting Health/Preventing Disease: Objectives for the Nation. J. Am. Diet. Assoc. 86:378, 1986.
5. Position paper of The American Dietetic Association: Nutrition education for the public. J. Am. Diet. Assoc. 90:107, 1990.
6. Baldyga, W.W.: Results from the 1981 census of The American Dietetic Association. J. Am. Diet. Assoc. 83:343, 1983.
7. Baird, S.C., and Armstrong, R.V.L.: The A.D.A. role delineation for the field of clinical dietetics. J. Am. Diet. Assoc. 78:370, 1981.
8. Kane, M.T., Estes, C.A., Colton, D.A., and Eltoft, C.S.: Role Delineation Study for Entry-Level Registered Dietitians, Entry-Level Dietetic Technicians, and Beyond-Entry-Level Registered Dietitians. Vols. I to III. Chicago, American Dietetic Assoc., 1989.
9. Kane, M.T., Estes, C.A., Colton, D.A., and Eltoft, C.S.: Role delineation for dietetic practitioners: Empirical results. J. Am. Diet. Assoc. 90:1124, 1990.
10. Martin, J.B., Holcomb, J.D., and Mullen, P.D.: Health promotion and disease prevention beliefs and behaviors of dietetic practitioners. J. Am. Diet. Assoc. 87:609, 1987.
11. Baird, S.C., and Armstrong, R.V.L.: Role Delineation for Entry Level Clinical Dietetics. Chicago, The American Dietetic Assoc., 1980.
12. Meyer, M.K., and Olsen, M.S.: Productivity of the clinical dietitian: Measurement by a regression model. J. Am. Diet. Assoc. 89:490, 1989.

13. Klevans, D.R., and Parett, J.L.: Continuing professional education needs of clinical dietitians in Pennsylvania. J. Am. Diet. Assoc. *90*:282, 1990.
14. Baird, S.C., and Sylvester, J.: Role Delineation and Verification for Entry-Level Positions in Community Dietetics. Chicago, The American Dietetic Assoc., 1983.
15. Sims, L.S.: Identification and evaluation of competencies of public health nutritionists. Am. J. Pub. Health *69*:1099, 1979.
16. Baird, S.C., and Sylvester, J.: Role Delineation and Verification for Entry-Level Positions in Foodservice Systems Management. Chicago, The American Dietetic Assoc., 1983.
17. Ericksen, K.: Communication Skills for the Human Services. Reston, Va., Reston Publ. Co., 1979.
18. Kinlaw, D.C.: Helping Skills for Human Resource Development. San Diego, University Associates, 1981.
19. Brammer, L.M.: The Helping Relationship: Process and Skills. 4th ed., Englewood Cliffs, NJ, Prentice-Hall, 1988.
20. Fletcher, D.J.: Self-care. How to help patients share responsibility for their health. Postgrad. Med. *78*:213, 1985.
21. Henderson, G.: Physician-Patient Communication. Springfield, Charles C Thomas, 1981.
22. Benjamin, A.: The Helping Interview. 3rd ed., Boston, Houghton Mifflin, 1981.
23. Peck, E.B.: The "professional self" and its relation to change processes. J. Am. Diet. Assoc. *69*:534, 1976.
24. Carruth, B.R., Mangel, M., and Anderson, H.L.: Assessing change-proneness and nutrition-related behaviors. J. Am. Diet. Assoc. *70*:47, 1977.
25. Mahoney, M., and Caggiula, A.: Applying behavioral methods to nutritional counseling. J. Am. Diet. Assoc. *72*:372, 1978.
26. Welch, L.B.: Planned change in nursing. Nurs. Clin. North Am. *14*:307, 1979.
27. Bryant, C.A., Courtney, A., Markesbery, B.A., and DeWalt, K.M.: The Cultural Feast. St. Paul, West Publ. Co., 1985.
28. Olendski, M.C., Tolpin, H.G., and Buckley, E.L.: Evaluating nutrition intervention in atherosclerosis. J. Am. Diet. Assoc. *79*:9, 1981.
29. Mason, M., Hallahan, I.A., Monsen, E., Mutch, P.B., Palombo, R., and White, H.F.: Requisites of advocacy. J. Am. Diet. Assoc. *80*:213, 1982.
30. Glanz, K.: Trends in Patient Compliance. Chicago, The American Dietetic Assoc., 1981.
31. Wylie, J.: Growth process in nutrition counseling. J. Am. Diet. Assoc. *69*:505, 1976.
32. Seidel, M.C.: The consulting nutritionist in an employee health office. J. Am. Diet. Assoc. *82*:405, 1983.
33. Hatten, A.M.: Nutrition consultant in home care services. J. Am. Diet. Assoc. *68*:250, 1976.
34. Etzwiler, D.D.: The patient is a member of the medical team. J. Am. Diet. Assoc. *61*:421, 1972.
35. Haynes, R.B. Introduction. In Compliance in Health Care. Edited by R.B. Haynes, D.W. Taylor, and D.L. Sackett. Baltimore, John Hopkins Univ. Press, 1979.
36. Glanz, K.: Strategies for nutritional counseling. J. Am. Diet. Assoc. *74*:431, 1979.
37. Glanz, K.: Dietitians' effectiveness and patient compliance with dietary regimens. J. Am. Diet. Assoc. *75*:631, 1979.
38. Schiller, M.R.: Current hospital practices in clinical dietetics. J. Am. Diet. Assoc. *84*:1194, 1984.
39. Dunbar, J.M., and Stunkard, A.J.: Adherence to diet and drug regimen. In Nutrition, Lipids, and Coronary Heart Disease. Edited by R. Levy, B. Rifkind, B. Dennis, and N. Ernst. New York, Raven Press, 1979.
40. Wedman, B., and Kahan, R.D.: Diabetes graphic aids used in counseling improve patient compliance. J. Am. Diet. Assoc. *87*:1672, 1987.

41. Hogan, S.E., Gates, R.D., MacDonald, F.W., and Clarke, J.T.R.: Experience with adolescents with phenylketonuria returned to phenylalanine-restricted diets. J. Am. Diet. Assoc. *86*:1203, 1986.
42. Ney, D., Stubblefield, N., and Fischer, C.: A tool for assessing compliance with a diet for diabetes. J. Am. Diet. Assoc. *82*:287, 1983.
43. Rosenstock, I.M.: Historical Origins of the Health Belief Model. Health Ed. Monographs, *2*:328, 1974.
44. Rosenstock, I.M.: Understanding and enhancing patient compliance with diabetic regimens. Diabetes Care *8*:610, 1985.
45. Morse, W., Sims, L.S., and Guthrie, H.A.: Mothers' compliance with physicians' recommendations on infant feeding. J. Am. Diet. Assoc. *75*:140, 1979.
46. Kouris, A., Wahlquist, M.L., and Worsley, A.: Characteristics that enhance adherence to high-carbohydrate/high-fiber diets by persons with diabetes. J. Am. Diet. Assoc. *88*:1422, 1988.
47. Remmell, P.S., Gorder, D.D., Hall, Y., and Tillotson, J.L.: Assessing dietary adherence in the Multiple Risk Factor Intervention Trial (MRFIT). J. Am. Diet. Assoc. *76*:351, 1980.
48. Remmell, P.S., and Benfari, R.C.: Assessing dietary adherence in the Multiple Risk Factor Intervention Trial (MRFIT). J. Am. Diet. Assoc. *76*:357, 1980.
49. Eckerling, L., and Kohrs, M.B.: Research on compliance with diabetic regimens. J. Am. Diet. Assoc. *84*:805, 1984.
50. Matejka, J.K., and Dunsing, R.J.: Opening doors: Good relationships as good management. Personnel J. *65*:74, 1988.
51. Position paper on the administrative dietitian. J. Am. Diet. Assoc. *67*:478, 1975.
52. Snyder, J.R., Schiller, M.R., and Smith, J.L.: A comparison of career-entry administrative competencies with skills required in practice. J. Am. Diet. Assoc. *85*:934, 1985.
53. Kirk, D., Shanklin, C.W., and Gorman, M.A.: Attributes and qualifications that employers seek when hiring dietitians in business and industry. J. Am. Diet. Assoc. *89*:494, 1989.

SUGGESTED ACTIVITIES

1. Divide the group into pairs for a 10-minute walk. For the first 5 minutes, have one person close his eyes and permit himself to be guided by his partner without speaking. After 5 minutes, reverse roles and have the other person become the helper. Discuss the feelings of the helper and those of the person being helped. What were the attitudes toward helping and the feelings of trust?

2. From the dietetic practice areas mentioned in the chapter, select a subspecialty area of practice, and interview a dietitian or nutritionist about his or her responsibilities, including the use of communication skills and education skills. Share this information with peers.

3. With someone trying to make changes in food practices (such as dieting), discuss the changes and the factors influencing change, including barriers. What are the factors influencing the person's adherence?

4. Select a dietary regimen, such as increased fiber, restricted sodium, low calorie, or low fat and cholesterol, and follow it for 7 days. Keep a daily record of all foods eaten. How easy or difficult was it to comply with the diet for a week? What factors helped or hindered your adherence?

2

Communication

American education has traditionally emphasized two communication skills, reading and writing, and ignored two others, speaking and listening. Consequently, many people today have grown up with the false assumption that speaking and listening are natural, that because one hears, one listens, and that because one speaks, one has speaking skills.

In all of the "helping professions," speaking and listening skills correlate with the professionals' effectiveness with their clients and staff. Regardless of the physicians', nurses', or dietitians' desire to help, if they are unable to relate well on a one-to-one basis with clients and staff, they are likely to be perceived as ineffective. The trust, cooperation, and confidence of helpees are positively related to their perceptions of the caring and interest, as demonstrated through the helpers' interpersonal communication.

A recent empirical study reported that both employers and dietitians ranked communication skills as essential to success in business and industry positions.[1] Other studies in the literature have stressed the need for professionals to develop communication skills, pointing out that individuals who develop these skills are able to establish better relationships with both clients and staff.[2,3] One recent study stressed the need for the managers and their employees of the nineties to learn how to learn, problem-solve, think creatively, listen, and, above all, communicate effectively.[4]

Communication Defined. The term "communication" is something of an enigma. Although everyone communicates, it is so expansive that it is difficult to define. In a broad sense, communication includes all methods that can convey thought or feeling between persons. The *Journal of Communication* has published no less than 15 working definitions of human communication.[5] From among the definitions, two common elements emerge: (1) Communication is the process of sending and receiving messages; (2) for a transmission of ideas to be successful, a mutual understanding between the communicator and the listener must occur.

Effective communication can be operationally defined for dietitians as the ability to use language that is appropriate to the clients' and staff's level of understanding, making sure that they have enough knowledge but are not overwhelmed; the ability to develop a relationship between themselves and their clients and staff; the ability to talk to them in a way that relieves anxiety; the ability to communicate to them in a way that assures their being able to recall information actively, and the ability to provide them with feedback.

This chapter discusses communication as a process, examines its components, and points out applications for dietitians. A model of the communication process is presented and discussed, followed by an explanation of the implications of the process for the verbal, nonverbal, and listening behaviors of the dietitian. The chapter concludes with a discussion of the barriers to communication.

Possessing only an intellectual appreciation of the various communication skills is of little use. Some sciences, such as mathematics, physics, chemistry, and biology, can be mastered by learning principles; the applied social sciences cannot. Being able to pass a test by explaining how one ought to interact with clients and staff, how to defuse their hostility, and how to create a supportive communication climate with them is not the same as actually being able to do it. Putting the principles into practice requires a conscious effort, repeated attempts, and months of trial. With practice, in a relatively short time, people can notice a difference in the way others respond to them. Honing the skills, however, needs to be an ongoing process, beginning with an understanding of the many elements included in the interpersonal communication transaction.

INTERPERSONAL COMMUNICATION MODEL

Complicated processes are easier to grasp when they can be visualized in a model. A model, however, is not the same as the actual phenomenon; rather, it is a graphic depiction to aid understanding. The elements included in the human communication model are the following: sender, receiver, the message itself—verbal and nonverbal, feedback, and interference. They are depicted graphically in Figure 2-1.

Components of the Communication Model. *Sender.* Senders of the messages are the first persons to speak, the ones who initiate the communication.

Receiver. Receivers of the message, listeners, usually interpret and transmit simultaneously. They may be listening to what is being said and thinking about what they are going to say when the senders stop talking. Even when silent, it is impossible for receivers in a two-way communication transaction not to communicate. They may be reacting physiologically with a flushed face or trembling hands, or in some other way, depending on their inferences from the message. Senders make inferences based on the receivers' appearance and demeanor and adjust subsequent communication accordingly.

Message. The receiver interprets two messages simultaneously: the actual verbal message and the nonverbal message inferred from the

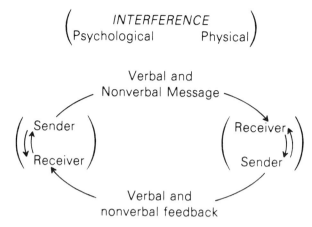

Fig. 2-1. A dietitian's communication model. (Adapted from Tindall, W.N., Beardsley, R.S., and Curtiss, F.R.: Communication in Pharmacy Practice. Philadelphia, Lea & Febiger, 1984.)

sender and the environment. Nonverbal inferences arise from the perceived emotional tone of the sender's voice, facial expression, dress, choice of words, diction, and pronunciation, as well as from the communication environment.

Feedback. The term "feedback" refers to the process of responding to messages after interpreting them for oneself. It is the key ingredient that distinguishes two-way from one-way communication. In two-way, face-to-face communication, the sender is talking, while looking at the other. The other's reactions to the sender's message, whether agreement, surprise, boredom, or hostility are examples of feedback. Unless the communication channel is kept clear for feedback, distortion occurs, leaving the sender unable to detect accurately how the message is received.[6]

In written communication, writers cannot clarify for readers because they do not see them. Even when writers carefully select words for the benefit of their intended readers, written communication is generally less efficient than one-to-one verbal communication because of its inability to re-explain and adjust language in response to the feedback from receivers.

Interpersonal communication, after the first few seconds, becomes a simultaneous two-way sending and receiving process. While senders are talking, they are receiving nonverbal reactions from receivers. Based on these reactions, they may change their tone, speak louder, use simpler language, or in some other way adjust their communication so that their message is better understood.

Interference. This term is used to denote multiple factors of the communicators (sender and receiver) and of their environment that affect the interpretation of messages. These factors include the unique attributes inherent in each of them; the room size, shape, and color;

temperature; furniture arrangement, and the physiological state of each communicator at the moment. The sophisticated communicator needs to understand these contingencies and to compensate for them, when possible, so that the intended message is the one received.

A crying baby, the sound of thunder, and low-flying planes, for example, not only can hinder the receiver in hearing the sender's message, but also can generate messages and interpretations in the receiver that were never intended by the sender. Another source of interference is the physiological state of the communicators at the moment. No two bodies are exactly alike. Because no one has shared in the exact life experience of another, no two people understand language in precisely the same way.

Distortions can stem from psychological interference as well, including bias, prejudice, and being closed-minded. Psychological interference in health care situations is often due to fear of illness and its consequences.[7] The job of senders is to generate in receivers those meanings for language that are closest to their own. Because meanings are not universal, they can be affected by external as well as internal influences. Communication environment, the distance between speakers, lighting, temperature, and colors are a few of the variables that can affect meanings ascribed to a message. These variables can be sources of interference and major factors in accounting for difficulty in generating in others the same meanings people intend. In the second half of this chapter, under the heading "Barriers to Effective Communication," additional physical and psychological forms of interference are discussed.

VERBAL AND NONVERBAL COMMUNICATION

Verbal communication includes the actual words selected by the sender and the way in which these symbols are arranged into thought units. Nonverbal communication includes the communication environment, the manner and style in which the communication is delivered, and the internal qualities inherent in the sender and receiver that influence their interpretation of external stimuli. Although verbal and nonverbal communication occur simultaneously during interaction, each is discussed separately here in the context of their influence on the communication process. The salient point to remember here is that the lack of clear communication by the dietitian is the most common cause of poor employee performance, and that conscious and clear communication is the key to every good relationship, with both clients and staff.[8]

Employees are often hesitant to approach their supervisors, even if the superiors have explicit open-door policies. In order to open real lines of communication, certain companies have begun "Operation Speakeasy." This new form of meeting brings a group of employees together once a month with two or three top managers. The employees, who change monthly, serve as presenters from their departments, bringing forth suggestions, concerns, and questions.[9] While this system is proving effective, it can only work in a supportive climate, which generally emanates from the management level.

To keep the communication channel open between the client or employee and the dietitian, the dietitian needs to know how to create a supportive climate. A supportive climate is one where as one person speaks, the other listens, attending to the message rather than to their own internal thoughts and feelings.

Although maintaining a supportive climate is always a concern, it becomes especially crucial when the professional is attempting to discuss a topic the client or employee views differently, or attempting to resolve conflict and defuse anger. The behavioral sciences offer suggestions on what one can do verbally and nonverbally to create a supportive climate under conditions of hostility or stress.[10]

Verbal Communication. The verbal guidelines for creating a supportive communication climate are: (1) to discuss problems descriptively rather than evaluatively; (2) to describe situations with a problem orientation rather than in a manipulative way; (3) to offer alternatives provisionally rather than dogmatically; (4) to treat clients as equals rather than as persons of lower rank than oneself; and (5) to be empathic rather than neutral or self-centered.

Descriptive Rather than Evaluative. Ordinarily, when approaching topics that tend to provoke defensiveness in clients, professionals should think through the discussion prior to engaging the client, so that the problem area is exposed descriptively rather than evaluatively. Whenever people hear others judging their attitudes, work, or behavior, they show an increased tendency to become defensive. Such comments as "You don't seem to be trying," "You don't care about cooperating," or "You are selfish" are based on inferences rather than facts. So when the other says, "I do care," "I am too trying," or "I am not selfish," the framework for an argument is set, with no way of proving objectively who is right or wrong. Instead of making judgments regarding another's attitudes, the safest and least offensive way of dealing with a touchy issue is to describe the facts as objectively as possible. For example, the professional tells a client that his continuing to eat four pork chops and a half pound of chocolates a day is frustrating to her as the client's diet counselor. The professional is confronting the problem honestly and objectively without being evaluative. The client can then address the topic of his overeating rather than argue the dietitian's negative evaluation of his poor attitude, lack of concern, or noncooperativeness.

Accusing an employee who has arrived late several mornings of being "irresponsible" and "uncaring" is likely to provoke a hostile refutation or cold silence. The employee may believe that his being late does not warrant a reprimand. There may, in fact, be a reasonable explanation. Describing how being late is frustrating you, causing problems to those who depend upon him, and causing work to back up, is honest, descriptive, and allows for non-defensive dialogue.

   Problem-Oriented Rather than Manipulative. Orienting a person to a problem rather than manipulating him promotes a supportive communication climate. Frequently, when people want others to appreciate their point of view, they lead them through a series of questions until the other reaches the "appropriate" insight. This is a form of manipulation and provokes defensiveness as soon as respondents realize they are being channeled to share the other's vision. It goes something like this:

"Three weeks ago I believe you told me you gained weight on the diet because your metabolism is slow, correct? Two weeks ago you told me that you gained weight because the diet itself was faulty, correct? We checked your metabolism, and it is normal, and I have assured you that someone of your size could not gain weight on 1200 calories a day. Today you tell me that you ate salty popcorn last night and that your weight gain for the third consecutive week is all water, correct? If you were dealing with a client like yourself, would you begin to get the feeling that this person is making a fool out of you?"

   A discussion with the client would probably be more productive if the dietitian took a direct problem-oriented approach:

"In 3 weeks on a 1200-calorie diet you have gained 1 pound per week. After checking the results of your laboratory tests, I am certain that the diet should have caused a weight loss of 4 to 5 pounds. There seems to be a problem here. Let's discuss what the other possibilities might be."

   Employees and clients respect professionals, even when they disagree with them, when they believe the professional is being straight-forward and authentic. A slick, manipulative style ordinarily can be seen through immediately and causes others to become disdainful.[8]

   Although opening remarks should be planned descriptively rather than evaluatively, the dietitian, after making them, should allow for spontaneous problem solving without preplanned solutions. Creative, superior, and long-lasting solutions are more likely to occur when each person hears the other out fully and is heard in return. If one is intent on "selling" a solution to the other, there is a natural disposition to block out conflicting opinions. The problem-solving process is discussed in detail in Chapters 4 and 6.

   In the example of the previous paragraphs, the dietitian's subsequent remarks depend on how the client or employee responds to the directive to explain the underlying problem. The dietitian might need to wait several minutes for an answer. Providing excuses or putting words into the other's mouth is a mistake. The dietitian needs to learn the discipline of sitting through the tension of silence supportively until the client or employee responds. Frequently, the first explanations are those that people believe will not upset or shock the professional. The "real" reasons, however, may not be revealed until the client or staff member feels secure enough to risk shocking the professional without fear of being humiliated or embarrassed. After the first explanations are offered, the dietitian would do best simply to repeat in her own words what she has understood. Only when the clients or employees are comfortable enough, will they be able to express their authentic reactions, questions, or answers, these ordinarily being less logical, more emotional and more risky to expose.

Provisional Rather than Dogmatic. When offering advice to clients or helping them to solve problems, the professional should give advice provisionally rather than dogmatically. "Provisionally" implies the possibility of dietitians changing their opinions, provided additional facts emerge. It keeps the door open for clients to add information. When advice is offered in a dogmatic way, it becomes threatening for clients or employees to challenge or to add their own information. A dogmatic prescription might be, "This is what you must do. I know this is the way to solve your problem." A provisional prescription might be, "Here is one thing you might consider," or "There may be other ways of handling this problem; perhaps you have some ideas too, but this is one thing you might consider."

Egalitarian Rather than Superior. In discussing problems, clients and dietitians should regard each other as equals. Whenever the possibility of defensiveness exists, even between persons of equal rank, any verbal or nonverbal behavior that the other interprets as an attempt to emphasize superiority generates a defensive response. In the relationship between dietitians and clients, or dietitians and employees, the dietitians' tendencies to emphasize status or rank may arise unconsciously from a desire to convince the other to accept their recommendations. Comments such as the following may cause the other to feel inferior, hurt, or angry: "As a lay person, you might not be able to grasp the theory, but it works," or "Just do what I ask; I've been doing this for 10 years." Certainly, there is nothing wrong with dietitians letting clients know that they are trained and competent. In fact, clients often need and appreciate the reassurance. The manner in which it is done is crucial, however. A more effective and subtle way to solve problems with a client is to say, "I have studied this problem and dealt with other clients who have similar symptoms. I am interested, however, in incorporating your own insights and plans into our solution. You must be satisfied and will have to live with the diet, so please express your views too."

An employee making a recommendation to a dietitian that the dietitian had tried unsuccessfully herself many years ago, might be told, "If I was in your shoes, I would think the same thing. Someday when you are more experienced, you'll know why it won't work." The subtle underscoring of the inferior relative status of the subordinate could be enough to cause a defensive battle. The dietitian would have done far better with a comment such as "I can understand why you say that. I have thought the same myself, but when I tried, it was not successful." Here the employee is left feeling reinforced and appreciated rather than humiliated. Showing respect for the clients' and employees' intelligence and life experiences and recognizing the human dignity in them facilitates receiving their cooperation.

In conflict resolution, problem solving, and the discussion of any issues that may be threatening to the client or employee, collaboration is far more effective than trying to persuade the individual to act according to the dictates of the professional. Collaboration has other virtues as well. People feel more obligation to uphold those solutions that they themselves have participated in designing. If individuals are trying the dietitian's solution, they may feel little satisfaction in proving the dietitian was right; however, if the solution is one that was arrived at through collaboration, there is genuine satisfaction in proving its validity. An additional reason for dietitians to involve others in problem solving is that often a valid solution that is superior to any the individual or dietitian would have discovered alone can be arrived at through collaboration. Two people sharing insights, knowledge, experience, and feelings can generate creative thought processes in each other, which in turn generate other ideas that would not otherwise have emerged.

Empathic Rather than "Neutral." Another verbal skill essential to maintaining a supportive climate is the ability to empathize. Traditionally, empathy has been defined as the ability to put oneself in the other's shoes. For a helping professional, however, that is not enough. To be effective in working with clients and employees, dietitians must be able to demonstrate in some way their desire to understand what it is those they are helping are feeling. This "demonstration" might be an empathic response to their comments. In an empathic response, the listener tells the other that he is attempting to understand not only the speaker's content, but also his underlying feelings. For example, a client might say, "For my entire life I have eaten spicy foods; they are a part of my culture. I don't know what my life will be like without them." The professional might then respond, "You feel worried that the quality of your life will change because of the severe dietary restrictions."

If the dietitian is accurate in her empathic remarks, the client will acknowledge it and probably go on talking, assured that he is with a helper who listens. If the dietitian is wrong, however, the client will clarify the judgment and continue to talk, assured that he is with a helper who cares. Thus, the dietitian need not be accurate in her inferences of the other's feelings as long as she is willing to try to understand them. In addition, empathic responses allow the professional to respond without giving advice, focusing instead on the individual's need to talk and to express his feelings and concerns. Before clients or employees can listen to the dietitians, they must express all of their concerns; otherwise, while the dietitians are talking, the clients or employees are thinking about what they will say when the dietitians stop.

An employee who has asked to be released from work on a busy weekend to attend a rock concert out of town might receive the following neutral response: "No offense, but a rule is a rule. If I make an exception for you, others will expect it." Alternatively, the employee would still feel sad about working but would feel less antagonistic toward the supervisor if he were to receive the following empathic response: "I realize how badly you feel about not being able to attend the concert, particularly because your girlfriend gave you the tickets as a birthday gift. I feel terrible myself having to refuse your request. I am truly sorry, but I can't afford to let you off." The supervisor, by letting the subordinate know that she has understood his underlying feelings and that she is sympathetic, uses the most effective means of defusing the subordinate's anger or antagonism. For further discussion of empathy, see Chapters 3 and 4.

Paraphrasing, a Critical Skill for Dietitians. Most people have not incorporated the skill of paraphrasing into their communication repertoire. Even after a person realizes how vital this step is, and begins to practice it, he may feel uncomfortable. Often the person just beginning to use paraphrasing in his interactions feels self-conscious and fears others may be insulted or think he is "showing off" professional communication skills. This fear itself, unfortunately, causes some people to alienate others, while trying to communicate with them. A hint for the dietitian feeling awkward about asking clients and staff to paraphrase would be to ask for the paraphrase by acknowledging her own need to verify that what she has heard is what the other intended. She might say, for example:

"I know that I don't always grasp everything immediately, and that frequently, I need to repeat what I think I have understood. My instructions today may be a bit complicated for someone who has never had to count food exchanges before. Just to be sure the instructions are understood as intended, would you mind explaining in your own words how you plan to manage this diet?"

Of course, it takes less time to ask, "Have you got it?" Asking this question is less effective, however. Because of the perceived status distinction between the helper and the person being helped, the latter may be ashamed to admit that he has not understood. Perhaps in the back of his mind, he is thinking that he can read about it later or ask the patient in the next bed for an explanation after the dietitian leaves the room. When persons of perceived higher status ask others if they "understand," almost always the answer is, "Yes." Another possibility is that the client or staff member honestly believes that he has understood, and for that reason has answered, "Yes." His understanding, however, may include some alteration of the original message, in the form of substitution, distortion, addition, or subtraction. The skill of paraphrasing needs to become "second nature" and automatic for the professional dietitian as she verifies important instructions and significant client/staff disclosures.

Because of the anxiety attached to being in the presence of another of perceived higher status, the client or staff member may be less articulate than usual when describing symptoms or explaining a problem.

The dietitian should paraphrase to verify that she is understanding the message according to its intended meaning, The professional should avoid sounding too clinical with such comments as "What I hear you saying is . . ." or "Let me repeat what you just said"; rather, she should keep the language clear, simple, and natural. A comment such as "I want to make sure I am understanding this; let me repeat what you are saying in my own words" is more natural.

Two points need to be emphasized regarding paraphrasing: (1) Not everything the other says needs paraphrasing. It would become a distraction if, after every other sentence, the dietitian interrupted with a request to paraphrase. Paraphrasing is essential only when the discussion is centered on critical information that must be understood. (2) Paraphrasing often leads to additional disclosure and therefore tends to cause longer interaction sessions. People are so accustomed to being with others who do not really listen that when they are with someone who proves he has been paying attention by repeating the content of what has been said, they usually want to talk more. For the dietitian, this additional information can be valuable. Another benefit is that after the client or staff member has expressed all his questions and concerns and has cleared his mental agenda, he is psychologically ready to sit back and listen, or to solve problems with the dietitian. By talking too much or too soon, the dietitian may not be able to convey all of her message to the other, who may be using the difference in time between how fast the dietitian speaks and how fast his own mind processes information (the human mind operates 5 to 8 times as fast as human speech) to rehearse what he is going to say next.

Nonverbal Communication. Of the two messages received simultaneously by receivers, verbal and nonverbal, ordinarily it is the nonverbal that is more influential. As receivers of messages, people learn to trust their interpretations of nonverbal behavior more than the verbal word choices consciously selected by the sender. Intuitively, they know that control of nonverbal behavior is generally unconscious, while control of verbal messages is usually deliberate.

Communication experts and social scientists feel that the image a person projects accounts for over half of the total message conveyed to another individual at a first meeting. Personal appearance, including clothing, hairstyle and accessories, is one of the most important elements of the image. Personal space variables should be experimented with to determine where an individual feels most comfortable and how that distance makes others feel.[11]

The chief nonverbal vehicles inherent in communicators are facial expression, tone of voice, eye contact, gesture, and touch. Receivers of communication perceive nonverbal behavior in clusters. Ordinarily one does not notice posture, eye contact, or facial expression isolated from the other nonverbal channels. For that reason, professionals need to monitor all of their nonverbal communication vehicles so that together the clusters are congruent with one another as well as with the verbal messages.

Facial expression is usually the first nonverbal trait noticed in interaction. A relaxed face with pleasant expression is congruent with a supportive climate. A supportive tone of voice is one that is calm, controlled, energetic, and enthusiastic. Supportive eye contact includes gazing at the other in a way that allows the communicator to encounter the other visually—to the extent of being able to notice the other's facial and bodily messages. Besides being an excellent vehicle for feedback, eye contact also assures the other of the dietitian's interest and desire to communicate. Attending to the other visually allows inferences of interest, concern, and respect. The dietitian's posture is best when leaning somewhat toward the person as opposed to away from him. Large expansive gestures may be interpreted as a show of power and, in general should be avoided.

Like eye contact, touch can work positively in two ways: (1) Through a gentle touch, a pat, or a squeeze of the hand, one can communicate instantly a desire to solve a problem without offending the other. Touch can communicate affection, concern, and interest faster than these messages can be generated verbally. (2) Like eye contact, touch is a vehicle for feedback. While an individual may look calm, controlled, and totally at ease, a touch can reveal nervousness and insecurity. These clues when monitored by the dietitian, often provide insight. She reacts to them by spending more time putting the person at ease; she has the individual paraphrase to make sure information is being understood, and she makes an effort to alter her communication style to be more overt in her support. People usually respond positively to touch, whether or not they are consciously aware of it.

Dietitian Must be Alert to Nonverbal Signals Emanating From the Other. Besides dietitians' concerns with the environment and their own verbal and nonverbal behavior in their attempt to create a trusting climate between themselves and others, they must also be sensitive to the nonverbal cues in other people. Even though the dietitian is being open, natural, caring, and attending to her own behavior and the environment, the internal anxiety, confusion, nervousness, or fear in people may be causing them to misunderstand or to react inappropriately. Two requirements for effective interpersonal communication, therefore, are that the professional observe the nonverbal cues in others and then respond to them in an affirming way.

If the client or employee is nodding his head to suggest understanding but looks puzzled, the dietitian needs to verify understanding by having the individual paraphrase important instructions or dietary recommendations. If the patient is flushed, has trembling hands, or tears rolling down his cheeks, the dietitian may need to deal directly with relieving anxiety before communicating instructions or explanations. Until the patient is relaxed enough to concentrate, optimal two-way communication between him and the dietitian is unlikely.

After talking with one another for only a few minutes, both the dietitian and the patient can sense the "warmness" or "coldness" of the other, as well as the degree of the other's "concern." Each person tends to generalize these impressions, while inferring additional traits in the other person. If the speaker has a gentle touch, pleasant expression, and looks directly into the eyes of the listener as he talks, he might be generating inferences in the listener of his being an excellent spouse, active church member, or loving mate. Once the initial positive impression has been created, the impression tends to spread into other areas not directly related to the originally observed behavior. The process can work in the reverse as well, negatively. If the dietitian does not look at the client as she talks, or touches the client in a rough way and has an unpleasant facial expression, the inferences being created now may be arrogance, lack of concern, indifference, and "coldness." Even though these initial reactions, both positive and negative, may be inaccurate, faulty first impressions are common. The helping professional might not be given a second chance to win the client's trust and cooperation; the client's inferences regarding the dietitian's concern and positive regard need to be anticipated and begun at the initial encounter.

Positive Affect Must be Consistent. Seeing employees daily gives the dietitian an opportunity to reinforce or alter the perceptions the other has of her. If one is cold, aloof, and uncaring on a daily basis, and suddenly, because it is time to conduct an appraisal or counseling session with an employee, acts differently, one will not be believed. The dietitian needs to be consistent in adding positive inferences to the impressions of her staff and clients. Dietitians must make a total commitment to the word-of-mouth process by listening and questioning effectively, taking appropriate action, focusing on a subordinate/client orientation, delivering on promises, and teaching people, both employees and clients, how to seek information efficiently.[12]

Not only is it important to attempt to generate concern through one's own nonverbal behavior, manner, and disposition, it is also essential to control, whenever possible, the communication environment so that it too leads to positive inferences with a minimum of "interference." Attractive offices, rooms in pastel colors, soft lighting, intimate and private space for counseling, and comfortable furniture can all add to the client's or staff member's collective perception, promoting inferences that one is concerned. One recent empirical study, for example, reported that because so much of the dietitian's counseling takes place in a hospital setting, more attention must be given to creating an inviting educational atmosphere within the hospital environment.[13]

Related indirectly to effective communication are the actual dress and physical appearance of the dietitian. Dress and appearance are usually consciously selected, and they are nonverbal communication vehicles. The female dietitian who is overly made up or too strongly scented, or the male dietitian who is wearing an earring or open shirt revealing a hairy chest, may be well meaning and competent; by their dress, however, they risk offending a more conservative person. Professional dietitians communicate their image best when they are clean, and wearing clean and pressed clothing and only a mildly scented cologne. Because any ostentatious show of material wealth or status tends to provoke a defensive reaction in others, items such as expensive jewelry and other valuable possessions should not be worn.

At work, the only real way to win an argument is to stop it as quickly as possible by settling the dispute rationally. This is not easy to do because generally people are programmed to respond to aggression in one of three ways: fighting back, running away, or becoming immobilized.[14] Sometimes, when dealing with a hostile client or employee, the dietitian may want to remain calm and supportive, but her body refuses to cooperate. Her face may turn red, her hands may begin to shake, and her voice may become loud and threatening. If this occurs, she should acknowledge that although she had wished to resolve the problem with the individual, she is feeling defensive and realizes that this might be upsetting the person. Because the individual sees the physical manifestations of the dietitian's defensiveness, the dietitian should acknowledge the reaction rather than attempt to feign control. Under these circumstances, the dietitian should avoid further immediate communication and should schedule another appointment after regaining composure.

Among the requirements for effective interpersonal communication is the need for the dietitian to send verbal and nonverbal messages that are congruent with one another. If a client hears a dietitian say, "I want to help you; I'm concerned about your health and any possible recurrence of your heart problem as a result of improper diet," but at the same time sees the dietitian looking down at her notes rather than at him, making no attempt to connect with him physically through handshake or gentle touch, or looking frequently at her watch, the incongruous second message of impersonality or impatience will be more intense then the stated message of concern. Although the professional has said all the "right" words, she is judged as insincere.

Helping professionals and managers who do not genuinely like working with people are destined ultimately to fail; often, however, professionals who do like people and care for their clients and employees fail as well. To be successful in working with others, the dietitian must develop congruent verbal and nonverbal communication skills. One can develop all the appropriate verbal skills and still be unsuccessful in calming a hostile employee or client or in securing an obstinate client's adherence to the dietary plan. Only when the professional treats others with respect, soliciting their opinions and responding to them, can an environment of trust and openness be created.[15]

LISTENING SKILLS

Well-developed listening skills are an essential requirement for effective interpersonal communication between dietitians and their clients and staff. An individual with average intelligence can process information at speeds that are approximately five times that of human speech. The higher the intelligence is, the faster the mind tends to process information. Some individuals can think at speeds of eight to ten times the rate of human speech. Thus, while dietitians are listening to their clients or staff members talk, they have time to be thinking about other things simultaneously. Everyone has had the experience of listening to a speaker and thinking about what he might be like as a person or letting the mind wander to other topics. From the speaker's clothes, shoes, jewelry, diction, speech patterns, etc., people tend to fill in details and develop an elaborate scenario while they listen, more or less, to his presentation. The process of good listening involves learning to harness one's attention so that one is able to concentrate totally on the speaker's message, both verbal and nonverbal. Development of these skills is not difficult, but it does require a conscious effort and perseverance.

Listening is taught as an academic subject in the department of communication studies in most colleges and universities. Research projects conducted at the University of Minnesota, however, indicate that listening ability can be enriched only when the individual desires such enrichment and is willing to follow the training with practice.[16] The following list of four of the most common poor listening habits is an excellent starting place for readers who desire to practice improving listening skills:[5]

1. Most people have a limited and undeveloped attention span.
2. People tend to stop listening when they have decided that the material is uninteresting and tend to pay attention only to material they "like" or see an immediate benefit in knowing.
3. Listeners tend to trust their intuition regarding the speaker's credibility, basing their judgments more on the speaker's nonverbal behavior than on the content of the message.
4. Listeners tend to attach too much credibility to messages heard on electronic media—radio, television, movies, tapes, etc.

Listening can be improved with practice. The most important step in such improvement is resolving to listen more efficiently. Simply being motivated to listen causes one to be more alert and active as a receiver. The following are specific suggestions for improving listening:[5]

1. Prior to engaging in the communication transaction, listeners should remind themselves of their intent to listen carefully.
2. The communication situation should be approached with the attitude of objectivity, with an open mind, and with a spirit of inquiry.

3. Listeners need to watch for clues. Just as one uses bold type and italics in writing, speakers use physical arrangement, program outlines, voice inflection, rate, emphasis, voice quality, and bodily actions as aids to help the listener determine the meaning of what is being said and what the speaker believes is most important.
4. Listeners need to make use of the thinking-speaking time difference and to remind themselves to concentrate on the speaker's message. They must use the extra time to think critically about the message, to relate it to what they already know, to consider the logic of the arguments, and to notice the accompanying nonverbal behavior—all simultaneously.
5. Listeners need to look beyond the actual words to determine what the speaker means, and to determine whether the clusters of accompanying nonverbal behavior are congruent with the verbal message.
6. Listeners need to provide feedback to the speaker, either indirectly through nonverbal reactions or directly through paraphrasing, to verify that what is being understood by the listener is what the speaker intends.

Giving accurate feedback is the only way to prove that another person's message has been heard and understood.[17] Ultimately, the most valuable listening skill is ongoing practice. Those who want to improve their listening must put themselves in difficult listening situations, must concentrate, and must practice good listening.[18]

BARRIERS TO EFFECTIVE COMMUNICATION

Thus far this chapter has dealt with what dietitians can do verbally and nonverbally to ensure accurate communication with others. Most people tend to underestimate the forces and variables likely to impede the process. There are myriads of barriers that often alter perceptions, increasing the likelihood of inaccurate communication. Only after individuals are aware of these barriers can they begin to alter their communication to safeguard against them.

Meanings Are in People, Not Words. The major barrier to communication, which probably accounts for about 90% of the misunderstandings between people, is based on the communication principle that meanings are in people, not words. Communication scholars have been attempting to make people aware of the implications of this principle for over 5 decades; however, it does not yet seem to be accepted and understood by most communicators. To comprehend the principle, one needs to understand the many ways in which humans differ one from another and how these differences account for the variations in the way they understand and use language. With the possible exception of identical twins at birth, no two people have the exact same physiological make-up. Although a person may think that he is experiencing objective reality as he moves from one life experience to another, he is in fact interpreting objective reality subjectively through his body and mind.

To understand this point better, the reader can try to remember a time when he was not feeling like himself, a time perhaps when he was under strong medication or severe stress. If the medication or stress accelerated the processes of his nervous system, he noticed that he was more nervous, less tolerant, and perhaps more depressed than usual. If the medication slowed down these processes, he noticed that he was more lethargic, less enthusiastic, and less motivated than usual. In both cases, the objective reality would be interpreted differently than if he were in his normal state. Even the "normal" range varies considerably. For some, being lethargic, moody, and slow-moving is normal. For others, being energetic, hyperactive, and tireless is normal. These two "normal" individuals might attend the same party, get married, or be involved in a helping relationship. Eventually, they will discover that each tends to interpret the same reality differently, with each assuming his interpretation is "correct."

In addition to an understanding and appreciation of the uniqueness of each person's physiological profile, there is a need to consider that over time, even the same person experiences a range of sensation, which affects inferences about reality. As people grow older, their senses change and begin to atrophy. Two people sitting at a baseball game eating hot dogs might be having different sensual experiences. One is enjoying and savoring every mouthful, while the other is lamenting, "They just don't make them like they used to." The senses of sight, hearing, touch, smell, and taste all diminish over time. These internal changes add to the problem of inferring that because two people have heard the same message or shared the same experience, they therefore have the same "meanings" in their interpretation.

Two people of identical intelligence may interpret the same external stimuli differently. Some people are dispositionally oriented toward seeing details, are introverted, and are less emotional, while others with similar intelligence tend to miss details, are more extroverted, and are more emotional. Although it is usually easier to communicate with someone who is cognitively similar to oneself, intelligence alone is not a predictor of ease of communication between individuals.

Culturally, people differ from one another, which causes them to have different interpretations of the same phenomenon. One of the authors (R.J.C.) is a second-generation Italian-American. When he traveled in Italy as a young student, he understood what it meant to be an Italian-American as opposed to a native Italian. He saw the world differently from his Italian-born cousins. Although he had never examined or challenged his values, he now realizes what it meant to be "acculturated." The kind of home in which a person is brought up and the values he learns as a child continue to influence the way in which he interprets the world.

Many writers have pointed out the advantages of writing in English, the language with more extant words than any other. Theoretically, the extra number of words ought to allow writers and speakers of English to express "meanings" more precisely than communicators using other languages. When the language is examined carefully, however, other limiting variables emerge. No language in the history of the world has as many words to express extremes. There are dozens of synonyms for "bad," "terrible," "evil," and "horrible," as well as of "good," "beautiful," "wonderful," "terrific," and "fantastic." English has, however, only a scant representation of words that describe intermediate feelings and thoughts, middle-of-the road positions, and other "gray" areas.

Philosophers have pointed out that thoughts are controlled to a great extent by vocabulary. One cannot think about something if one has no words for it. The inability to verbalize vague or intermediate areas of thought or feeling may distort one's perceptions of objective reality, increasing one's tendency to overreact, and hindering the likelihood of easy collaboration.

Another idiosyncrasy of the English language involves its many words with multiple meanings. *The Oxford English Dictionary,* for example, includes some 15 definitions for the word "fast." A "fast" horse, for example, is one that runs with great speed, while a "fast" color is one that does not run at all.

Generating one's own meanings in others, which involves trying to arouse those meanings in the other that are closest to one's own, is an extremely difficult process. Because we are each unique physiologically, psychologically, socially, and culturally, and because we speak a language that is susceptible to many interpretations, the process of communicating accurately to one another is complicated.

In addition to the variables previously discussed, numerous other phenomena affect the accuracy of person-to-person transmission of messages. One such factor evolves from the predictable phenomena of substitution, addition, and simplification that occur as messages are passed from person to person. As messages are sent from sender to receiver, each receiver tends to alter the message unconsciously when he becomes a sender and passes it on to another.

While distortion of messages is predictable, additional complications arise from status distinctions between the interactants. When people who have the power to reward or punish others attempt to give instructions, teach a procedure, or merely relate a series of facts, their perceived higher status often makes understanding the message more difficult for receivers who perceive themselves to be of lower status.

Sensations similar to the tension, stress, and side effects of the adrenal secretions of prehistoric humans fighting for survival still exist in people today. When an employee is called before his boss, who wishes to explain the importance of the employee's task or a complicated procedure, the employee might become nervous, experience trembling hands, begin to perspire, feel his face become flushed, or develop the feeling of "butterflies" in his stomach. These "fight-or-flight" symptoms often make it even more difficult to think clearly. At the very time when one needs to be most alert, he may be subject to a physiological handicap.

The most salient implication for the dietitian engaged in helping clients or training staff is the need to compensate for this phenomenon by assisting her clients and employees in developing the appreciation and ability of paraphrasing. In the presence of health professionals, clients and staff members often experience tension and anxiety, which make it difficult for them to grasp messages. The dietitian needs to learn communication skills to compensate for this tendency. In addition to being natural, deemphasizing status distinctions, using clear, concise language, and showing concern, the dietitian must consistently paraphrase the other, as well as have herself paraphrased, to verify that what was explained or taught was understood.

Selective Perception is Rampant, Although "Selectors" are Unconscious of it. A final barrier to communication is the human tendency to perceive information selectively, and to be intolerant of others who interpret the information differently. General Motors, for example, did a study several years ago to determine who reads Pontiac advertisements. The corporation learned that the major consumers of information about Pontiac automobiles are Pontiac owners. Each person tends to tune in to information that supports his already existing attitude and tends either to distort or not to hear information that refutes his existing attitudes.

Count the "F's" in the following statement:

FASCINATING FAIRYTALES ARE THE
RESULT OF YEARS OF SCIENTIFIC
STUDY COMBINED WITH THE
EXPERIENCE OF CREATIVE MINDS.

Most people looking at the message above for the first time, and told to count the number of "F's" see three. Even after being told that there are actually six, some people continue to see only three. How many do you see? Although many people believe themselves to be open-minded, unprejudiced, and able to see all sides of an issue, this simple test provides some evidence that there is the tendency in each of us to lock onto an expected view of reality and miss the objective truth.

This tendency to perceive reality selectively is unconscious. In general, people are unaware of which stimuli their minds are selecting to attend to and which stimuli are being ignored. For this reason, stereotypes, biases, and prejudices are likely to emerge and distort interpretations of messages. Such distortions carry implications for professional dietitians. The increase in foreign-born and minority employees and clients in the United States will further challenge the management and client skills which had been effective with "traditional" Americans. In dealing with clients or staff members, dietitians must consciously attempt to verify perceptions as a safeguard against selective distortion. One of the best ways to accomplish this is to listen actively, paraphrasing and making empathic responses. If the empathic response or paraphrasing is inaccurate and represents selective perception, the other person has the opportunity to clarify. To maintain organizational cohesiveness and effectiveness, dietitians must become conscious of their own biases and stereotypes and must develop, stretch, and risk in the process of developing appropriate techniques for dealing with the actual differences among foreign-born, minority, and nonminority employees and clients.[19]

This chapter has presented numerous suggestions for improving the dietitian's communication competence with clients and staff. One can read and reread this chapter, pass a quiz on the material with a grade of A+, and still be ineffective in practicing communication skills. To develop communication skills, readers must begin immediately to put into practice what has been read. They should not be discouraged if they cannot employ all skills immediately. Months of conscious attention to these skills are needed before they become a part of one's natural approach to clients and staff.

Nothing is as frightening to humans as the fear of uncertainty and ambiguity. When people have the opportunity to try out new communication behavior, forces within them tend to pull them toward their past behavior. Even if their old methods have been unsuccessful, they are comforted by having produced predictable results.

The dietitian who is serious about increasing her communication competence needs to swallow hard and stretch, forcing herself to attempt the new behavior. The time to begin is now. One need not have access to clients or staff. People can exercise these skills just as effectively in their personal as in their professional lives. Despite all the problems, improved communication is possible, and the professional who is aware of the problems and the recommended safeguards to minimize them is going to be more effective.

REFERENCES

1. Kirk, D., Shanklin, C., and Gorman, M.A.: Attributes and qualifications that employers seek when hiring dietitians in business and industry. J. Am. Diet. Assoc., *89*:494, 1989.
2. Owen, A.: Challenges for dietitians in a high tech/high touch society. J. Am. Diet. Assoc., *84*:285, 1984.
3. Eckerling, L., and Kohrs, M.: Research on compliance with diabetic regimens—Applications to practice. J. Am. Diet. Assoc., *84*:805, 1984.
4. Carnevale, A.P., Gainer, L., Meltzer, A., and Holland, S.: Workplace basics: the skills employers want. Training and Development J., *42*:22, 1988.

 5. Samovar, L., and Mills, J.: Oral Communication, Message and Response. Dubuque, IA, William C. Brown Company, 1986.
 6. Fielden, J.S.: Why can't managers communicate?. Business., *39*:41, 1989.
 7. Tindall, W., Beardsley, R. and Curtiss, F.: Communication in Pharmacy Practice. Philadelphia, Lea & Febiger, 1984.
 8. Matejka, J.K.: Opening doors: good relationships as good management. Personnel J., *67*:74, 1988.
 9. Anderson, J.S.: Blueprint for real open-door communication. Personnel J., *68*:32, 1989.
10. Gibb, J.: Defensive communication. J. Communication, *11*:141, 1961.
11. Davidson, J.: Shaping an image that boosts your career. Marketing Communication, *13*:55, 1988.
12. Haywood, K.M.: Managing word of mouth communication. J. Services Marketing., *3*:55, 1989.
13. Picus, S.S.: Evaluation of the nutrition counseling environment of hospitalized patients. J. Am. Diet. Assoc., *89*:403, 1989.
14. Bernstein, A.J. and Rozen, S.C.: How to cool it when things heat up. Sales and Marketing Management., *141*:66, 1989.
15. Field, L., and Knowles, L.: Can we talk? The key to a productive management pattern. Canadian Manager., *14*:21, 1989.
16. Nicholas, R., and Stevens, L.: Are You Listening? New York, McGraw-Hill Book Co., 1957.
17. Lewis, D.V.: The art of active listening. Training and Development J., *43*:21, 1989.
18. Buher, P.: What attributes does the better manager possess?. Supervision., *50*:8, 1989.
19. Ballard, L. and Kleiner, B.: Understanding and managing foreign-born and minority employees. Leadership and Organization Development J., *9*:22, 1988.

SUGGESTED ACTIVITIES

1. After filling out the questions below, join with classmates in groups of three to share and discuss your responses with one another.

A. What types of nonverbal signals from your instructor or supervisor indicate to you that he is getting angry?

    a.
    b.
    c.

B. What nonverbal cues indicate that you are getting angry?

    a.
    b.
    c.

C. List some of the nonverbal signals that you send when you are talking and someone interrupts you.

    a.
    b.
    c.

D. List some of the nonverbal signals you send when you want to signal confidence or approval of the other person.

    a.

b.

c.

E. List changes you might make in the room where you are reading to alter its climate positively.

a.

b.

c.

2. Write a two-paragraph description of a current interpersonal conflict you are experiencing. Be sure to indicate: (1) the behavior on the part of the other that has caused you a problem and (2) what "feelings" you are experiencing as a result of that behavior. Do not sign your name unless you want to be acknowledged. After the instructor has collected the descriptions, he may read them and either invite students to participate in role-playing of the situations, using the guidelines for supportive verbal and nonverbal behavior, or engage the class in a case study discussion of how the communication skills might be employed to resolve the conflict.

3. The following is an exercise that the reader might try with friends. The first person expresses the message to the second, who in turn expresses it to the third, and so on until six people have heard it. Ordinarily, the message is audiotaped and played back. This allows the participants to see the many ways in which messages are altered as they pass from person to person.

Message:

There has been an accident, and I must report it to the police. It is necessary, however, for me to get to the hospital as soon as possible.

The cement truck, heading east, was turning left at the intersection when the sports car, heading west, attempted to turn right. When they saw that they were turning into the same lane, both honked their horns, but each continued to turn without slowing down. Actually, the truck appeared to be speeding up just before the crash.

3

Interviewing

Most people have engaged in the interviewing process at one time or another. A person applying for a new position interviews the employer concerning the job opening and in turn, is interviewed by the employer. Interviewing is a skill used frequently in some occupations, including health professions. When one seeks medical care, the physician takes a medical history using interviewing techniques. The client or hospitalized patient may be interviewed at great length and by more than one person. A considerable amount of time is spent in gaining information from an individual in order to advise, counsel, or assist him. Dietitians apply interviewing skills with their patients, clients, and employees.

Interviewing may be defined as a guided communication process between two people with a predetermined purpose and an exchanging or obtaining of specific information. The interview is more than a question-and-answer session, although questions are the means of determining the subject matter of the interview. The goal of the interview is to collect valid data from the respondent while maintaining an interpersonal environment conducive to disclosure. These data include both rational and emotional reactions of the respondent.

Development of interviewing skills requires practice and repetition over time. Anyone conducting an interview for the first time may expect to feel quite uncomfortable. While some advance planning concerning the content and process of interviews is important, the warm human relationship that develops between two people differs each time, and no two interviews are exactly alike. Knowing the principles and process of interviewing, using them, and frequently evaluating the results can help students and practitioners to improve their skills. Developing listening skills is also important, as an effective interviewer must be a good listener. Skillful listening requires concentration on the verbal and nonverbal behavior and perception of what is important in the respondent's behavior. One listens not only for facts, but also for attitudes, feelings, and values.

This chapter examines the principles and process of interviews, the conditions which facilitate interviews, the three parts of an interview, the use of different types of questions, and the types of interviewer responses.

TYPES OF INTERVIEWS

For the purpose of illustrating the interviewing principles and process, two examples of interviews are referred to in this chapter—the diet history and the pre-employment interview. Although a full delineation of the content of these types of interviews is beyond the scope of this book, a brief explanation of each follows. For more detailed information on content, other sources should be examined.[1-8]

A diet history, obtained by interview, is an account of a person's food habits, preferences, eating behaviors, and other factors influencing food intake. (A diet history form is presented in Appendix A.) It may be used along with other data to assess the nutritional status of the individual prior to establishing a nutrition care plan or may be used to check for appropriate and inappropriate eating habits prior to nutrition counseling. Approaches utilized frequently are the 24-hour recall, the record of usual daily food intake, and the food frequency checklist.

In the 24-hour recall, the dietitian asks the client to recount, qualitatively and quantitatively, all foods and beverages consumed in the previous 24-hour period. The second method, the usual daily food intake, elicits a record of what the client usually consumes during one day. In both approaches, the portion sizes, the methods of food preparation, the between meal snacks, the times of day food is consumed, and the alcoholic beverages consumed require consideration. Neither method is considered to have a high degree of accuracy in assessing the nutritional status of the individual, and each suffers certain deficiencies. For example, the previous 24-hour period may not have been typical of what the person normally eats, and the usual daily intake this week may differ considerably from previous weeks and may undergo seasonal variations. An additional point is that the food intake Mondays through Fridays often differs from that of weekends. One method to increase the accuracy of the diet history is to use a food frequency checklist. A food frequency checklist determines the daily or weekly frequency of consuming basic foods, such as meats, milk, breads, cereals, fruits, vegetables, fats and oils, sweets and desserts, beverages, and snack foods. With the previously mentioned methods, skillful interviewing obtains more accurate and usable information than unskilled interviewing.

In the management of personnel, the dietitian uses interviewing skills with prospective employees. Several applicants for the same position may be interviewed to obtain information on which to base the hiring decision. The same basic interviewing principles are utilized, but for a different purpose. Federal legislation outlaws discrimination in hiring based on race, color, religion, national origin, sex, age, and physical handicap. Pre-Employment Interview Questions give examples of some interview questions that are permissible and others that are not recommended. Those responsible for pre-employment interviews should con-

sult additional resources to determine the content of questions that may
be considered discriminatory.[1-5]

PRE-EMPLOYMENT INTERVIEW QUESTIONS
Permissible Questions and Their Significance

In general, questions asked in pre-employment interviews should be job-related or
predictive of success on the job. The following are examples with their significance:
1. "Tell me about yourself." Gives general impressions.
2. "Why do you want to work for our company?" Tells what the person knows and
whether or not there is a fit with the company's needs.
3. "Tell me about your previous work experience." Gives knowledge, skills, abilities.
4. "What are your greatest strengths and weaknesses as a worker?" Gives skills and
abilities.
5. "What kind of work interests you?" Tells interest and motivation.
6. "What subjects in school did you like most? Least?" Shows interests.
7. "What was your grade point average? Class rank?" Shows mental ability.
8. "While in school, what extracurricular activities did you participate in that have a
bearing on this job?" Shows diversity of interests, interpersonal skills, teamwork.
9. "What organizations do you belong to which are relevant to the job you are applying
for?" Shows interests, interpersonal skills.
10. "What offices have you held?" Shows leadership ability, acceptance of responsibility.
11. "Where do you see yourself in five years?" Shows any short or long range plans and
whether or not they are congruent with those of the company.

Questions That Should Not Be Asked

Certain subjects can be the basis for complaints of discrimination on the basis of race,
color, sex, marital status, national origin, religion, age, and physical handicaps. For this
reason, the following questions are examples of ones that should be avoided in pre-
employment interviews:
1. "Are you a citizen of another country?"
2. "What is your religious faith?"
3. "Are you married? Single? Divorced? Expecting?"
4. "What is your maiden name?"
5. "Where does your spouse work?"
6. "Who will babysit for you?"
7. "Do you have plans to start a family?"
8. "What is your date of birth? Date of graduation from school?"

PURPOSE OF THE INTERVIEW

Prior to the interview, the purpose should be clearly identified and
communicated. A diet history may serve one of several purposes. The
dietitian may use it as a basis for calculating the individual's daily
nutrient intake, comparing it with anthropoemetric and laboratory data
in nutritional assessment. It may be initiated by a dietitian who has
identified a patient as being at high risk for nutritional deficiencies prior
to establishing a nutrition care plan. The history may be used prior to
initiating nutrition education to identify what nutritional problems the
client has, and to provide a baseline for gauging change. A history can
also help to determine a person's current food habits and the necessary
changes when instituting counseling on a modified diet, such as a sodium-restricted diet.

In the case of a job opening, the purpose of the interview is to
determine which applicant best meets the qualifications for the position,
and whether the opening is suited to the person's talents. The decision

of which applicant to hire is based on the interview and other sources of information, such as the application form, references, and physical examination. A secondary purpose is to "sell" the company and to give applicants information about the position and the organization on which to base their own decisions regarding possible employment with the company. The interviewer both gives and gathers information.

The dietitian should communicate the purpose of the interview to the interviewee. With clients and patients, one can also stress that the interview is necessary to provide better advice, service, or health care to the individual, and with job applicants, that it is important to find an employee who will be satisfied with the company and the position. If the purpose is clear and understood, better cooperation from the interviewee may be anticipated.

CONDITIONS FACILITATING INTERVIEWS

For effective interviewing, a number of conditions should be considered. They include the following:[9,10]

(1) attentiveness including attending to nonverbal behavior
(2) rapport
(3) freedom from interruption
(4) psychological privacy
(5) physical surroundings
(6) emotional objectivity
(7) personal context of the respondent
(8) note taking

Attentiveness. Attentive listening helps to create a climate in which the interviewee can communicate more easily. The professional needs to develop listening skills and to listen with empathy rather than to talk extensively. Listening is an active, not a passive skill. The professional assists interviewees in gathering and communicating their thoughts and feelings. To understand the complete message, the interviewer must listen to the verbal message while observing the nonverbal behavior, such as facial expressions and tone of voice. At the same time, the interviewee observes the nonverbal behavior of the interviewer. Frequent looking at one's watch, failure to maintain eye contact, sitting back in too relaxed a posture, frowning, yawning, and tone of voice all may convey a negative message and inhibit effective interviews.

Rapport. Rapport should be established early in the interview. Rapport is the personal relationship established between the interviewer and the respondent and is a key to a good interview. It deals with emotional aspects, the building of a warm and supportive climate, the release of stress, and the smooth flow of conversation in a nonjudgmental atmosphere. The interviewee should be put at ease and relieved of anxiety and uncertainty of what is planned, since people react more favorably in situations that they understand and accept. Examples of positive nonverbal behaviors include smiling, when appropriate, having an approving facial expression, nodding approval, giving undivided attention, speaking confidently, and making people feel that one is interested in what they are saying. When the individual has been seen previously, less time is needed to develop rapport; a comment on something from a previous visit may be sufficient. Excessive deference, although it may be flattering to the professional, may actually inhibit the development of rapport with patients. Patients, overwhelmed by the professional's expertise, may give information they think is being sought instead of medically useful information. Building trust in the relationship is the key to rapport.

If the person has been kept waiting for a long time, negative feelings may occur, and the person may appear angry, belligerent, or unfriendly. Recognizing that these emotions interfere with establishing a good relationship, the dietitian should apologize and attempt to reduce these feeling by saying, for example, "I'm sorry you had to wait so long. I was busy with another patient, and it took longer than I expected. I can understand if you are annoyed."

Rapport may be inhibited by addressing people by their first names, a practice usually restricted to close friends and family. This may be interpreted as lack of respect by some people, especially those who like the tradition of formal address or who are older. When in doubt, use both names, such as "Mary Smith" or "Mrs. Smith." A first name should be used only with permission of the interviewee, after an inquiry, such as "Do you prefer to be addressed as 'Mary' or 'Mrs. Smith.' "[11] Using the person's preferred name does not show excessive concern with tradition, but is simply another tool for promoting rapport.

Freedom from Interruptions. Freedom from interruption furthers the impression that one is genuinely concerned about the person being interviewed. The dietitian should arrange to have phone calls held, and if a phone call should come despite such an arrangement, the dietitian should explain to the caller that a conference is in progress, and should ask to return the call later. Upon hanging up, the dietitian should apologize for the interruption, and then resume the interview.

Psychological Privacy. Psychological privacy is enhanced by geographical privacy, but is not absolutely necessary for psychological privacy to exist. Since they may discuss private matters, the interviewer and interviewee should be alone. A quiet office without interruption is preferable. At the patient's bedside in a hospital setting, however, others may be present in the room. Whenever possible, arrange the setting so that the interview cannot be overheard, is not interrupted, and promotes the giving of undivided attention. The interviewee should understand that the conversation will not be repeated later. In a professional relationship, the confidentiality of patient, client, and applicant information must be respected. Anecdotes and stories should not be shared with others over coffee breaks, lunch, or at social gatherings.

Physical Surroundings. Other variables related to the location of interviews include comfort, distance between parties, and seating arrangements. These may either help or hinder an interview, and may or may not make the other person feel more like communicating. Comfort concerns proper furniture, lighting, temperature, ventilation, and pleasant surroundings. A comfortable setting where eye contact can be maintained should be arranged. Preferably the parties should be at the same head level, since standing over a patient lying in bed may trigger deference behavior.[11] According to Stewart, the optimum distance between people involved in an interview is 3 or 4 feet, or about an arm's length.[12] The most formal seating arrangement is for one person to sit across the desk from one another, while a chair along the side of the desk is less formal and makes people feel more equal in status to one another. Two parties seated without a table is informal, but when it is necessary to view materials, a round table is less formal since it avoids the head-of-the-table position. In general, the fewer the furniture barriers, the better. A clean desk top also removes distractions.

Emotional Objectivity. Emotional objectivity is another essential for effective interviewing. Personal feelings and preferences should be controlled and not revealed to the interviewee. The client should feel free to express all feelings and attitudes and in the process, may express some which are contrary to those of the professional. An attitude of acceptance, self-control, and concern for the interviewee should be maintained, with a desire to understand behavior, rather than judge it.

Interviewers should be aware that a professional relationship is most easily established with persons of similar socioeconomic status, ethnic group, and age, while barriers to the relationship may arise when these factors differ. The professional needs to learn about, understand, and accept the cultural differences, value systems, and lifestyles of other groups. Exploration of one's own attitudes towards those who are different may be necessary. The interviewee should feel free to discuss all matters without fear of condemnation, since any such expression will block the progress of the interview. A raised eyebrow, a look of shock or surprise, or an incredulous follow up question, (e.g. "You had three pieces of pie and two milkshakes for lunch?") may cause an obese woman to change or end her story. The dietitian should seek to understand the circumstances, not to pass judgment on them. The respondent who does not find the professional an understanding person is unlikely to converse freely.

Interviewers should develop an awareness of their own conscious and unconscious prejudices. These include not only racial or religious preferences, but also exaggerated dislikes of people and their characteristics, such as obese, poorly dressed, or uneducated people, aggressive women, meek men, highly pitched voices, redheads, and weak handshakes. Interviewers who identify their areas of intolerance may be better able to control their expression and avoid nonverbal behaviors revealing prejudices.

Personal Context. Interviewees bring to the interview their own personal contexts or systems of beliefs, attitudes, feelings, and values which must be recognized.[11] Concerns about perceived threats to health can be so frightening, for example, that they preoccupy and block conversation. The dietitian would do well to recognize that the respondent's situation may have both subjective and objective aspects. That a man has had a heart attack is a medical fact, but his subjective feelings about his illness may be equally important. Fear, resentment, anger, anxiety, dependence, or regression may be underlying emotions that interfere with cooperation. The dietitian's understanding of the psychological reactions to illness and ways of dealing with them may be necessary, and a sense of caring and concern is helpful. The dietitian may need to facilitate the venting of feelings and to acknowledge them before going on to the interview.[11] A job applicant may have been laid off recently from a position held for 10 years, which is a fact. The subjective way the individual feels about the situation, however, is as important as the situation itself. Anxiety, nervousness, and depression may be evident. The dietitian should be alert for nonverbal and verbal clues about the person which give a frame of reference for understanding.

Usually, the dietitian has some information about the person in advance, which may prove helpful in understanding the personal context of the interviewee. In the hospital setting, the medical record is a source of information on the social and economic circumstances which may influence the treatment—marital status, number in household, age, occupation, economic status, religion, level of education, physical health, level of activity, medications, weight, height, and medical history. In pre-employment interviews the application form should be examined in advance, since it contains information on education and previous work experience.

The professional should keep in mind that people may be suffering from problems of which they are not consciously aware or problems that they are unable to express. Job applicants may be nervous or apprehensive about the impression they are making. Patients may be worried about their medical problems and how these will affect their jobs or lifestyle. While the dietitian may be focusing on obtaining a diet history and giving diet instructions, the patient may be thinking about adjusting to a new disease or completing arrangements for hospital discharge by 2:00 p.m. By putting people at ease, by encouraging them to talk freely, by assisting them to organize their thoughts and feelings, the empathetic, skilled listener may ease or eliminate these problems.

Note Taking. Another factor to consider is the impact of note taking. The inexperienced interviewer may find it necessary to take notes, which may raise suspicion on the part of the interviewee and hamper the flow of communication. To avoid such concern, the dietitian should ask for the interviewee's permission to jot down a few notes, and should explain why they are necessary and how they will be used. The dietitian can ask, for example: "Is it all right if I take a few notes so that later I can review what we said?" Writing constantly throughout an interview interferes with both parties. The interviewee may be distracted, and the professional has less time for listening carefully and developing continued rapport with the person. Attention should be concentrated on what is said, not on writing. Notes should be as brief as possible, and eye contact with the interviewee should be maintained while writing. Interviewers should train themselves to remember conversations from a limited number of key words, phrases, or abbreviations. A breakfast of orange juice, cereal, toast, and coffee with cream and sugar, for example, may be abbreviated, "OJ, cer, tst, C-C-S" while a pineapple cottage cheese salad may be noted as "P/A-CC sld." Taking brief notes during an interview may be difficult initially for students who are accustomed to taking notes during classroom lectures, sitting passively and filling notebooks with what is said; however, this skill can be developed with time.

Comprehensive notes should be dictated or written immediately after the person has departed. Waiting 15 minutes or longer, seeing another client or job applicant, or accepting phone calls may cause the interviewer to forget essential information.

PARTS OF THE INTERVIEW

Each interview can be divided into three parts. They include the following:
(1) Opening
(2) Exploration
(3) Closing
The initial phase or opening involves introductions and establishing rapport, a process of creating trust and good will between the parties.[12] The exploration phase includes the use of questions to obtain information while maintaining the personal relationship, as the interviewer guides and directs the interview with responses. In the final phase, the interview is closed and any future contacts are planned. Table 3-1 summarizes the interview process.

Opening

The opening sets the tone of the interview—friendly or unfriendly, professional or informal, relaxed or tense, leisurely or rushed. Introductions may establish several conditions. Interviewers should greet the client, and state their name and job title, e.g., "Good morning. I'm Judy Jones, a registered dietitian." A smile, eye contact, a handshake or

Table 3-1. The Interview Process

Phases	Tasks
Opening	Introductions
	Establish rapport
	Discuss purpose
Exploration	Gather information
	Explore problems
	Explore both thoughts and feelings
	Continue rapport
Closing	Express appreciation
	Review purpose
	Ask for other comments/questions
	Plan future contacts

placing a hand on the other's hand or arm, and friendly face and tone of voice are supporting nonverbal behaviors. It is possible to be professional without being cold, distant, and formal. In the hospital setting, it may be necessary to verify who the patient is. The dietitian may ask, "Are you Mary Johnson?" If answered affirmatively, one may respond, "I'm glad to meet you, Mrs. Johnson." If the person's physician has requested the contact, the dietitian may mention this. "Did Dr. Smith tell you that he asked me to visit you?" If the client answers, "No," the dietitian should explain the fact that the physician requested the contact. A discussion of the nature and purpose of the interview may follow, along with how the interviewee will benefit from the interview. Stating one's name and immediately unleashing a barrage of questions should be avoided.

Discussion may center initially on known information from the medical record or from the application form of job applicants. Alternatively, the weather, baseball scores, a national or international event, or any topic of joint interest may be appropriate for opening the discussion. When the conversation appears to be artificial or merely small talk, however, the interviewee may become uncomfortable.

When interviewees initiate the appointment, it is preferable to let them state in their own words their problem or purpose for coming. The dietitian may ask "What brought you to the Friendly Company to seek employment, Mrs. Johnson?" or "How have things been going since we last talked?" or "When we talked on the phone, Mrs. Smith, you mentioned that your doctor told you that you have borderline diabetes." When interviewees are given the chance to express themselves first, the interview begins with their agenda, which is preferable.

Although it may be time-consuming for the busy dietitian, the opening exchange of either information or pleasantries is important and should not be omitted. Rapport, a degree of warmth, a supportive atmosphere, and a sense of mutual involvement are critical components in the interview.[12] Willingness to disclose information about oneself is influenced by the level of trust established in the relationship, and cooperation and disclosure are crucial to the success of interviews. Interviewees quickly develop perceptions of the situation and make decisions about the amount and kind of information they will share. Mrs. Johnson and Mrs. Smith form impressions of the dietitian just as the professional does of them. The purpose should be clearly stated prior to directing the conversation to the second stage.

Exploration Phase

In the second stage the interviewee is asked a series of questions. A good interviewer has preplanned and prepared an "interview guide," an outline of information desired or topics to be covered. The guide should not only tell what questions will be asked, but also how questions will be phrased in order to elicit the most information in the least amount of time. Topics should be arranged in a definite sequence. In a diet history, for example, the interviewer may desire information about beverages consumed, eating in restaurants, portion sizes, meals, methods of food preparation, and snacks. Put in sequence the list includes meals, portion sizes, methods of food preparation, snacks, beverages, and eating in restaurants. See Questions and Directives for Diet Histories. In a pre-employment interview the sequence may be previous work experience, education, present activities and interests which are job-related, and personal qualifications. Refer to p.42 for Pre-Employment Interview Questions.

QUESTIONS AND DIRECTIVES FOR DIET HISTORIES

1. "Tell me about any diet you have followed previously or are currently following."
2. "Can you tell me about any problems you have had with your diet and what caused them?"
3. "Tell me about the people in your family who eat together and any dietary problems they have."
4. "Who is responsible for grocery shopping, meal planning, and meal preparation?"
5. "I need to get an idea of what you are eating now. Please start with your first meal of the day and tell me what you eat with the amount."
6. "Tell me about your second meal of the day—what you eat including the amount."
7. "What about your third meal?"
8. "How are your meats and vegetables usually prepared?"
9. "We haven't talked about snacks between meals. What do you have between each of your meals and during the evening or before bed?"
10. "What times of day are your meals?"
11. "What about alcoholic beverages?"
12. "What about meals in restaurants? How often do you eat out and what would you eat?"
13. "To summarize what you have told me, can you tell me how many servings you eat daily or weekly of these foods? Milk? Cheese and other daily products?" (Continue with food frequency checklist)

While it ensures that information is gathered in a systematic manner, the interview guide does not have to be followed strictly. The interviewer should be thoroughly familiar with the questions and not have

Table 3-2. Advantages and Disadvantages of Questions

Kind of Question	Advantages	Disadvantages
Open	Gives interviewee control Communicates trust/interest Less threatening Tells what person thinks important	Time consuming May get unneeded information
Closed	Gives interviewer control Provides quick answers	May get incomplete answers Short answers force more questions
Primary	Introduces new topics	
Secondary	Elicits further information	
Leading		Reveals bias of interviewer Directs person to one answer
Neutral	More accurate answers	

to refer to them constantly. Knowing the purpose and significance of each question is important so that questions are not asked in a perfunctory manner, and so the interviewer does not accept superficial or inadequate answers. Asking a job applicant about offices held in organizations, for example, is an attempt to seek information about leadership ability and the acceptance of responsibility, while inquiring about plans over the next 5 years is an attempt to learn about short- and long-range goals.[13] Refer to p.42 for a review of Pre-Employment Interview Questions. To answer fully, interviewees must see how the questions are relevant to their needs. With patients or clients, the dietitian can explain that the answers to questions are a basis for nutrition counseling or education. Appendix B contains supplementary information on questions to ask and to avoid in nutrition interviews.

Using Questions. Questions play a major role in interviews. The wording of questions in interviews is as important as one's manner and tone of voice. A friendly approach in asking the questions communicates the desire to understand and be of assistance. The kind of questions asked should require the other person to talk 60 to 70% of the time. Questions that are highly specific or may be answered with one word or with "Yes" or "No" should be avoided initially, but may be necessary later to follow up on specific information. Knowledge of the kinds of questions to use and skill in using them are important to successful interviewing. Stewart classifies questions in three ways: open or closed, primary or secondary, and neutral or leading.[12] Table 3-2 summarizes the advantages and disadvantages of different kinds of questions.

Open and Closed Questions. Open questions are broad and give the interviewee great freedom in responding while giving the professional an opportunity to listen and observe. Two examples of open questions are:

"Can you tell me a little about yourself?"
"Can you tell me about your eating habits?"

At the beginning of the interview, open questions are less threatening, communicate more interest and trust, and reveal what the interviewee thinks is most important. Disadvantages are that they may involve a greater amount of time consumed, the collection of unnecessary information, and lengthy, disorganized answers.

Additional examples of open questions, but with moderate restrictions, are:

"What about your meals?"
"What diet have you been following?"
"What did the doctor tell you about your diet?"
"Can you tell me about your job responsibilities in your previous position?"
"How did you become interested in this position?"

Closed questions are more restrictive, that is, they limit answers. Some closed questions are more limiting than others, as for example:

"Who cooks the meals at home?"
"Can you tell me about any snacks you eat?"
"What skills do you have which are important for this job?"

Closed questions give the interviewer more control, require less effort from the interviewee, and are less time consuming. Disadvantages include the inhibition of communication, which might result if the interviewer shows little interest in the answers, taking more questions to obtain the same information, and getting answers that may not reveal why the respondent feels as he does.

Primary and Secondary Questions. Questions may also be classified as primary or secondary. Primary questions are used to introduce topics or new areas. The following are examples:

"Now that we have discussed your most recent position, can you tell me about your former job with Smith & Co.?"
"Now that we have discussed the food you eat at home, tell me about what you eat in restaurants."

Note that mentioning what was just said shows that one has been listening.

Secondary questions attempt to obtain further information or explanation which primary questions have failed to elicit; they may be referred to as "follow-up" questions. Interviewees may have given an inadequate response for many reasons, including poor memory, misunderstanding of the question or amount of detail desired, and the feeling that the question is too personal or irrelevant, or that the professional would not understand the response. Specific follow-up questions, such as the following, may be asked:

"How much orange juice do you drink?"
"What do you use in your coffee?"
"In your previous position, how many people did you supervise?"

Neutral and Leading Questions. Neutral questions are preferred to leading questions. Leading questions direct the respondent to one answer in preference to others, an effect that may be unintentional on the part of the interviewer. Leading questions reveal the bias of interviewers which they themselves may not realize. Listed below are examples:

"You eat breakfast, don't you?" "Yes, of course."
"You aren't going to eat desserts anymore, are you?" "No."
"What do you eat for breakfast?" "An egg and toast."

Two of these questions assume the client consumes breakfast, and in these instances, people will probably answer as they feel they are expected to, even if they usually omit the meal. Clients may change their answers on the basis of nonverbal appearances in the dietitian of surprise, disgust, dislike, or disagreement with what clients are saying. To receive uninhibited responses from clients, the interviewer should try to avoid these appearances.

The dietitian's language and wording must be understood by the client if successful communication is to take place. One does not need to impress people with medical and dietetic vocabulary. Complex terminology should be avoided, or used sparingly, and only when one is sure that the client understands. The following may be misunderstood:

"People with the type of hyperlipidemia you have should avoid eating foods containing saturated fatty acids and emphasize polyunsaturates instead."

When the interviewer senses that too many questions are being asked and the respondent may be developing a "feeling of interrogation," one may introduce some questions as a statement or directive.[1] For example: "How has your diet been going?" may be changed to "I'd be interested in hearing how your diet has been going." "How did you become interested in this position?" may be changed to "I'd be interested in some of the reasons you decided to apply for this position." This makes the interview more conversational.

Questions should be asked one at a time, and the interviewer should concentrate on listening carefully to the answers rather than thinking ahead to the next question to be asked. Further discussion of questions is found in Chapter 4.

Sequencing Questions. Questions are often arranged in a "funnel" sequence.[12] A funnel sequence begins with broad, open questions and proceeds to more restrictive ones. For example:

"Tell me about the food you eat during the day."
"What do you have for snacks between meals?"
"We haven't discussed alcoholic beverages—what about them?"

Beginning with open-ended questions poses the least threat to the client and induces a response. The person then volunteers much information, making it unnecessary to ask additional questions. At times, an inverted funnel sequence may be preferable. In pre-employment interviews, for example, applicants may feel more comfortable dealing with a specific question than with a broad, open one, such as "Tell me about yourself," when they are apprehensive and unsure of what to say or what the interviewer expects.

In taking a diet history, questions or statements starting with "What" or "Tell me about" elicit better responses than "Do you. . . ?" Examples include the following:

"I'd like to get some background about your daily food intake starting with when you arise in the morning. Tell me about the first meal or food you eat during the day—what you eat, and in what amounts."
"Tell me about the next meal or food you eat. What would it be like?"
"Now that we have discussed your meals, can you tell me about coffee breaks or the types of snacks you eat between meals and the times of day you eat them."
"We haven't talked about beverages. What about beer, wine, and alcohol?

These questions or statements allow people to tell their stories in their own way.

Questions that do not require a sufficient answer or may be answered with one word or "Yes" or "No" are less productive, such as the following:

"Do you eat breakfast?" "Yes."
"Do you drink orange juice?" "Yes."
"Do you eat cereal for breakfast?" "No."
"Do you like milk?" "No."
"How often do you eat meat?" "Once a day."

A series of short, sequential, dead-end questions from the professional's list of information to be gathered prevents people from telling their stories their way, and information may be omitted as a result.

In the follow-up visits, open questions should be broad to allow the client to determine the focus of the interview. Examples are, "Tell me how the diet is going," and "What progress have you made since we last talked?" The dietitian should begin discussion with whatever is of current concern to the patient. For opening questions, the dietitian should also refer to the records regarding the client's background and problems.

Bernstein and Benjamin recommend avoiding questions beginning with "Why."[9,10] While asking "why" may seek information, it may also indicate disapproval, displeasure, or mistrust and appear to ask for justification or explanation, for example:

"Why don't you follow your diet?"
"Why don't you eat breakfast?"
"Why did you resign from your job?"
"Why were you late for your appointment?"

Clients may react defensively or explain their behavior in a manner they believe is acceptable to the dietitian.

"Because I don't understand my diet."
"I'll start eating breakfast tomorrow if you think I should."
"Because there was no chance for advancement."
"Because the traffic was heavy."

If threatened by a "why" question and unwilling to reveal the answer, the individual may answer in an evasive manner, in which case nothing is gained.

Responses. In the verbal interaction of medical interviews, interviewer responses may be divided into six categories:[9]

(1) evaluative
(2) hostile
(3) reassuring
(4) probing
(5) understanding
(6) confrontation

Confrontation should be used only by an experienced interviewer. In the discussion of each type, responses to the following statement by Mrs. Jones, an obese woman, are compared: "I haven't lost any weight this week. I ate just a few cookies. The diet doesn't work."

Evaluative Response. In the evaluative response, the interviewer makes a judgment about the person's feelings or responses or implies how the person ought to feel. The evaluative response leads to the offering of advice by the professional for the solution to the client's problem. An example is, "I suggest that you stop buying those cookies." Note that the evaluative response leads to the giving of advice, not information. Little attempt is made to understand the psychological needs of the patient or the reasons that the cookies were eaten. The recipient of the advice has the choice of following it or not. At times, some people ignore advice as a means of maintaining their independence.

Hostile Response. In the hostile response, the professional's anger is uncontrolled, and the response may lead to antagonism or humiliation of the client. The following response is an example: "You're not acting very mature, Mrs. Jones. I've told you before to avoid all sweets and desserts if you want to lose weight." The hostile response may lead the client to a reply that retaliates: "How would you know about dieting? Look how thin you are." A vicious cycle of angry, hostile responses results, destroying the professional/client relationship. The fact that the client is anxious about the inability to follow the diet has been ignored by the professional. The dietitian who is frustrated by the client who is not following the diet should avoid responding with anger.

Reassuring Response. With a reassuring response, the client is prevented from working through her feelings since the interviewer suggests that there is nothing to worry about. Frequently, a client's expressions of anxiety are followed by the dietitian's reassuring response that things will improve and that the person should not worry, as illustrated by the following: "Don't worry about it, Mrs. Jones. It takes time to adjust to new eating patterns. You'll do better next week." This response suggests that the problem does not exist, or that the professional does not want to discuss it. Such responses make it difficult to solve the client's problem or to discuss it further. Admission of failure with the diet may have been difficult for the client, but it indicated a desire to discuss the problem.

Probing Responses. The probing response is an attempt to gain additional information. It implies that the person should give more information so that the professional can assist in solving the problem. "So you think the diet doesn't work, Mrs. Jones. I wonder if you could tell me a little more about that." This helps the person to tell her story, and further information can be obtained.

There are a number of probing techniques, which may be used to facilitate better interviewee responses in addition to secondary or follow-up questions. They should be nonthreatening and nonjudgmental. A brief silence may be effective, as may repetition of the last phrase spoken by the client or a summary sentence. Closing probes may elicit important additional information. Probing further in the case of superficial and vague responses, as well as probing for feelings about events, is suggested in the following paragraphs.

When a more detailed response is desired in the case of superficial answers, the following may be asked:

"Can you tell me more about that?"
"What do you do next?"
"Please explain a little more about . . ."
"Anything else?"

To obtain clarification if the answer is vague one may respond:

"Could you clarify for me what did you mean by. . . ?"
"I don't think I quite understand. . . ."

Paraphrasing is another technique to ensure that the information is clear and correct. By repeating, summarizing, or rewording what was said, interviewers show that they are trying to understand.

When the person seems hesitant to go on, the interviewer may remain silent, pausing for the respondent to gather her thoughts and continue. The professional should appear attentive, with perhaps a thoughtful or expectant look, but should avoid eye contact for the moment. While the inexperienced interviewer may find silence uncomfortable and embarrassing and push on too quickly, a more experienced interviewer realizes that too hasty a response may cause part of the story to remain untold or change what is disclosed. If the interviewee does not go on within 30 to 60 seconds, however, she may perceive the silence as disinterest or disapproval; the interviewer should commence before that impression can occur.

A technique useful in breaking a silence is to repeat or echo the last phrase or sentence the person has said raising the tone of voice to a question. For example:

"I follow my diet except when I eat out."
"Except when you eat out?"

Repetition, however, should not be overdone, or it has a parrot-like effect. If this is noticed by the respondent, it will inhibit conversation.

A summary sentence stated as a question also elicits further elaboration. For example:

"You say you already know the exchange system for diabetic diets?"
"You think this company is the one you want to work for?"

Other probes are:

"Go on."
"I see."
"I understand, Mrs. Jones. Please continue."
"Un huh."
"Hmmmmm."
"And next?"
"Oh?" or "Oh!"
"Really?"
"Very good!"
"That's interesting!"

"I see," "I understand," and "that's interesting" may give a feeling of acceptance and encourage conversation or elaboration of a point of view. "Very good" gives the person a pat on the back, and is another kind of acceptance comment. Nonverbal probes include giving a quizzical look, leaning forward in the chair, and nodding of the head.

Understanding Responses. In the understanding response interviewers try to understand the person's message and re-create it within their own frame of reference. People have more rapport with those who try to understand them, and this may lead to more cooperation on the part of the client. "You are feeling concerned because you haven't lost any weight, Mrs. Jones, and you are wondering if it was something you ate, or a problem with the diet." The understanding response assists the person to clarify what was stated. The person also feels accepted even if her behavior has not been perfect. The client will feel safe in expressing her sentiments, and exploring them further. The client who believes that the professional is an understanding person may cooperate more fully in the interview.

Note that the professional should focus on the client's feelings and attitudes, rather than only on the content of what is said. In the example given, the client may be expressing her feelings of disappointment with the diet, her dissatisfaction with lack of progress in weight loss, her frustration in changing eating habits, or her fear of the dietitian's response to the fact that no weight has been lost. The understanding response should be most helpful in assisting the client to recognize problems and to devise her own solutions. She may progress from initial negative feelings to more neutral ones and finally to more positive attitudes and solutions Expressions of sincere sympathy may assist in building bridges in personal relationships, especially in response to information about death, prolonged illness, discomfort, or other problems. A quick response may be "Oh, my!" or "I'm very sorry to hear that."

It is necessary to differentiate and understand both the content of a message and the feelings. To determine the content, one may ask oneself, "What is this person telling me or thinking?" Feelings may be classified as positive, negative or ambivalent, and these may change as the interview progresses.[9] In identifying feelings, ask, "What is this person feeling, and why is he feeling that way?" One may use the following sentence in paraphrasing the person's statement to verify one's understanding. The answer may be inserted into a format, such as "You feel ... because ..." Although one may have an incorrect impression, such as a feeling that a person is bored when the person actually is fatigued, the interviewee will usually provide the correct interpretation, thereby furthering the interviewer's understanding; this process demonstrates that one is trying to understand. To avoid overuse of the same phrase and sounding mechanistic, the phrase can be varied, as for example: "Do I understand correctly that you feel. . . ?" or "You seem to be saying that you feel. . . ."

Interviewee responses that suggest feelings about an event may provide an important key to the person's behavior. How patients or clients feel about their lifestyles, their diets, or their health is critical to dietary adherence. Food behaviors may be influenced by psychological, cultural, and environmental variables that are important to understand. Job applicants may also express feelings about previous work experience, relationships with superiors and subordinates, and activities and interests. Preceding a statement with "I think," "I feel," or "I believe" gives a signal that the statement expresses opinions, beliefs, attitudes, and values. Follow-up probes may be the following:

"Can you explain more about your feelings?"
"What do YOU think about that?"
"What do you think causes that?"

Confrontation. Confrontation is an authority-laden response in which the interviewer verbally calls to the person's attention some startling aspect of verbal or nonverbal behavior that the client may not have recognized. For example:

"You seem to have a lot of difficulty following your diet."
"It sounds like you didn't get along well with your previous supervisor."

This response challenges the person to recognize and cope psychologically with some aspect of behavior which is self-defeating, or to examine the consequences of some behavior. Confrontation should not be used by an inexperienced interviewer or when good rapport and a supportive atmosphere are missing. Otherwise such responses can become threatening or appear punitive, and will inhibit conversation.[11,14]

During the interview, one can examine not only what the person says, but also what she does not say. Are there gaps in the information which the interviewer should try to fill? One should also note nonverbal behaviors, such as tension, inability to maintain eye contact, hand movements, fidgeting, and facial expressions of discomfort, nervousness, anger, or lack of understanding. The nonverbal behaviors may be inconsistent with the verbal message, or may add to it.

While interviewers should adjust the pace of the interview to that of the respondent, they are also responsible for the direction of the interview. When the topics for discussion are inappropriate, the skilled interviewer brings the conversation back to appropriate areas. The patient talking about his wife or his children, for example, must be brought gently back to the diet history. A job applicant discussing a recent visit to Spain must be brought back to relevant topics. People who are especially talkative may ramble frequently, requiring more leadership on the part of the interviewer. In these cases, restating or emphasizing the last thing said that was pertinent to the interview and asking a related question may be helpful.

Closing

The third part or closing of the interview takes the shortest amount of time, but should not be rushed or taken lightly. A word of appreciation sincerely expressed, such as thanking the person for his or her time and cooperation, is a common closing. Another suggestion is to review the purpose of the interview and declare its completion. One may ask if there are any questions they would like to ask or any other comments they want to make, which may elicit important new information for which adequate time should be available. For example, "What else would you like to ask or tell me about?" The time, place, and purpose of future contacts should be mentioned. To a hospitalized patient, the dietitian may say, "I'll stop by to see you tomorrow to discuss your diet with you." With a client, arrangements for a future appointment may be made. To make sure that each has understood the other, plans may be paraphrased.

As a courtesy to job applicants, they should be told approximately when the employment decision will be made and how they will be notified if selected, for example, "We are interviewing additional candidates, but if selected, you'll hear from us in about a week by telephone." For those not selected, a letter may be sent thanking them for their applications and interest in the company and telling them the position has been filled. This letter is a public relations effort which may be handled by the human resources department. The applicant who hears nothing after an interview may react negatively or telephone again for information. One may signal the close of the interview by breaking eye contact, placing hands on the arms of the chair, standing up, offering to shake hands, smiling, and walking the interviewee to the door.

Interviewing is a skill, and as with other skills, it takes practice to develop. The inexperienced interviewer needs to plan in writing what topics need to be covered and in what sequence. Various types of questions can be prepared in advance in an appropriate sequence for the three parts of the interview. Physical surroundings and freedom from interruption should be planned. These conditions put the professional in a better position to concentrate on the interviewee and on the process of developing rapport, noting the verbal and nonverbal responses, and providing understanding responses with empathy. The interview session should be following by a self-evaluation to determine areas which went well, as well as those which could be improved for the next interview. Appendix D contains an interview evaluation form.

REFERENCES

1. Morgan, J., and Cogger, J.: The Interviewer's Manual, 2nd ed., New York, Drake Beam Morin, Inc., 1980.
2. Chruden, H.J., and Sherman, A.W.: Managing Human Resources, 8th ed., Cincinnati, South-Western Pub. Co., 1988.
3. Mathis, R.L., and Jackson, J.H.: Personnel: Human Resource Management. 5th ed., St. Paul, West Pub. Co., 1988.
4. Umiker, W.: Selection interviews of health care workers. Health Care Superv., *6*:58, 1988.
5. Olson, R.: Managing the Interview. New York, John Wiley & Sons, Inc., 1980.
6. Dikovics, A.: Nutritional Assessment: Case Study Methods. Philadelphia, George F. Stickley Co., 1987.
7. Jasmund, J.M.: The Diet History: A Tool and a Process. East Lansing, Michigan State Univ. Press, 1981.
8. Mason, M., Wenberg, B.G., and Welsch, P.K.: The Dynamics of Clinical Dietetics. 2nd ed., New York, John Wiley & Sons, Inc., 1982.
9. Bernstein, L., and Bernstein, R.S.: Interviewing: A Guide for Health Professionals. 4th ed., Norwalk, Conn., Appleton-Century-Crofts, 1985.
10. Benjamin A.: The Helping Interview. 3rd ed., Boston, Houghton Mifflin, 1981.
11. Wiese, H.J.C.: The Diet Interview: A How-To Guide. ACS 8. Chicago, The American Dietetic Assoc., 1984.
12. Stewart, C.J., and Cash, W.B.: Interviewing: Principles and Practices. 4th ed. Dubuque, Iowa, Wm. C. Brown Pub., 1985.
13. Lozez, F.: Personnel Interviewing. 2nd ed., New York, McGraw-Hill Book Co., 1975.
14. Engen, H., Iasiello-Vailas, L., and Smith, K.: Confrontation: A New Dimension in Nutritional Counseling. J. Am. Diet. Assoc., *83*:34, 1983.

SUGGESTED ACTIVITIES

1. Watch an interview on television noting the parts of the interview, techniques used, and verbal and nonverbal responses. Use the evaluation form in Appendix D, if appropriate.

2. Observe a television interview show. What types of questions are asked? What kinds of responses does the interviewer obtain?

3. Plan an interview guide specifying content and sequence. Write examples of various kinds of questions, such as open and closed, primary and secondary, neutral and leading. Which kinds of questions do you prefer to answer?

4. Divide into groups of two for role playing with each person interviewing the other in turn. When this is completed, use the evaluation form in Appendix D to complete an evaluation. If three people are available, the third may serve as evaluator.

5. Make an audiotape of a simulated or actual interview, if participant's permission is granted. Complete an evaluation.

6. Make a videotape of a simulated or actual interview, if participant's permission is granted. This will show both the verbal and nonverbal behaviors as well as any personal idiosyncrasies. Complete an evaluation.

7. Turn on the television set without the sound. Try to interpret the nonverbal behavior you are seeing.

8. Arrange the furniture in a room or office for an optimum interviewing setting.

9. Change the following words which are used by professionals into terms that a client can understand:

Fiber	Saturated fatty acids
Sodium	Polyunsaturated fatty acids
Protein	Monounsaturated fatty acids
Carbohydrate	Hypertension
Exchange lists	Fluid intake
Colitis	Osteoporosis
Gastric ulcer	

10. Directions: Read each statement. Identify both the thought the person is expressing and the feelings the person may be experiencing. Write a paraphrase statement reflecting the content or thought.

Write a second paraphrase statement reflecting the feelings, such as:

"You seem to be *feeling* (angry, depressed, lonely etc) *because* . . . ."

"It sounds like you *feel*. . . ."

"I hear you saying that you *feel*. . . . Tell me if I'm understanding you accurately."

Example: Client: "My friend and I are both dieting. She has lost weight, but I haven't even though I have been trying."

Counselor: "You seem to be *feeling* upset *because* your friend has lost weight and you haven't."

After writing your own paraphrase, discuss your paraphrase with others.

A. "I've had diabetes for 6 years. They put me on a diet and insulin injections when I first found out about it, and I check my blood sugar sometimes. The diet isn't too bad."

B. "I'm expecting my second baby. I never paid any attention to what I ate during my first pregnancy and my baby was healthy."

C. "The doctor told me that I can go home tomorrow, but I live alone so I have no one to help me with a diet, and I'm in no hurry to leave."

D. "Joan talks to people all day long and doesn't get her work done. The rest of us have to finish for her or we get yelled at."

E. "I've been working here for 10 years. Now you come in as a new supervisor and want to change everything around. What's wrong with keeping things the way they are?"

F. "How do you expect me to get all this work done? First you tell me to do one thing, and then you tell me to do another."

Note: An additional paraphrase exercise may be found in Appendix E. Role plays for practicing interviewing may be found in Appendix F.

4

Counseling

In recent years, the profession of dietetics has experienced profound changes as the scope of practice has broadened. As the roles and responsibilities of dietitians have changed, so has the need for knowledge and skills in different subjects. According to the Study Commission on Dietetics, one area of educational preparation of dietitians that needs greater emphasis is communication skills.[1] Role delineation studies conducted by the American Dietetic Association in the areas of clinical dietetics, community dietetics, and food service systems management confirmed the need for dietitians to be knowledgeable of the process of communication in general, and the techniques of counseling in particular.[2-6]

Today a considerable portion of the dietitian's time may be spent counseling. For a professional member of the health care team in clinical practice, counseling skills are applied in nutrition counseling, and for an administrative dietitian, they are utilized in counseling staff. Counseling can be defined as a process that assists people in learning about themselves, their environment, and methods of handling their roles and relationships. It involves problem solving, identifying goals, and change. Counselors assist individuals with the decision-making process, resolving interpersonal concerns, and helping them to learn new ways of dealing with and adjusting to life situations.

This chapter presents an overview of the counseling process as it applies to dietitians. Counseling may be considered a four-stage process, with the first stage involving the development of a trusting, helping relationship between counselor and counselee, and the next three stages concentrated on problem solving. In addition, approaches to counseling, classified as either nondirective or directive, are compared. The nondirective or "client-centered" approach originated by Carl Rogers is described and applied to the nutrition counseling of clients and patients. Guidelines for directive counseling are also provided and applied to the counseling of subordinate staff regarding job-related problems.

ROGERIAN CLIENT-CENTERED COUNSELING

The nondirective approach to counseling is often called "client-centered" and is best represented by the writing of its originator, Carl

Ransom Rogers. Dr. Rogers' theory was first presented in his book *Counseling and Psychotherapy* (1942), and was further refined in subsequent publications.[7-8] Although the theory is constantly developing, changing with experience and research, there seems to have been no basic change in its assumptions. The theory is one of the more detailed, integrated, and consistent theories currently existing and has led to, and is supported by, a greater amount of research than any other approach to counseling.[9] Rather than providing a complete description of the theory, the following discussion is intended to acquaint the reader with some of its more salient assumptions, particularly those related to the counseling techniques described later in this chapter.

Contrary to the common concept that people are by nature irrational, unsocialized, and destructive of themselves and others, a basic assumption in the client-centered point of view is that humans are basically rational, socialized, and realistic. All people, if their need for positive regard from others and for positive self-regard are satisfied, possess an inherent tendency toward realizing their potential for growth and self-actualization. Counseling releases the potentials and capacities of the individual.

One of the most important characteristics of this theory is the relationship it suggests between the counselor and the client. The underlying assumption is that the client cannot be helped simply by listening to the knowledge the counselor possesses or to the counselor's explanation of the client's personality or behavior. Prescribing "cures" and corrective behavior are seen as being of little lasting value. The relationship that is most helpful to clients, that enables them to discover within themselves the capacity to use the relationship to change and grow, is not a cognitive, intellectual one. Rogers states: "I believe the quality of my encounter is more important in the long run than is my scholarly knowledge, my professional training, my counseling orientation, the techniques I use in the interview."[10] There are four specific characteristics that Rogers suggests the counselor possess for the therapy relationship: acceptance, congruence, understanding, and the ability to communicate these to the client.

The counselor needs to be accepting of clients as individuals, as they are, with their good and bad points, their conflicts and inconsistencies. Only after clients are convinced that they are accepted unconditionally and nonjudgmentally can they begin to trust the counselor. Recent research, moreover, has indicated that trust is not a nebulous feeling that people have about other individuals; instead, it is focused on predictability, genuine concern, and faithfulness.[11]

Ideal counselors are characterized by congruence within the counseling relationship. They are unified, integrated, and consistent, with no contradictions between what they are and what they say. These counselors are able to express outwardly to their clients what they are feeling within themselves. Their verbal and nonverbal behaviors are consistent.

The counselor must experience an accurate, empathic understanding of the client's world as seen from the inside, sensing the client's world as if it were his or her own, but without losing the "as if" quality. This empathy is essential to nondirective therapy. The understanding enables clients to explore freely and deeply, and develop a better comprehension of themselves.

It is of no value for the counselor to be accepting, congruent, and understanding if the client does not perceive or experience this. The acceptance, congruence, and understanding need to be communicated to the client verbally and nonverbally. Rogers is definite in his belief that these not be "techniques," but a genuine and spontaneous expression of the counselor's inner attitudes.[9]

If the counselor has these characteristics and attitudes and is able to communicate them to the client, then a relationship develops that is experienced by the client as safe, secure, free from threat, and supportive. The counselor is perceived as dependable, trustworthy, and consistent. This is a relationship in which change can occur.

The administrative dietitian, moreover, working with staff, must be able to make the transition from technical professional to helping professional with a priority-oriented, tightly focused coach/counselor approach. This requires being a good listener, having intuition, providing feedback on both data and feelings, and providing inspiration.[12]

Understanding One's Need to Be a Counselor. Because one's own needs for being a counselor affect the helping interactions, it is essential that counselors become aware of their own motivations in choosing to help others. Generally these include doing good, having contact with people, earning a living, and fulfilling a personal commitment. Often, however, there may be deeper motivations as well. Helping satisfies basic needs; it may provide a salary, but it also satisfies psychological needs. For example, counselors may become involved in helping others to resolve problems or to satisfy personal needs for power, prestige, and the dependency of others. A counselor's needs do affect the process of helping others. For example, a counselor with a strong need to be needed might extend a helping relationship unnecessarily to gratify the need. Counselors with a need for power may take too much control over their counselee's situation or give too much advice. Counselors who have a need to be seen as competent can also interfere with the process of helping. If they tend to take personal responsibility for their counselee's successes and failures, they will become upset when counselees do not change. Counseling is influenced by the counselors' personal needs and motivations; therefore, it is crucial that counselors understand these needs prior to engaging in counseling to ensure that their personal needs do not interfere with their efforts to help.[13]

COUNSELING AS A FOUR-STAGE PROCESS

In accordance with the theoretical assumptions of nondirective counseling, many counselors, trainers, educators, and theoreticians consider counseling to be a four-stage process, with the first stage, "involving," including the development of rapport, empathy, and a trusting relationship, and the three subsequent stages referred to as "exploring," "resolving," and "concluding," dealing with the implementation of specific behavioral change strategies and techniques directed at the client's problem. Counseling deals simultaneously with both content and feelings. Trained counselors realize that only after the client's underlying feelings have been exposed and talked about can the content behind those feelings be discussed. Each stage requires special counseling skills that may have a particular utility and relevance at that stage.[14]

The first stage, involving, may be initiated by either the client or the counselor, but the goals of this stage remain the same—to give clients clear expectations of the counseling process and a level of comfort and trust enabling them to interact authentically and effectively with the counselor. The counselor's sincere concern and caring must be established during this stage or the remainder of the counseling process is likely to be ineffective. Concern and caring are often expressed in ways other than words. The old adage is valid: actions speak louder than words. If the counselor seems uninterested, the counselee is likely to feel uncomfortable and confused. Attentive nonverbal behavior allows one to infer caring and concern and creates the impression that the counselor is capable and effective. Counselors need to be conscious of eye contact, body posture, hand and arm movements, facial expressions, and vocal quality because these are the signals by which clients infer the degree of attentiveness, caring, and concern. A counselor's words can make a difference, however. They can encourage the counselee to discuss a concern with greater openness or they can limit the counselee's disclosures. One must learn a new set of verbal responses, each of which is useful for a specific purpose.

Stages II, III, and IV relate more specifically to the recognition and initiation of specific behavior-change strategies. Stage II, exploring, can begin once trust has been established. The goal is to discuss the nature of the specific problem in concrete rather than vague terms. The counselor's role is to encourage the counselee to enlarge on all issues and provide details related to the problem. In stage III, resolving, the counselee's goal is to begin planning some actions to resolve the problem. The counselor, mostly through the use of questions, attempts to collaborate, suggest alternatives, and serve as a resource to the counselee. The final stage, concluding, is intended to verify for the counselee the plan for subsequent actions. The counselor may reinforce the proposed actions of the counselee, but the primary task is to make certain that both counselor and counselee agree on what has occurred during the session and on all subsequent actions that are to take place.

DIRECTIVE AND NONDIRECTIVE COUNSELING

The remainder of this chapter focuses on the general applications of directive and nondirective counseling strategies as they might be used in nutrition counseling and in employee counseling. Counselees perceive the two counseling strategies differently, and their responses, consequently, to the two strategies differ as well. Directive counseling tends to be most appropriate when the counselor is aware of the problem and/or is concerned about the behavior of the counselee but the counselee is unaware of the problem or is avoiding acknowledging it. Nondirective counseling tends to be most appropriate when the counselee has insight and calls on the counselor to assist in the problem solving.

In the first instance, directive counseling, the counselor initiates discussion or summons the counselee. In the second instance, nondirective counseling, the counselee is aware of the problem and seeks help from the counselor. Counselees tend to be far more likely to become defensive and resist problem solving under the conditions of directive counseling. For this reason, counselors employing the method need to be especially sensitive to all verbal and nonverbal behavior, being supportive while attempting to explore the problem areas.

Unresolved employee complaints and concerns, for example, can result in formal grievances, serious performance difficulties, or legal disputes. Complaints fall into two categories: verbal and nonverbal. The latter may be expressed through careless or late to work habits, absenteeism, sleeping on duty, and horseplay. The administrative dietitian needs to be receptive and alert to complaints and concerns and defuse them before they become more serious. Feedback from and to employees can be obtained through regularly scheduled staff or work unit meetings, the company's performance appraisal system, or counseling sessions.[15]

Directive counseling probably occurs most often in the manager/subordinate relationship rather than in the dietitian/client relationship. In general, directive counseling techniques are used to expose poor employee performance when employees are unaware or unwilling to expose it themselves. Nondirective counseling is ordinarily the preferred counseling method when dealing with clients who need to plan and set wellness goals or with employees who have sought out the help of their manager or supervisor. Frequently, counselors employ a combination of both methods, but for discussion purposes, each is described separately, with the directive method described first.

Applications of Directive Counseling

Directive counseling is the method used for discussing job-related problems with subordinates when the employee is unaware of the problem, has already been warned about the problem and has not corrected it, or is aware of the problem but hopes that the manager is not. Often, managers tolerate abusive and inappropriate behavior from subordinates, rather than confronting and counseling them directly to improve. Among the reasons this often occurs are the following: managers may be afraid of handling the counseling poorly and making matters worse; they may be afraid of losing an otherwise good employee if the employee objects to being called in for counseling; they may be afraid of being confronted in return and becoming defensive themselves; they may be afraid of retaliation from the employee, either by his spreading stories to the other staff members or by his engaging in some kind of subversive activity on the job; or they may be worried about losing the friendship and respect of the employee. Because directive counseling has the potential to make matters worse, these fears are legitimate for managers who have not had training in directive counseling or in conflict resolution.

Training in directive counseling is essential for managers. Often, individuals who are extraordinary in their professional expertise or ability to perform a professional task are selected to manage others. Promoting technical professionals into management without first providing them with adequate training for the job is like sending individuals to bat with two strikes against them. Directive counseling, like nondirective counseling, can bring two people closer interpersonally, but only when the counselor understands the underlying principles and is sensitive to the need to preserve the self-concept of the counselee.

Managers who fear confronting employees directly and who tolerate poor work behavior may be creating additional morale problems among the rest of the staff. Resentment swells in those who are cooperating and attending to their occupational obligations. When they see others of equal rank and salary doing less or doing poorly and getting away with it, their own morale sags.

Directive counseling of employees is a form of discipline, and those administering it need to understand the concept. The root of the word "discipline" comes from Latin and means "to train" or "to mold." The attitude of the counselor needs to be that of a caring teacher who wishes to assist the other in improving. The objective of employee counseling is to change workers' behavior and develop productive members of the organization. After a supervisor has assembled and reviewed the facts surrounding a problem, these must be presented to the worker in detail. Next, the worker should be told how to modify the behavior. Finally, the worker should be informed of the penalties for further problems.[16]

As pointed out earlier, counselees are far more likely to become hostile and defensive in directive counseling than in nondirective counseling, because in directive counseling, they are "called in" rather than doing the "calling," and they may be more concerned with exonerating themselves of blame than with collaborating to solve the problem.

Employee Counseling. Employee counseling can be defined as the discussion of a work-related problem to eliminate or reduce it. Problems might include such things as performance and discipline on the job as well as the need for professional and/or skill development. Unless dietitians have advanced degrees with appropriate clinical counseling experience, counseling their staff should be limited to the job-related concerns mentioned previously and should not include probing into personal problems such as depression, drug abuse, alcoholism, and mid-life crisis. For such personal problems, the dietitian should provide referrals, recommending professional therapists, psychologists, or psychiatrists. When employee counseling loses its problem-performance orientation, it runs the risk of being interpreted as meddling or an invasion of privacy.

The administrative dietitian has an obligation to conduct work-related counseling sessions with employees. These should be held as often as necessary, assisting the staff in their professional development as well as dealing with career problems as they occur. Counseling employees can be considered a form of staff development and training. Recent studies indicate as the American work force moves on into the 1990s, that increased and ongoing training will become critical. In the future, a broader range and increased proficiency of skills will be needed by dietitians, including listening and speaking skills, creative thinking, learning and problem-solving skills. These can be taught and modeled during counseling.[17]

Above all, the administrative dietitian should not postpone employee counseling until the annual or semi-annual performance appraisal interviews. Allowing problems to accumulate and handling them all at one time may seem more time-efficient, but in the long run this strategy is generally ineffective, for problems may accumulate beyond easy resolutions. Dealing with issues one at a time as they occur is highly advisable.

Guidelines for Directive Counseling. Many well-meaning managers do more harm than good when they try to ignore the unsatisfactory performance of their employees. The best way to address and improve poor performance involves a 3-step process. The first step is to be ready to face the facts and recognize that waiting for things to change simply will not work. It is essential to make sure that the employee understands that management is seriously dissatisfied with work performance, that the need for change is urgent, and what specific changes in performance are needed. If the employee has objections, they should be carefully considered, and modifications in the requirements should be made if merited. The second step is to establish clear objectives and a timetable to meet them. The third step and, last resort, is to terminate the employee in an honest and straightforward manner.[18]

Except in rare cases, such as theft or intoxication at work, progressive discipline should precede discharge and should always be documented. New laws and recent court decisions have radically altered acceptable reasons for and methods of discharging an employee. There are several simple, preventative techniques by which employers may lessen the possibility of a lawsuit or position themselves to defend successfully against such action at a much reduced cost. A detailed account of directive counseling sessions, however, still remains the most effective safeguard.[19]

Involving Stage. In opening the discussion with the counselee, the counselor must be explicit in the desire to solve a problem rather than to punish. The dietitian's aim is to improve the subordinate, not to get an apology. One way of keeping the conversation from becoming threatening is to keep remarks performance-centered rather than to make judgments about the staff member. It is more supportive and factual to say, "You have been late 6 times in the past 2 weeks," for example, than to say, "Lately you don't seem to care about your job; your attitude is poor." Inferences are not facts. The manager could not possibly know the quality of the employee's "caring" for his job or the condition of his "attitude," but she does know the objective facts—that the employee has been late 6 times in 2 weeks.

Exploring Stage. Throughout the interview, the counselor focuses on objective facts, being specific about what she has seen, what she wants in terms of improved behavior, and what action she will take if she does not get it. If others have been complaining, and if the administrative dietitian is unable to document the examples from personal observation, it would be best to postpone the session until she has personal examples. Saying such things as "Some of the staff members have been complaining about your behavior" or "Word has gotten to me" will make the employee suspicious of co-workers and hinder the possibilities for future trusting relationships among the staff.

Resolving Stage. As in nondirective counseling, the counselor should provide adequate opportunity for employees to tell their side of the story, and their remarks should be paraphrased as well. As pointed out in the "Count the 'F's' " exercise in Chapter 2, not only do people not know what they do not know, but they easily fall into traps of seeing, hearing, and selectively perceiving what they expect to see and hear. Giving employees an opportunity to tell their side of the story and then paraphrasing it, and empathizing with what the employee is feeling, usually leads to collaboration in the conflict-resolution process. There may be extenuating circumstances that no one on the staff is aware of that account for the dysfunctional behavior of the employee. Having employees explain the problem from their own perspective may add significant insight and understanding.

When attempts at collaboration do not work, administrative dietitians can shift to another mode of solving the problem. They can use a win/lose mode, insisting that it be their way "or else." They may win the battle but lose the war if they use this mode too often. They can back down when they see the employee becoming defensive and allow the employee to continue the poor performance. They can attempt to compromise with the employee and agree to some exceptions if the employee agrees to improve soon. Too often, however, managers rush to compromise and negotiate behavior change with employees because this approach is less stressful than collaboration. The problem with compromise is that neither party leaves fully satisfied. Employees resent being called on a problem and being asked to change, and the managers resent that they have been unable to bring about the optimal behavior they had originally hoped for. In "real life," there may be times when the best approach is any one of the four discussed previously. Collaboration is not always possible, and so it may be necessary on occasion to use one of the others. Managers, however, need to understand that their first approach should be to try to collaborate on solutions with employees as a first and preferred mode of problem solving.

Concluding Stage. After an agreement on a solution has been reached, the counselor should describe as specifically as possible what the consequences will be if the agreed upon changes in the employee's behavior are not actualized. At the moment, less tension and a shorter discussion might result from simply saying, "You had better straighten up or else"; however, in the long run, it is far more effective to be exact. One might say, for example, "If you are absent without notice again, I am going to file a warning notice with personnel." The administrative dietitian needs to remember at this point not to exaggerate the consequences or to mention consequences she has not the authority or intention to carry out. If the employee does continue the dysfunctional behavior and the administrative dietitian fails to implement the consequences, the dietitian is implicitly fostering a norm that the others will expect to be applied to them. She is giving one extra chance beyond the final warning. Also, she risks developing the reputation of being "all bark and no bite," and of being an ineffective manager.

If administrative dietitians have been too lenient in the past, tolerating poor work behavior from the staff and avoiding confrontation in the form of directive counseling, they will encounter resistance if they suddenly insist that everyone must perform optimally. Staff members tend to assume that supervisors are partially to blame because they did not object to their behavior in the past. In such cases, counselors need to admit their share of the blame for lax supervision in the past. They need to acknowledge their own responsibility for not attending to the problem sooner, and then to work with the staff on ways of correcting the poor performance.

While verifying understanding is important in nondirective counseling, it is even more important in directive counseling. The tendency for employees to experience physiological stress symptoms from the threat of being called in by the manager heightens the possibility of their misunderstanding some of the communication. Both the administrative dietitian and the staff members need to paraphrase one another to verify that each has understood the other and that they agree on the final solution.

A final step that is appropriate for directive counseling of subordinates is for administrative dietitians to assure subordinates that they really do want them to succeed. An expression of confidence and support can help ensure successful implementation of an action plan that both parties have agreed upon. Rather than saying, "Well, let's see what will happen," the dietitian provides more motivation by saying, "I think these are the kinds of ideas that can make a difference." Employees should be reminded that they are an important part of the unit, that the manager does indeed care for them personally, and that their contributions to the staff are valued. If the action plan includes a multi-step process for improvement, it would be wise to set follow-up dates for meeting with the subordinate. Doing so not only confirms commitment, but also adds incentive to begin changes.

The processes of both directive and nondirective counseling are far more effective if a trusting relationship exists between the counselor and counselee. In the case of directive counseling between a manager and a subordinate, there is an ongoing and consistent relationship before the counseling as well as after it. The manager cannot vacillate between being unfeeling, bureaucratic, officious, and cold toward subordinates most of the time and being suddenly supportive, caring, and trustworthy during the counseling session. Subordinates begin inferring the degree of trustworthiness and caring on the part of managers from the time of their first encounter with them, with each subsequent encounter adding to their perceptions. Being a manager of other people is actually a "helping profession" in itself. The manager needs to lay the foundation for that trust early and continuously. Directive counseling is characterized by both a caring and a determined effort to correct dysfunctional behavior affecting work performance.

As in nondirective counseling, managers must attend to the supporting nonverbal behavior throughout the directive counseling interview. They should select a private place free of interruptions. The spatial dynamics of the location should allow the two people to feel close and intimate as feelings are being shared and help is being given to solve the problem. The manager needs to act, talk, look, and gesture in a manner that allows the subordinate to infer that the purpose of the counseling session is to change dysfunctional behavior, not to reject or punish him. Finally, the manager has to remember to allow adequate time for full expression of thoughts, scheduling multiple sessions when appropriate.

Applications of Nondirective Counseling

Involving Stage. When a client seeks out a dietitian directly, or when a dietitian has been recommended by a physician, the dietitian should first allow clients to expose their own concerns fully before giving any suggestions. The dietitian may be rushed and anxious to prescribe a diet regimen, but the regimen is likely to be ignored unless the patient has participated in the plan and has developed trust and a sense of confidence in the dietitian. An earlier chapter has elaborated on the necessity for clients to vent all of their concerns so that they are mentally receptive to listening. It is the nondirective counselor's responsibility to encourage "venting." Sometimes patients are ill-at-ease with professional helpers and hesitate to talk. Dietitians may need to learn to tolerate some silence and to be reassuring and supportive when they attempt to induce clients to reveal underlying concerns.

Because underlying problems are frequently emotional rather than logical and are not likely to be revealed until the counselee trusts the counselor, the counselor's learning to respond without giving advice or passing judgment is essential. This response is especially important in the case of the administrative dietitian working with a staff member. Employees' reasons for occasional abruptness with patients or apparent lack of interest in their jobs may be due to some illogical prejudice rather than laziness. They may be aware of the problem and may want to correct it, but before they reveal their underlying rationale they will certainly want assurance that they will not be humiliated or embarrassed for doing so. An employee who is frequently late to work because of family problems, for example, may have underlying emotional and illogical explanations for this behavior. Revealing these reasons to a counselor usually occurs, if it occurs at all, only after less honest but more logical reasons have been presented and the counselee is confident he or she can be honest without being belittled.

Exploring Stage. There is little value in counselors making recommendations until they have first fully understood the client's perspective and gained the client's trust. Clients become far more receptive to hearing their counselor's advice when they are certain that they have said all they want to say and that their words have been understood. During the exploring stage, the dietitian attempts to provide insight for the counselee by clarifying perceptions and attempting to discuss the problems in concrete terms.

Several techniques can be used to motivate clients or staff to contribute to the counseling session during the exploring stage. Small talk at the beginning of the interview can help relax the interviewee. The location of the interview, as well as the physical surroundings, can create different moods and should, therefore, be carefully selected. All interruptions should be eliminated during the entire interview period, and note-taking should not interfere with the client-interviewer relationship. If there are forms to be filled out, they too should be personalized as much as possible.[20]

In reality, not all clients, whether patients or subordinates, are articulate and able to express themselves. Although they may want to express themselves, they may have a difficult time exposing their concerns. The counselor can offer assistance by asking questions that stimulate full explanations. Two kinds of questions used in counseling are "open-ended questions" and "closed-ended questions." Understanding the distinction between the two is important because each tends to elicit a different response from the counselee. The use of directives or "encouragers" and active listening are helpful.

Closed-Ended Questions. Closed-ended questions are designed to be answered by brief responses (often by one or two words, or by "yes" or "no"). They are good for eliciting specific data quickly. Examples include questions such as "When did you notice you were gaining excess weight?" or "How many times have you asked to leave early in the past two weeks?" One of the limitations of closed-ended questions is that they do not promote any explanation or elaboration on the question asked and are controlled totally by the questioner. Also, they tend to be characterized by the concepts "who," "where," or "when," or they are statements turned into questions. Additional examples include "Who is responsible for your department's high turnover?" "Where do you tend to do most of your eating?" and "When do you find yourself craving sweets most?"

Open-Ended Questions. Open-ended questions are designed to encourage longer answers. They are good for eliciting responses in the other's own words, and for encouraging the other to enlarge on an idea and to reveal all concerns. The major difficulty with open-ended questions is that they take longer to answer and can be frustrating when specific data are needed and time pressures are present. They tend to be characterized by the words "how," "what," and "why." "How did you initially try to lose weight on your own?" "What sorts of treatments have you tried in the past?" and "Why do you want to be a size three?" are examples of open-ended questions.

The skill of asking specific closed-ended questions when a short and concise direct answer is desired and open-ended questions when a fuller and more subjective answer is desired is not natural for most people. The explanation and examples given previously may make it seem simple. It is not! Developing this ability takes practice, and both students and professionals wishing to increase their competence in question formation should make a conscious effort to practice it whenever possible. Over time, the skills become automatic and one begins to frame questions easily, either to elicit specific answers or to allow the counselee to move the discussion subjectively into other areas.

Use of Directives. There will be times when even open-ended questions fail to lead the client to expand on an idea or give additional information. The response may be a simple shrug of the shoulders, or "I don't know" or "I don't remember." When this occurs, there is an additional verbal response possible from the counselor that is often effective. It is called a "directive." A directive involves the use of a command rather than a question. It should not, of course, sound like a command and put the client on the defensive, but when delivered in a gentle, supportive manner, directives often do what open-ended questions cannot do with hesitant clients—get them to talk more. Examples of directives include comments such as "Talk more about . . ."; "I want to know what you think of . . ."; "Tell me your ideas on . . ."; "Expand on your thoughts regarding. . . ."

Use of Encouragers. In addition to the use of open-ended questions, closed-ended questions, and directives, counselors need to develop their ability to use nonverbal "encouragers." Encouragers are sometimes verbal utterances such as "Yes, yes," "Ah, ha," or "Hmmmm," or some other sound that indicates to the client that the counselor is listening and comprehending. These utterances should be accompanied by such nonverbal signs as nodding the head, leaning forward toward the client, and making other facial expressions that suggest interest, understanding, and the desire for the client to go on speaking. Frequently, the best way to get the client to talk more is for the counselor to remain silent when the client stops talking. After a few moments of silence without the counselor filling in the awkward moments, the clients are apt to go on talking if they have more to add.

Active Listening. It has been mentioned that prior to the counselors' asking questions, probing into specific areas, giving advice, passing judgment on the rightness or wrongness of the client's behavior, or disclosing their own experiences, they must first be certain that they have understood the problems as the client intends. This is done through the use of active listening—paraphrasing and responding empathically. After the counselor has understood the original problem to the counselee's satisfaction, and at each subsequent stage in the counseling process, the counselor needs to repeat the verification process through paraphrase and empathic responses. Communicators need to remember that they don't know what they don't know. Everyone is subject unconsciously to selective perception and communication distortion. For that reason, a summary paraphrase and an empathic reaction are appropriate at each stage in the counseling process. Besides verifying that she is understanding the counselee as intended, the paraphrase summary often provides real insight for the counselee. Just hearing the same comments in another person's words can help the counselee to see new possibilities and to provoke new insight.

The underlying principle governing the use of nondirective counseling is that when clients seek help, they are often the people in the best position to solve their own problems and to suggest corrective behavior. The job of the counselor is to help counselees to understand their problems more clearly and, in nutrition counseling, to make them aware of alternatives available for solving the problem. In nondirective counseling, the technique for doing this is called "mirroring." The counselor "mirrors" or reflects back to the counselee what has been said. When this is done in a supportive manner, without the subjective values and judgments of the counselor added, the process tends to stimulate creative thinking and understanding in the counselee. Part of the "supportive manner" for counselors includes the ability to make responses without sounding clinical. A comment such as "What I hear you saying is . . ." may be interpreted as sounding clinical and officious. It is more supportive to say, "I just want to be sure I'm understanding. Is this what you are saying . . .?"

Resolving Stage. Once the total problem has been explored and understood, the counselor and counselee can move on to examine the criteria for solving the problem, which form the framework for any solution. The specific purpose of this stage is to assist the counselee in setting goals and identifying resources for resolving the problem. As mentioned earlier, all stages of the process are primarily interrogative for the counselor. The dietitian moves through the stages by asking questions, not by judging. The counselor might say to someone with high blood pressure and a problem of eating too many high-sodium foods, for example, "What are some low-sodium snacks that could be substituted for potato chips?" To someone whose problem is eating too many high-calorie desserts and whose goal is to lose weight, she might ask about the possibility of selecting fruit for dessert for the next 7 days or the possibility of purchasing lower-fat meats for the next week.

Throughout the process, discipline is required of counselors. Often, they will be tempted to say, "Can't you see, this is what you need to do!" or "This is what you must do." The problem in being prescriptive, that is, telling the counselee what he or she must do to solve the problem, is that the solutions arrived at in that manner are not really the counselee's; they are the counselor's. Solutions that people have struggled to form themselves are more likely to work than ones "given" to them by another person. If the solution prescribed by the counselor does not work, the counselee can always say, "I told you so," or "You didn't really understand what I meant." Also, when counselors dictate solutions to counselees, they are likely to receive the response, "Yes, but . . ." from the counselee. The counselee tends to rationalize a reason for rejecting whatever the counselor prescribes. Although the alternative method takes longer and requires more discipline, counselors will be more effective in the nondirective process if they coach the counselee to make all decisions, whenever possible.

After the criteria for a solution are made clear, the counselor needs to help the counselee formulate several alternative solutions. This process may take time, discipline, and patience. Frequently, one solution is obvious, while other possible solutions remain in the client's unconscious. Counselors with discipline and patience can bring other potential solutions to the consciousness of their clients by helping them to focus on other possibilities and not allowing them to rush off on refining the single first alternative. Some open-ended questions useful at this stage are "What solutions have you tried already?" "What are some things that might help?" "Are there other possibilities you haven't yet thought of?" Allowing time for silent reflection on the part of the counselee during this process is critical.

After several alternatives have been listed, the counselor may add other possibilities. As the nutrition expert, the dietitian has knowledge and insight to suggest alternatives unknown to the client. It is important, however, to add additional suggestions in a way that leaves the counselee free to reject any and all. The difference between "Here is one thing you might consider" and "Here is what you need to do" is that if the former is accepted as the solution, the counselee considers it his or her own idea and will be committed to making it work; if the latter is selected, the counselee considers it the counselor's idea and is less committed to making it work.

There will also be times when the alternative selected by the counselee is obviously a poor choice. Here the counselor may be tempted to say, "Can't you see what a poor solution that is?" or even worse, "That is a terrible idea." Rather than pass negative judgments, the counselor would do better to assist the counselee in understanding the weaknesses in the solution. This can be done through the use of open-ended questions that will foster the counselee's involvement in evaluating the solution. The counselor might ask, for example, "What would happen if you tried that? Would the situation get better or worse?" In this way, the counselee, not the counselor, is rejecting the solution.

Concluding Stage. It is possible for a client, whether employee or patient, to go through the entire process previously described and not internalize the agreed upon solution and action plan. Because most people are not accustomed to being counseled, and because of the status distinction between the counselor and counselee, the counselee may feel a heightened anxiety, which causes him or her to distort meanings and block clear understanding. The client may be agreeing and nodding understanding when, in fact, nervousness is hindering clear perception. Another possibility is that while the counselee is nodding and agreeing, and the counselor is nodding and agreeing, each thinks he or she is in consensus with the other; however, as pointed out in Chapter 2, meanings are in people, not in words. It is possible that each person has interpreted the agreed upon solution differently. For those reasons, closure of the counseling session needs to include a final paraphrase by the counselee that includes action plans. As a result of the session, the counselee should have plans to do something to correct the problem, and both the client and the counselor need to be in agreement on what that action is to be.

For nondirective counseling of an employee who has sought out the manager to assist in solving a problem, a written summary including action plans is often useful. Counseling subordinates is a primary responsibility of managers and supervisors, and when they do it well, their subordinates feel closer to them, receive reinforcement, and tend to want to repeat the positive experience. Although counseling subordinates is an important part of the administrative dietitian's job description, there are other critical job responsibilities to be done as well. There must be some way for staff to distinguish between which matters are severe enough to take up the manager's time in nondirective counseling and which matters staff members can settle and solve themselves. Insisting that subordinates write up a summary of the counseling session, including specific action plans in the report, not only assures that the agreed upon solution and action plans have begun to be implemented, but also gives employees enough additional work to cause them to consider carefully the consequences prior to scheduling any subsequent appointments for counseling.

COMPONENTS OF NUTRITION COUNSELING

The overall process of nutrition counseling may be divided into two separate functions: interviewing and counseling. Interviewing, discussed in Chapter 3, involves the gathering of information and requires considerable training to elicit accurately the selective information vital to the counseling process. Counseling, per se, is a process involving listening, accepting, clarifying, and helping clients to form their own conclusions and develop their own plans of action. The dietitian guides the client's thinking to focus on goals, interprets and evaluates information, and translates for the patient the regimen prescribed by the physician.

Nutrition counseling is a process that assists individuals in learning about themselves, about their eating habits as a part of their total environment, and about methods of coping with their dietary problems. The purpose of counseling is to change behavior, which requires both learning and motivation. In the person with diabetes, for example, the purpose of nutrition counseling would be to change from current to diabetic eating patterns. For the pregnant woman, the purpose might be to add to the diet foods which meet the nutrient needs of pregnancy while maintaining appropriate caloric levels. Nutrition counseling involves deliberation and collaboration between two parties (the dietitian or counselor and the client or counselee) during which values may be examined, knowledge imparted and acquired, new ways of dealing with life situations learned, goals set, and decisions made. The counselee is assisted in setting goals and planning new and different actions.

Since the purpose of counseling is to promote change, or to select and implement new food-related behaviors, the counselor should note that change is never easy for people. Continuing with one's current, comfortable lifestyle and avoiding change represent the path of least resistance. The client's resistance to change may occur at an unrecognized, subconscious level and should be expected and probed by the counselor. Changing one's eating patterns is probably one of the most difficult lifestyle changes an individual has to make owing to the fact that dietary habits are of long-standing, have been associated with pleasure from the time mother offered the bottle or the breast, and may provide psychological relief for emotions, such as boredom, frustration, and stress. At the same time, food may be associated with status, comfort, security, and celebration.

A number of models of the nutrition counseling process may be found in the literature.[21-28] Models help one to examine and understand the steps in a complex process. The following model is a composite of those available. For further examination of nutrition counseling, which is beyond the scope of this book, other sources are recommended.[24,27,29] The components of nutrition counseling include the following:

1. preparation
2. assessment: dietary, behavioral, and physical, social, and cognitive environments
3. treatment
4. evaluation
5. follow-up

Preparation. The first step is to gather in advance data or information about the client that may have an impact on treatment and to arrange the physical environment for effective counseling. The physical environment was discussed earlier in the book.

In a hospital or clinic setting, the medical record is the source of data about the patient. Height, weight, results of laboratory tests, and medical problems should be noted. Mason suggests a number of factors which may impact upon eating patterns, including family status, occupation, income, educational level, ethnicity, religion, physical activity and recreation, physical disabilities or impairments (seeing, hearing), and place of residence.[25] Information that is unavailable from the medical record may be obtained during the interview. Dietary counselors are expected to know their clients physiologically, psychologically, socially, and economically; i.e., they should know what factors make their clients what they are.[21] The counselors must view their clients as individuals living and interacting in an environment that influences their motivation and capabilities for change.

A second source of data is one's own records kept from previous counseling sessions or previous contact with the client. These records should be reviewed prior to follow-up counseling.

Assessment. Since the purpose of counseling is to promote change, the dietitian needs to collect and assess data that indicate what changes need to be made and what personal and lifestyle factors may promote or interfere with changes in eating patterns. After informing the client of the purpose of the interview and after having established good rapport with the client, the dietitian may collect data from the client by using the interviewing skills discussed in Chapter 3.

The assessment may have a number of important functions. These include making both parties aware of the current dietary habits and health history, providing baseline information from which to gauge progress, alerting both parties to the demands placed on the patient so that realistic goals can be set, providing both parties with ideas for making changes, providing an opportunity to continue rapport, and enabling the counselor and client to work together on a plan for gradual changes that is congruent with the client's lifestyle.[27]

The dietitian may collect data on current eating habits as described in Chapter 3, and on the physical, social, and cognitive environments.[27,29] Behavioral assessment and cognitive assessment are discussed in later chapters. The physical environment includes where meals are eaten (at home or in restaurants and in which rooms of the home), and events which occur while eating (watching television or reading). The social environment, which may or may not be supportive, includes family members, friends, social norms and trends involved with eating behaviors (e.g., popular food customs of a bridge club, drinking buddies).

The cognitive or mental environment involves the client's thoughts and feelings about food, self-image, and self-confidence. It concerns what clients say to themselves about their food habits and life, since personal thoughts may or may not promote successful change. Some thoughts may be positive, such as "I love a steak and baked potato," or "My favorite snacks are potato chips and beer." There may be negative and self-defeating thoughts, or thoughts of failure, boredom, stress, and hunger. Examples include "It's too difficult," "It's not worth it," "I can't do it," "I've been on diets before, always failed, and regained all of the weight I lost," or "I'm happy the way I am and don't want to change." Further information on cognitions is found in a later chapter. Since behavior is influenced by beliefs and attitudes, one may need to explore these in relation to the medical condition, nutrition, diets, and health.

After the data are gathered, they should be analyzed and interpreted. Influences on eating patterns should be identified, and recommended changes noted. Changes may be thought of as problems to be solved with the client. This information is baseline data on the client prior to counseling and should be recorded later and referred to in future counseling sessions.

Treatment. Treatment involves a number of substeps, which include the following:

1. explaining the counseling relationship
2. identifying the problems—The difference between what is eaten and what should be eaten determines what the client is doing right and where changes are needed

3. exploring the problems, conditions, and circumstances, and setting of priorities for change with the client
4. setting goals for change with the client and eliciting a commitment.

The counseling relationship was described earlier in the involving
stage of the counseling process previously in the chapter. Counselors
may wish to clarify that the responsibility for change rests with the
client, but they are willing to be of assistance in solving problems and
making new plans.

Before problems are explored in the exploring state of the counseling
process, it is advisable to discuss with the client, show approval for,
and reinforce those current food choices that do not need changing,
i.e., what the individual is already doing right according to the diet
prescription. Problems—foods that should be omitted or foods or cooking practices that should be changed—may be discussed next, perhaps
starting with the dietitian's estimation of what is most important. The
conditions and circumstances surrounding food behaviors need to be
explored. This stage of counseling requires the skills of the helping-
process model discussed earlier: listening, questioning, accepting, clarifying, and helping clients find solutions to their problems and develop
their own plan of action.[21] Counseling should not be directed solely at
the client's knowledge, but also at feelings, attitudes, beliefs, and values,
which have strong and powerful influences on dietary behaviors.
Knowledge is a tool only if and when an individual is ready to change.[30]

At the resolving stage, one or two priorities for change should be
selected for the next week or so. Clients who are enthusiastic about
making total changes immediately are setting themselves up for frustration and possible failure which may lead to abandoning the dietary
changes altogether. The counselor should guard against this. Slow,
steady changes that will persist over time are preferable. The session
with a client needing a sodium-restricted diet, for example, may uncover
the following problems:

1. uses salt in cooking and at the table
2. uses some high sodium spices and flavorings
3. snacks include crackers and potato chips
4. likes bacon, ham, and salami
5. eats lunch in a restaurant
6. no one else in the family is on a sodium-restricted diet
7. wife does the grocery shopping and does not read labels

The problems can be reinterpreted into positive goals for change.
Laquatra and Danish suggest four steps to using goal setting with clients:
(1) goal identification, (2) goal importance assessment, (3) goal road-
block analysis, and (4) goal attainment.[31-33]

The first step is goal identification. Because clients will be more
committed to changes they select, the counselor may inquire what one

or two of the problems the individual wants to address first, by saying "What one or two changes do you think that you can you make this week?" When people play a significant role in selecting goals, they hold themselves responsible for progress and engage in self-evaluative mechanisms in the process. If goals are imposed by others, individuals do not necessarily accept them or feel personally responsible for fulfilling them. If these goals impose severe constraints and burdens, they can render the pursuit aversive and breed dislike rather than nurture interest.[34]

Goals selected by the client should be positively stated as concrete behaviors. Goals should be specific, reasonable, and attainable. A goal should specify what the individual will do or what one is trying to achieve. For example: "I will eat fruit instead of baked desserts today." The degree to which goals create incentives and guides for action is partly determined by their specificity. Clear, attainable goals produce higher levels of performance than general intentions to do the best one can, which may have little or no effect.[34] When goals are set unrealistically high, performance may prove disappointing. If the client selects problems numbered one and three from the earlier list, for example, these can be reinterpreted into goals for change as follows:

"I will use low sodium seasonings in cooking and pepper at the table."
"I will eat fruits and low sodium crackers for snacks."

Note that the positive statement of using low sodium seasonings is preferable to the negative goal of avoiding salt. It is easier to do something positive than not to do something.

Goals should provide a degree of challenge, and are standards against which performance attainments are compared.[34] To be realistic and reasonable, goals should be based on one's past and current behavior. The first challenge should be only a small step away from one's current behavior, not a major change, and be matched with one's perceived capabilities for achievement. The counselor may wish to guide the individual toward those goals which the client believes it is possible to accomplish. Hopefully, the client will have a successful change experience, not failure, if first assignments are not difficult, before returning for follow-up counseling. This is especially important when the individual has negative thoughts or a previous disconfirming experience. Each succeeding subgoal should present new challenges in the mastery of new subskills. Small steps lead to major gains.

A distinction must be made between short-term goals and distal or end goals. The relationship between the problem of goal attainment and effort expenditure differs for each.[34] Short-term subgoals that are challenging, but attainable with effort, are likely to be more motivating and self-satisfying. Self-motivation can be increased by progressively raising subgoals even though the long-range goals are difficult to realize. For example, individuals need to commit themselves to the goal of following the dietary regimen or goal today, rather than a long-term goal of never eating disallowed foods again. When the distant future is the focus, it is easy to put off the goal and decide to start tomorrow. Persistence that leads to eventual mastery of an activity is thus ensured through a progression of subgoals, each with a high probability of success. When self-satisfaction is contingent upon attaining challenging goals, more effort is expended than if easy goals are adopted as sufficient.

Secondly, after identifying goals, the counselor assesses the goal importance by asking, for example: "On a scale of 1 to 10 with 10 being the highest, how important is that goal to you?" Goals which are not perceived as important are unlikely to be achieved. Perhaps other goals should be set instead.

Most of the activities which we now enjoy at one time held little or no interest for us. Subgoals, if valued, can cultivate people's intrinsic interest, enlist sustained involvement in activities which will build new skills and competencies, and increase motivation and self-percepts of efficacy.[34] Those who do not set any goals achieve little change in performance. Strength of goal commitment is affected by several factors. The value the person places on the activity, the perceived attainability of the goals, and binding pledges people make to others concerning their future performance make a difference.[34] The practitioner needs to inquire about these.

In the third step, obstacles to achieving the goals are examined. "What problems do you see in achieving this goal?" "What might interfere?" "How do you feel about this change?" may be asked. It is important to discuss the problems thoroughly along with the impact of physical, social, and cognitive environments on the goals selected for change. Roadblocks may be lack of knowledge, lack of skills, inability to take risks, and lack of social support.[31-33] It is advisable to tell the client to expect some problems since some things may come up which were not thought of during the counseling session. If aware of the possibility of problems, the client may avoid abandoning the diet with the first lapse or obstacle. Supplying a phone number for questions may resolve this problem.

Finally, if the obstacles are overcome, clients can discuss what specific steps they plan to take in achieving the goals. For example, the goal of using low sodium seasonings may require their identification, their purchase, the acquisition of new recipes for using them, and the modification of favorite recipes to use them.

By selecting a level of performance, individuals create their own incentives to persist in their efforts until their efforts match the standards of the goals. They compare results against the goals continuously so that they know when they are succeeding. The personal standards against which performance attainments are compared affect how much self-satisfaction is derived from the subgoal. Feedback on progress of how one is doing is provided by cognitive comparison and self-evaluation. By making self-satisfaction conditional on a selected level of performance, individuals create their own incentives to persist in their efforts until their performances match their internal standards.[34,35]

The attainment of subgoals builds motivation, competencies, interest, and self-percepts of efficacy. Motivational effects do not derive from the goals themselves, but from the fact that people respond evaluatively to their own behavior.[34] When individuals commit themselves to goals, perceived negative discrepancies between what they do and what they seek to achieve create self-dissatisfactions that serve as incentives motivating enhanced effort. Without standards against which to measure performance, people have little basis for judging how well they are doing nor do they have a basis for judging their capabilities. Subgoal attainments increase self-percepts of efficacy, and self-satisfaction sustains one's efforts. Attainments falling short of the goals lowers perceived self-efficacy and the way one feels about oneself.

The dietitian may wish to know if there are others with whom the client can discuss the goals since a public commitment may make it more likely for goals to be accomplished.[29] Dietitians may ask their clients to keep records of food intakes and environments, which they should bring to the next appointment as a way for them and the counselor to learn about factors affecting eating behaviors, and as a demonstration of their commitment to change.[23] Clients' personal records, observations, and analysis of their environments will contribute to their personal understanding. The chapter on "Behavior Modification" discusses this matter in more detail. By the end of the counseling session, the client should not only know what to do and how to do it, but also be committed to doing it.[36] The client has to perceive and accept the need for change. Motivation for change should be explored as well as the dangers in continuing the current dietary patterns. Solely providing information about a dietary regimen is frequently not enough to interest or enable people to improve their eating habits. Counseling involves much more than distributing printed diet materials to clients.

Evaluation. Diet counselors may wish to evaluate both the success of the client in following the goals set and in implementing new dietary behaviors as well as their own personal skills as counselors. Counselor self-evaluation forms may be found in the literature.[27] Rethinking the session may be helpful. Records of the problems and goals, and of the factors influencing them, should be kept by the dietitian for future measurement of client change, and documentation of the counseling is completed on the medical record. A measure of success such as weight lost in an obese person is obvious. Changes in laboratory tests, such as blood sugar levels in people with diabetes or cholesterol and lipid levels of cardiovascular patients are more difficult to evaluate since they depend on factors beyond dietary adherence.

Follow-up. Frequent follow-up for reassessment and support is essential until the client is self-sufficient. Discussion at subsequent sessions should focus first on what went well, i.e., the successful experiences and subgoals reached. Such positive focus helps clients feel that they can have some control over their eating, health, and life, and builds a sense of personal mastery and coping ability. Records kept by the client should be examined jointly and discussed, and problems should be solved. Overlooking the records indicates to the client that they were not considered important. If things are going well, new subgoals for change may be established jointly. Support and reinforcement to strengthen desirable habits along with gradual, planned changes should continue as long as necessary.

Enthusiasm for change may decline the first week and even more in the second week, as problems develop. Therefore, frequent follow-up appointments should be scheduled. Dietitians in tertiary care settings who do not have the opportunity for follow-up may need to refer patients to dietitians in outpatient clinics or in private practice since one session with a client is insufficient to promote long-term change in health counseling. The minimal requirements for a successful nutrition counseling program and long-term change are active patient participation in the planning, execution, and evaluation of various nutrition change strategies, continuity of care over an extended period, and treatment strategies tailored to the individual's needs.[23]

COUNSELING AS A SPECIALIZATION FOR DIETITIANS

The concept of the intervention specialist is emerging as a challenge to dietitians who want to expand their role to include counseling patients on therapeutic regimens in matters other than diet. Articles have begun to appear in the dietetic literature suggesting that the dietitian can prepare to counsel clients in other areas. The concept originated in clinical trials, where dietitians effectively counseled study participants on adherence to taking drugs as well as on adherence to diet. Counseling in areas of stress management, exercise, and smoking cessation are other examples. Requirements of education and experience for intervention specialists are essentially the same as those for registered dietitians; the only difference is that additional training in interviewing and behavior counseling may be needed.[22] Intervention specialists do require, of course, more time with the patient than the usual one or two counseling sessions afforded to clinical dietitians. The dietitian needs extra time in this counseling approach to achieve long-term health behavior in cases of adherence problems.

Dietitians need to train for this role and to promote it as being of significant benefit to private physicians and their patients. One writer urges dietitians to educate the medical community about their qualifications as intervention specialists and their entitlement to increased professional responsibility.[22] The intervention specialist can also coordinate several different prescribed treatments that require behavior changes by the patient. Currently, drug, diet, exercise, stress management, smoking cessation, and physical therapy treatments are often prescribed with no provision for monitoring success of their incorporation into a client's lifestyle. Close cooperation and coordination between the patient, the intervention specialist, and other members of the medical team can help improve the quality of medical care.[37]

All dietitians need to be knowledgeable in the concepts, processes, and techniques of counseling, although they may apply them in different situations in professional practice. Some clinical dietitians, with added training, are expanding their roles to those of intervention specialist dealing with long-term health behavior problems in addition to diet, and they are counseling to achieve patient adherence. Chapter 5 discusses another approach to counseling, that of behavior modification.

REFERENCES

1. A New Look at the Profession of Dietetics. Chicago, American Dietetic Assoc., 1985.
2. Baird, S., and Armstrong, R.: Role Delineation for Entry-Level Clinical Dietetics. Chicago, American Dietetic Assoc., 1981.
3. Baird, S., and Sylvester, J.: Role Delineation and Verification for Entry-Level Positions in Community Dietetics. Chicago, American Dietetic Assoc., 1983.
4. Baird, S., and Sylvester, J.: Role Delineation and Verification for Entry-Level Positions in Foodservice Systems Management. Chicago, American Dietetic Assoc., 1983.
5. Kane, M.T., Estes, C.A., Colton, D.A., and Eltoft, C.S.: Role delineation for dietetic practitioners: Empirical results. J. Am. Diet. Assoc. *90*:1124, 1990.
6. Kane, M.T., Estes, C.A., Colton, D.A., and Eltoft, C.S.: Role Delineation Study for Entry-Level Registered Dietitians, Entry-Level Dietetic Technicians, and Beyond-Entry-Level Registered Dietitians. Vols I to III. Chicago, American Dietetic Assoc., 1989.
7. Rogers, C.: Client-Centered Therapy. Boston, Houghton Mifflin, 1951.
8. Rogers, C.: On Becoming a Person. Boston, Houghton Mifflin, 1961.
9. Patterson, C.H.: Theories of Counseling and Psychotherapy. New York, Harper & Row, 1966.
10. Rogers, C.: The interpersonal relationship: The core of guidance. Harvard Educational Review, *32*:416, 1962.
11. Johnson, K.: How to Create Trust. Broker World, *9*:100-104, 1989.
12. Luzaszewski, J.: How to Coach Executives. Communication World. *6*:38-41, 1989.
13. Danish, S., D'Augelli, A., and Hauer, A.: Helping Skills: A Basic Training Program. Trainee's Workbook. 2nd ed., New York, Human Sciences Press, 1980.
14. Kinlaw, D.: Helping Skills for Human Resource Development: A Facilitator's Package. San Diego, University Associates, 1981.
15. Pratt, H.: Employee Complaints: Act Early and Be Concerned. ARMA Records Management Quarterly, *23*:26, 1989.
16. Pizzano, J., and Pizzano, R.: The Key to an Effective Client Interview. Legal Assistant Today, *5*:61, 1988.
17. Cook, G.: Employee Counseling Session. Supervision, *50*:3, 1989.
18. McClenahen, J.: Training Americans for Work: Industry's Monumental Challenge. Industry Week, *237*:52, 1988.
19. Herman, S.: Ready, Aim or Fire? Personnel Administrator, *34*:132, 1989.
20. Kaplan, A.: How to Fire Without Fear. Personnel Administrator, *34*:74, 1989.

21. Ling, L., Spragg, D., Stein, P., and Myers, M.: Guidelines for diet counseling. J. Am. Diet. Assoc., 6:571, 1975.
22. Pace, P., Russell, M., Probstfield, J., and Insull, W.: Intervention specialist: New role for dietitians' counseling skills. J. Am. Diet. Assoc., 84:1357, 1984.
23. Zifferblatt, S., and Wilbur, C.: Dietary counseling: Some realistic expectations and guidelines. J. Am. Diet. Assoc., 70:591, 1977.
24. Snetselaar, L.G.: Nutrition Counseling Skills: Assessment, Treatment, and Evaluation. 2nd ed., Rockville, MD, Aspen Publications, 1989.
25. Mason, M., Wenberg, B., and Welsch, P.: The Dynamics of Clinical Dietetics. 2nd ed., New York, John Wiley and Sons, 1982.
26. Schrott, H., and Snetselaar, L.: Building Nutrition Counseling Skills, Vol. II. Washington, DC, U.S. Dept. of Health and Human Services, 1984.
27. Rabb, C., and Tillotson, J. (eds): Heart to Heart. Washington, DC, U.S. Dept. of Health and Human Services, 1983.
28. Wiley, J.: Growth process in nutrition counseling. J. Am. Diet. Assoc., 69:505, 1976.
29. Wilbur, C.: Nutrition Counseling Skills, ACS 5. Chicago, American Dietetic Assoc., 1980.
30. Hay, A.: Factors influencing the counseling behavior of clinical dietitians. Doctoral Dissertation, University of Tennessee, Knoxville, 1983.
31. Laquatra, I., and Danish, S.J.: A primer for nutritional counseling. In Frankle, R.T., and Yang, M.U.: Obesity and Weight Control: The Health Professional's Guide to Understanding and Treatment. Rockville, MD, Aspen Publications, 1988.
32. D'Augelli, A.R., D'Augelli, J.F., and Danish, S.J.: Helping Others. California, Brooks/Cole Publishing Co., 1981.
33. Laquatra, I., D'Augelli, A.R., and Danish, S.J.: Helping Skills II: Life Development Intervention Leader's Manual. New York, Human Sciences Press, 1983.
34. Bandura, A.: Social Foundations of Thought and Action: A Social Cognitive Theory. Englewood Cliffs, NJ, Prentice-Hall, 1986.
35. Bandura, A., and Cervone, D.: Self-evaluative and self-efficacy mechanisms governing the motivational effects of goal systems. J. Personality Social Psych 45:1017, 1983.
36. Mahoney, M., and Caggiula, A.: Applying behavioral methods to nutritional counseling. J. Am. Diet. Assoc., 72:372, 1978.
37. Franz, M.: The dietitian: A key member of the diabetes team. J. Am. Diet. Assoc., 84:285, 1984.

SUGGESTED ACTIVITIES

1. During the next week, make arrangements to view dietitian's counseling session, noting particularly what occurs during Stage I, "Involving." What behavior on the part of the dietitian facilitates the building of rapport and trust?

2. During the following week, make three efforts to express caring for another, using nonverbal behavior. What do you do, and how does the other respond?

3. Using a videotape recorder, meet with another individual and record 10 minutes of interaction and conversation. Comment on the quality of your verbal and nonverbal behavior. What kind of messages might one infer from your demeanor?

4. In groups of three, develop a conversation around the topics presented in this chapter. Before one person can respond to what another

has said, however, he will need to paraphrase to the other's satisfaction what the other has just said.

5. During the next week, practice paraphrasing after others talk. What reactions do you get? Does you paraphrasing tend to cause the other to go on talking?

6. In round-robin groups of 5, each person expresses a statement, and the person to the right should attempt to identify a feeling expressed in the statement. After three rounds, discuss the reactions of the group to the attempts at empathizing.

7. Write both a paraphrase and empathic comment to the following comments made by a counselee:

A. I feel awkward discussing my eating habits. I feel I must be disgusting to you.

B. People tend to think I'm jolly, but I don't believe they take me seriously.

C. I am at a point now where I don't believe I will ever lose the weight.

8. Form triads consisting of a counselor, counselee, and observer. Each individual should take a turn in each of the roles for 7 minutes. The counselee should play the role of an obese client, and the counselor should use paraphrasing and empathizing, along with open and closed questions, to facilitate disclosure and problem solving. After each round, the observer should share his reactions to the counselor's approach and encourage feedback from the counselee to the counselor. From the counselee's perspective, what did the counselor do that helped their interaction; what did he do that hindered it?

9. Write an open-ended question for each of the statements below:

A. I never have any fun at a family gathering anymore. Being on this diet has taken the fun out of my life.

B. I dislike my supervisor at work. No matter what I do, he criticizes me.

C. Since I developed these health problems, it seems that all I do is think about my diet.

10. After each of the statements below, write responses in the form of a closed-ended question, an open-ended question, or a directive.

A. My work situation is impossible. It seems that I'm the scapegoat for everybody. I'm beginning to wonder if I should consider looking for another job.

B. It doesn't seem fair to me that I should have to work weekends when the staff members who have been here only 2 years longer don't have to.

C. It seems easy every morning to promise myself that today I will stick to the program you designed for me. By noon, however, I begin thinking that I'll never be able to comply with the diet for the rest of my life, so why bother?

11. In groups of two, take turns discussing a life-style problem and restating it as a goal for change.

A. Think of a life-style problem the counselee would like to change, such as eat too much, eat the wrong foods, exercise too little, doesn't study enough, need to budget better, drink too much, smoke too much, and the like.

B. Help the person discuss the problem and the conditions and circumstances surrounding it. Then have the counselee restate the problem as a positive goal for change, i.e., "I will. . . ."

C. Assess the importance of the goal on a scale of 1 to 10, with 10 being the highest importance. Revise the goal if necessary.

D. Ask about and discuss the obstacles and barriers to accomplishing the goal and try to have the person resolve these.

E. Have the person list the steps to achieving the goal. What will the person do, and when will it be done?

Note: Appendix F contains role plays that may be used to practice counseling.

5   Ann B. Williams, Ph.D.

Behavior Modification

There is one characteristic that is common to all living organisms—behavior. The behavior of some organisms is simple, limited, and to many of us, quite unexciting. The behavior of other organisms, such as human beings, is complex, sophisticated, extensive, and to most people, quite exciting and interesting, however difficult it may be to understand. One of the first questions that a scientist asks in order to understand an organism is, "What does it do?"

Interesting and complex behaviors usually are based on a combination of inherited and acquired characteristics. The inherited characteristics cannot be changed—one does not have the option of choosing one's biological parents and thus, one's genetic inheritance. The acquired characteristics, those shaped by one's environment and experience, however, are amenable to change.

According to Stunkard, "People are best described by their behavior—what they think, feel, and do in specific situations."[1] Since some behaviors are learned or acquired, these behaviors can be changed or modified. One of the challenges of the discipline of psychology is to establish the principles that underlie the process of behavioral change or modification.

The approach of psychologists to this task has been primarily based on environmental analysis. Certain behaviors are thought to be acquired or learned through interaction with the environment. Because of this strong environmental orientation, much attention has been devoted to the study of the basic principles of learning. The position taken is that if many behaviors could be, and indeed, are learned, then these same behaviors could also be unlearned. There is tremendous potential for behavioral change.

This chapter reviews the principles of learning and behavior modification that have evolved from research studies. Included are classical conditioning, operant or instrumental conditioning based on positive reinforcement or rewards, and observational learning or modeling after others. The role of cognitions, the individual's mental perceptions of events, and their effect on behavior, a newer area of research, is mentioned and covered in more detail in the next chapter.

In behavior modification the therapist attempts to alter previously learned behavior or to encourage the development of new behavior.

Food preferences and eating behaviors have deep roots within the individual and may be highly resistant to change. Furnishing information concerning what to eat frequently is insufficient in promoting alterations in eating behaviors or adherence to modified diets. In addition to information on nutrition, behavior modification principles may be used as they offer the dietitian another approach to counseling.

Applications of behavior modification principles as part of the treatment of various nutritional problems are examined in this chapter. One of the earliest and the most frequently used application, was in the treatment of obesity. Therapy for eating disorders, such as anorexia nervosa and bulimia, and inappropriate eating behaviors related to diabetes mellitus and cardiovascular diseases are other potential uses of behavior modification.

In human resource management, supervisors may be interested in altering the behavior of subordinates and encouraging the development of new behaviors. More effective interaction between peers and superiors may also be a goal. Although the term behavior modification in the context of human resource management may sound manipulative, the principles may be used by an honest and understanding supervisor who has shared with employees the goals of the process. These learning principles are the basis for the advice in the book, *The One Minute Manager*.[2] Modeling is a technique that frequently is used in employee training programs.

CLASSICAL CONDITIONING

The methods of behavior modification are based on principles of learning that, for the most part, have been discovered in the experimental laboratory. According to Hill, the best known animals in the history of psychology were the dogs housed in the laboratory of Ivan Pavlov, the Russian physiologist, who was conducting research on digestive processes.[3] Serendipitously, Pavlov noted that his laboratory animals salivated not only when food was presented, but also when the laboratory assistant, who regularly fed them, came into the room; at times they even salivated at the sound of the laboratory door opening. Pavlov spent the rest of his life investigating a type of learning based on association, now known as classical conditioning.

Pavlov realized immediately that the response of salivation to laboratory assistants and noisy doors was not a part of the physiological makeup of the dog. The dogs were salivating when events occurred that had regularly and repeatedly come before the presentation of their food. An association was apparently being formed between some event and the future appearance of food.

Pavlov noted that certain environmental events or stimuli would reliably trigger or elicit a particular behavioral response. For example, food in a dog's mouth would reliably produce saliva. The triggering event (food in the mouth) became known as the unconditioned stimulus (US) while the response triggered (salivation) was called the unconditioned response (UR). This relationship was built into the organism, and hence, unconditioned. Conditioning occurs, then, when some other stimulus (a neutral stimulus) that originally does not trigger the particular response (salivation), eventually comes to produce that response. This occurs by pairing the originally neutral stimulus with the unconditioned stimulus. When conditioning has occurred, the conditioned stimulus (CS), which was originally neutral, produces the same, or a very similar, response as the US. In the example, the CS was the presence of the laboratory assistant. Pavlov showed that bells, tones, lights, and many other stimuli could serve as the CS and could come to elicit the response of salivation, which is labeled a conditioned response (CR) once it is triggered by or produced by a CS.

Many different types of responses have been found to be responsive to classical conditioning principles. Not only reflexive responses, such as salivation and eye blink, but complex emotional responses can be classically conditioned, as illustrated by the following example. The heart pounds and beads of perspiration appear on the forehead as one hears the siren of an ambulance approaching a neighbor's home. The same phenomenon may occur when the teacher passes out examination questions. Try to construct a scenario to account for this response in terms of classical conditioning principles, or think of other situations where classical conditioning might play a part in human behavior or emotional responses.

OPERANT CONDITIONING

At about the same time that Pavlov was delineating the principles of classical conditioning, a young American scientist, Edward Thorndike, was pursuing the investigation of learning principles from another perspective. Thorndike used many types of animals in his research and designed and constructed "puzzle boxes" for cats. A hungry cat was placed inside the box with food located outside. To have access to the food, the cat had to solve the puzzle of how to escape from the box. Thorndike observed that the cats made trial-and-error responses until escape was achieved and the food consumed. Gradually, the time required to solve the puzzle decreased, and the behavior that achieved success in solving the puzzle became dominant, while nonsuccessful behaviors were eliminated.

Thorndike proposed an explanation for this phenomenon based on a principle he called the Law of Effect. The Law of Effect stated that behaviors could be changed by their consequences. Responses that were followed by satisfying consequences would be stamped in or strengthened. Behaviors not followed by satisfying consequences, or behaviors followed by annoying consequences, would be weakened and less likely to occur in the future. Thorndike's Law of Effect led to much research in principles of learning and formed the foundation for the study of operant or instrumental conditioning, which is learning or conditioning based on reinforcement or reward.

The focal point of research on the Law of Effect is the relationship between responses, or behaviors, and the consequences of those behaviors. Schwartz described four types of response-consequence outcomes.[4] First, responses or behaviors may produce positive outcomes, a consequence known as positive reinforcement. An example would be the lavish praise and attention one receives after achieving a svelte new figure. Second, responses may produce negative outcomes; this consequence is known as punishment. Punishment decreases the future likelihood of a response. Examples of punishment include the receipt of a traffic ticket for an improper left turn and the inability to fit into a favorite, expensive outfit after gaining weight. Third, responses may result in the elimination or removal of aversive stimuli that are already present. This consequence is known as negative reinforcement or escape, and it is similar to positive reinforcement in that it increases the future likelihood or probability of a response. Examples include escaping devastating cold by going into a heated building, escaping a poor television show by changing channels, and escaping unfavorable comparisons with others by shaping up and trimming down. Finally, responses may prevent an aversive event from occurring. Examples include avoiding the cold by staying indoors and avoiding unfavorable comparisons with the figures of others by maintaining a trim figure. The avoidance of aversive events increases the future likelihood of the response, as does positive reinforcement. Behaviors that are not positively reinforced or negatively reinforced, leading to escape or avoidance of aversive stimuli, should not increase in strength, and with continued nonreinforcement, should decrease in strength.

Later behaviorists continued where Thorndike concluded. B.F. Skinner is best known for his championing of a set of methods and terms to explain behavior on the basis of the principles of operant conditioning. Skinner developed a situation in which behavior could be observed in discrete units and subsequently recorded. This situation was an operant chamber, which has been dubbed a "Skinner box." The lever presses of rats and key pecks of pigeons have been the most frequently studied responses. Skinner's enthusiasm for the behavioristic approach was not limited to lower animals, however, for he proposed wide application for the principles that were established. In recent years, the behavioristic approach has become an increasingly important practical technique in many settings, such as classrooms, mental hospitals, prisons, clinics, the work place, and self-management situations.

MODELING

In addition to classical and operant conditioning as modes of behavior change, a third form of learning is known as observational learning, or modeling. Learning by modeling involves the observation of some behavior or pattern of behaving, which is followed later by the performance of either the same or some similar behavior. Albert Bandura is associated with this method of learning by modeling.[5]

The model being observed may be either another person or a representation of the pattern of behaving. The model, then, could be another human, an animal, or some symbolic representation that uses verbal stimuli, such as films, television, or other media presentations.

The effectiveness of learning by modeling appears to be directly related to certain characteristics of the model. The two characteristics found to be most relevant are the observer's similarity to the model and the status of the model. The more similar the characteristics of the model are to those of the observer, the higher is the probability that learning by modeling will occur. Research has shown that models with greater status, prestige, or expertise are more likely to be imitated by the observer than models lacking these characteristics. Golfers, for example, are more likely to imitate the stance and swing of a player of the caliber of Hale Irvin, (1990 U.S. Open champion and now a three time winner of the U.S. Open) than the techniques of an unknown player. Certainly, this fact has been noted and capitalized on by movie and television stars and other well-known persons who have produced books and videotapes of their fitness/exercise/nutrition programs. Many people will model their behavior after the person with "status" even though equally effective or superior programs could be developed by relatively unknown, but professionally trained, nutritionists and exercise physiologists.

To take advantage of modeling, clinical dietitians may try sharing success stories of people who have made permanent dietary modifications for the benefit of their health. In group therapy, clients who have followed their diets may serve as models for others. The dietitian may be viewed as a model by the client. As a result, in counseling obese people, the counselor should be of normal weight, and dietitians should be following the normal nutrition recommendations that they give to others.

Behavior modeling is used in employee training programs to teach basic supervisory techniques, selling skills, and a variety of other verbal skills through observation of films and videotapes. In assigning a new employee to work with a current employee, the latter serves as a model. Managers should make sure that their own behaviors are exemplary of what they expect of subordinates.[6] If the supervisor adds an extra 10 minutes to the allowed time for a coffee break, for example, employees may model after the example set.

There is no doubt that a great deal of human learning or behavior change is due to modeling, even though traditionally, emphasis has been placed upon the stimulus-response (or behavior-consequence) approach to explaining changes in behavior, or the acquisition and extinction of responses.[3] These three approaches—learning through classical conditioning, operant conditioning, and modeling form the basis for behavior modification. The behavioristic position is that many behaviors are learned or alterable through utilization of these three learning principles.

COGNITIVE PSYCHOLOGY

In behavior modification one attempts to alter behaviors that previously have been learned or to encourage the development of new behaviors. More recently the importance of cognitive psychology has been recognized. Researchers have considered the role of cognitions and have emphasized the role of cognitive and symbolic processes in influencing behaviors. It has been noted that an individual's perception of external events, rather than the events themselves, often will account for behaviors.[7] The client's thought patterns, beliefs, attitudes, opinions, and thoughts about himself may affect change.

Modifying views about food and food consumption may be critical. Establishing the right mindset is an effective step. The counselor needs to explore cognitions, which may be defined as what the person says to himself. Since many overweight individuals have had previous unsuccessful experiences with dietary control, they may have feelings of low self worth, personal failure, or guilt, which can interfere with successful dietary change and weight loss. The person may have self-critical thoughts, such as "I'm a pig," "I look so fat," or "I can't lose weight and am a failure." With all clients, the dietitian should look for negative cognitions, such as "This diet is too difficult," "I can't do it," "I don't see why this is important," or "I'd rather eat what I want and die happy." When the dietitian discovers negative cognitions, the dietitian should discuss these with the client. Cognitive restructuring is used to modify negative, self-defeating, or pessimistic thoughts into more positive ones that will assist the patient with dietary adherence. Clients should be encouraged to "accentuate the positive," congratulate themselves for any progress—however small—and counter negative thoughts with constructive ones that will help them to cope. Further information is found in the next chapter.

CHANGING EATING BEHAVIORS

As the principles that govern behavior and behavior change became more clearly defined, it became increasingly apparent that nutritionists and behavioral scientists should work together to provide methods of using these principles in applied settings where changes in dietary habits are the primary goal. The National Heart, Lung, and Blood Institute has been one of the leaders in encouraging this type of collaboration.[8] The most frequent application has been the behavioral management of obesity, but cooperative programs have led to application in such diverse areas of concern as cardiovascular diseases, eating disorders, and diabetes mellitus.

Dietary behaviors must be studied in terms of the client's total environment, which includes physical, social, psychological, physiological, and environmental factors as well as all conditions and events which precede and follow eating. Several behavioral scientists have referred to this framework as the ABCs, derived from analysis of the Antecedents (stimuli or cues) of behavior, the Behavior (response) itself or eating, and the Consequences (reinforcement or reward) of the behavior.[1,9] For example, seeing a package of cookies left on the kitchen counter may be the antecedent or cue. The behavior is eating half a package of cookies in the kitchen when one is home alone at 4:00 p.m. The consequences may be pleasure from the taste of the cookies and reduced feelings of hunger or frustration with increased feelings of happiness and satisfaction, which reinforce the behavior. The dietitian and the client must find ways to decrease undesirable eating behaviors and increase new, desirable ones.

Antecedents. Behavior modification techniques work by regulating the antecedents, the behavior of eating itself, and the consequences or rewards. Analysis of antecedents of behavior seeks to control or limit the stimuli or cues to eating. For example, a cue may be seeing or smelling food, watching television, arriving home from work or school, attending a social event, or noticing the presence of extra food on the table at mealtime. Behavior may be influenced by both internal and external factors. There may be internal cues, such as physiological feelings of hunger or psychological feelings of loneliness or boredom. A number of external variables may cue eating, such as noting the time of day or passing an ice cream shop in the street. Both internal and external factors may be mediated by cognitive factors, such as not caring about current weight levels or not wishing to dull one's appetite for the next meal.[10]

The strategy involves decreasing the number of times the person is exposed to situations where he consumes food. A list of suggestions for changing behavior that have been recommended by various authors for persons desiring to lose weight is found in Table 5-1.[1,11,12] To modify antecedents, the dietitian may suggest removing negative cues (not buying improper foods), introducing new, more positive cues (exercising instead of eating), restricting behavior to one set of cues (eating only at designated times), cognitive restructuring discussed previously, and role-playing new responses to old antecedents (telling a friend you would rather go to a movie than out for pizza). Breaking response chains and preplanning behavior are other strategies.[13]

Table 5-1. Techniques for Behavior Modification

I. PROVIDE INCENTIVES TO AID PATIENTS IN MAINTAINING COMMITMENT
   A. Determine ways to focus attention on successful experiences. A positive comment by the counselor is helpful, and one can always find something positive to say.
   B. Encourage people to tell others about dietary goals. This public commitment often will aid in maintaining one's course of action.
   C. Have the person anticipate problems that might come up and consider possible solutions before a problem arises. Having a plan ready will make focusing on the goal easier.
   D. Concentrate on allowed foods and portions, rather than the disallowed. Be positive.
   E. Keep reminding the person that dietary change is a gradual process. Dietary habits were not developed in a brief period of time and probably will not be significantly changed in a short time. Set realistic goals for immediate and long-term change. Encourage successive approximations to the desired behavior.

II. LEARN EATING HABITS (AND EXERCISE HABITS) BY RECORD KEEPING
One cannot change a habit until one knows what it is. Self-monitoring with accurate records of the foods consumed is necessary for behavioral control of eating. Information to consider recording would be:
   A. What food was eaten
   B. Quantity of each food
   C. What the person was doing just prior to eating (to help identify cues)
   D. Place of eating (cue providing)
   E. With whom eating occurs, or alone (cue providing)
   F. How the person felt (cue providing)
   G. Time of eating (cue providing)
This record keeping exercise can identify the person's patterns of food intake and those cues that are associated with food consumption as well as the emotional outcome of eating. The person will become more aware of the environmental stimuli that are associated with eating behavior.

III. CONTROL THE STIMULI (CUES) AND RESTRUCTURE THE ENVIRONMENT
   A. Physical environment:
      1. Based on the records kept, have the person identify physical stimuli in the environment that are associated with, and therefore are cues to, inappropriate eating behaviors. Different stimuli become associated with the act of eating and can become signals for appropriate or inappropriate food consumption.
      2. Ask the person to identify physical stimuli that could remind him to eat properly. Examples of these would be charts or graphs, cartoons, signs, and the like. The presence of appropriate foods in the home will probably be the best cue to appropriate eating, supplemented by the elimination of inappropriate foods.
      3. Have the person specify a special place where food should be consumed, such as at the dining table, and not in front of the television set or kitchen sink.
      4. Make those foods that are acceptable in the nutrition plan as attractive as possible. Use good dishes, crystal, and so forth to make dining a pleasant event.
      5. Set up shopping trips based on the following suggestions:
         a. shop for food only after eating
         b. use a shopping list
         c. avoid ready-to-eat foods
         d. do not carry more money than needed for shopping list

Table 5-1. Techniques for Behavior Modification (Continued)

      6. Set up specific plans and activities
        a. substitute exercise for snacking
        b. eat meals and snacks at scheduled times
        c. do not accept food offered by others
        d. store food out of sight
        e. remove food from inappropriate storage areas in the house
        f. use smaller dishes
        g. avoid being the food server
        h. leave the table immediately after eating
        i. discard leftovers
      7. Regarding special events and holidays
        a. drink fewer alcoholic beverages
        b. plan eating before parties
        c. eat a low calorie snack before parties
        d. practice polite ways to decline food
        e. do not get discouraged by occasional setbacks
   B. Social environment
      1. Have the person identify the types of social situations which contribute to poor eating habits. Examples of stimuli in the social environment that might contribute to difficulty for the person would be negative statements from family members or friends, social situations where there are expectations for eating inappropriate or disallowed foods.
      2. Have the person identify the kind of social interactions that would be supportive of good eating habits and following the nutrition plan. Role playing can be useful with the person practicing how he will ask others to help him change his eating habits.
   C. Cognitive or mental environment
      1. Have the person identify what thoughts and feelings are likely to make attempts to change eating habits unsuccessful.
      2. After the person has identified possible negative thoughts that could lead to discouragement, help him develop some positive thoughts that can be used to counteract the negative ones.
      3. Avoid setting unreasonable goals.

IV. CHANGE ACTUAL EATING BEHAVIOR
   A. Slow down
      1. Take one small bite at a time
      2. Put the fork down between mouthfuls
      3. Chew thoroughly before swallowing
      4. Take a break during the meal. Stop eating completely for a short period.
   B. Leave some food on the plate
   C. Make eating of inappropriate foods as difficult as possible
   D. Control snacks
      1. Save allowable foods from meals for snacks
      2. Establish behaviors incompatible with eating
      3. Prepare snacks the way one prepares meals—on a plate
      4. Keep a quantity of low calorie foods, such as raw vegetables, on hand to use. Have them ready to eat and easy to get.
   E. Instruct the person that when he eats, he should not be performing any other act. The cues associated with eating should be restricted to that act, so one should not eat while reading, sewing, watching television, and so on.
   F. Have the person continue monitoring himself

V. CHANGE EXERCISE BEHAVIOR
   A. Routine activity
      1. Increase routine activity
      2. Increase use of stairs
      3. Keep records of distance walked daily

Table 5-1. Techniques for Behavior Modification (Continued)

B. Exercise
   1. Begin supervised exercise program under specialist's direction
   2. Keep records of daily exercise
   3. Increase exercise gradually

VI. SET UP A REWARD AND REINFORCEMENT SYSTEM
   A. Have family and friends provide this help in the form of praise and material rewards.
   B. Clearly define behaviors to be reinforced
   C. Use self-monitoring records as a basis for rewards
   D. Plan specific rewards for specific behaviors. Use written contracts.
   E. Gradually make rewards more difficult to earn
   F. Use creative reinforcers, such as dropping quarters in a bank, putting money away for each goal reached, and earmarked for something desirable. Take money back as a punishment if the goal is not reached.

Adapted from: Stunkard, A., and Berthold, H.: What is behavior therapy? Am. J. Clin. Nutr., *41*:821, 1985; Rabb, C., and Tillotson, J.L. (eds): Heart to Heart. Washington, D.C., U.S. Dept. of Health and Human Services, 1983; and Fensterheim, H., and Baer, J.: Don't Say Yes When You Want to Say No. New York, Dell Pub. Co., 1975.

Some antecedents may be controlled by preplanning. Preplanning meals and snacks and having only proper foods in the house is preferable to expecting self-control when hungry. Preplanning social occasions and exercises is also helpful. Small portions of favorite foods may need to be included in the diet to avoid feelings of total deprivation and potential abandonment of dietary changes. Doing the right thing is enhanced by stimulus control. The goal is to decrease the number of times the person is exposed to tempting situations so that self-control is tested as rarely as possible.[14]

In some instances responses occur in chains in which each response produces the stimulus for the next response. An example of a chain would be feeling tired, looking at the clock, realizing that it is bedtime, turning off the television, going to the kitchen, getting a snack, eating the snack, feeling satisfied (reinforcer), and going to bed. The components of the chain should be identified, and then a break in the chain should be planned, such as adding 5 minutes of stretching exercises after turning off the television.

Behavior. After identifying antecedents, one should explore the eating behavior itself, investigating the speed of eating, the presence of others, and activities carried on during meals or snacks, such as watching television. Breaking a chain of eating too rapidly, for example, is accomplished by introducing delays in eating. Members of the "clean plate club" need to leave some food on the plate. Concentrating on the act of eating and enjoying the flavors of the foods are recommended.

Consequences. Consequences of eating are described as reinforcements or rewards. According to Stunkard: "Since behavior is believed to be maintained by its consequences, efforts are made to arrange consequences that will maintain desirable behaviors, such as adherence to the weight control program."[1] The consequences of eating may be positive, negative, or neutral. In general, positive consequences are more effective in promoting change than negative or punishing consequences. Alternatives to eating may be included, such as walking or exercising, writing a letter, cleaning a part of the house, a hobby, and so on. One recommendation related to sodium restriction was for the client to set aside a quarter (or dollar) as a reward for using a spice or flavoring in place of salt.[11]

The client's current eating habits are pleasurable, and if food is considered its own reward, then new and different rewards must be established. Eating is a powerfully motivated behavior, the occurrence of which is necessary to maintain the homeostasis of the organism. Without food consumption, the organism dies, so that eating provides reinforcement of a powerful biological drive. The dietitian needs to identify new reinforcers with clients. Eating changes should be pleasurable to be self-reinforcing. If new patterns are a chore and are disliked, they will fail to provide self-reinforcement.

The counselor can work with the client to establish reinforcers. Activity reinforcers may be identified by asking, "What do you like to do with your leisure time?" Reinforcers may be walking, attending movies, plays, or sporting events, taking a bath, gardening, hobbies, playing cards, reading, or whatever the individual prefers. Social reinforcers may be found by asking, "Who do you like to be with?" Reinforcers may include visiting family or friends or phoning. Other questions are, "What do you find enjoyable?" and "What do you like to buy when you have extra money?" (other than inappropriate foods, of course).[14] Table 5-2 summarizes the identification of reinforcers.

The counselor is also part of the reinforcement, and rather than focusing on failures, should emphasize what the person has done right with verbal reward and praise. Remind clients to reward themselves cognitively by telling themselves they are making progress and have done something right. For the obese, the ability to fit into smaller-sized clothes hanging in the closet and the weight loss itself are reinforcing. New reinforcers, such as enjoyable activities, need to be established

Table 5-2. Identifying Reinforcers

1. Make a list of leisure time activities and hobbies that you enjoy.

2. Make a list of people you like to be with.

3. Make a list of things you would like to purchase with small amounts of extra money.

4. What do you find relaxing?

5. What do you do for fun?

6. What are your favorite possessions?

and introduced for weight maintenance, however. The reinforcement provided by significant others and self-monitoring are discussed later in the chapter.

After one or two eating changes or goals are identified, a schedule of reinforcement needs to be discussed and established. The schedule specifies which behaviors, if any, will be reinforced and how frequently reinforcement will be provided. Continuous reinforcement is the simplest method, but this may lose its effectiveness if the reinforcer is used excessively. An alternative is intermittent reinforcement, such as reinforcement 3 times a day, or once a day. Eventually the time may be lengthened between reinforcements. The schedule should be appropriate to the behavior one is trying to strengthen, convenient for the person to apply, and applied immediately for the greatest effect. Never reinforcing a behavior leads to its extinction.[15]

In some cases, contracts may be desirable. Contracts are clear statements of target behaviors of the individual; they specify the type of reinforcers to be used, the person who will deliver the reinforcers, and the frequency of reinforcement. They are signed and dated by the counselor and the client. Contracts ensure that all parties agree on the goals and procedures, and provide a measurement of how close the client is to reaching the goals. The signatures help to ensure that the contract will be followed, since signing is a commitment and may provide added motivation to change.[11]

Completion of behavioral assessment is needed prior to counseling. Examination of the ABCs by the dietitian and the client assists both parties in understanding current eating behaviors and allows discussion of what can be changed. The role of the dietitian is to provide an integrated plan for the total nutrition program of each client. The dietitian serves as a guide or facilitator of change rather than a director or controller of change, by suggesting behavioral techniques that are appropriate to the situation. The counselor should assist the client in learning to analyze the eating problems and should suggest possible goals, strategies, and techniques to deal with them.[16]

Since clients are not in daily contact with the counselor (unless the telephone is used for follow up), they must be ready to assume personal responsibility for sound dietary changes, and must eventually become independent. They must learn to analyze and solve their own eating behavior problems. Have the client start with small, easy changes, which are most likely to be successful, and progress incrementally to more difficult ones in later sessions. To be self-reinforcing, the eating changes should be pleasurable ones. If clients enjoy potato chips, ice cream, pizza, and beer, they have to find substitutes they enjoy, such as crisp apples, fresh grapes, unbuttered popcorn, and dietetic beverages. It may be sufficient to start by reducing the quantity of favorite foods consumed. Needless to say, strategies must be highly individualized, and what is appropriate for one client may be inappropriate for another.

The client should be told to expect problems and some inappropriate eating binges, especially when under physical or emotional stress. Expecting total control over change is unrealistic and may lead to diminished self-esteem in clients who have problems following diets, with eventual abandonment of the dietary changes. Learning any new skill requires practice over a period of time. Repetition of the same new behaviors gradually becomes reinforcing. Support and forgiveness should be provided during any lapses. Enthusiasm for change may be expected to drop rapidly after the initial period, especially if frustration and disappointments arise, and weekly appointments with the counselor are needed in the beginning.

SELF-MONITORING

Self-monitoring, or keeping records of eating behaviors to be controlled, was intended originally as a means of supplying the counselor and client with data for analysis. Clients record what, where, when, and how much they eat; the circumstances, (e.g. watching television or feeling bored); and the persons present. See Table 5-3 for an example. The exercise of keeping records, however, was determined to have additional value of its own. It increased client awareness and understanding of current eating behaviors and the influences on them, and led to such realizations as "I'm eating too much during evening hours while I read." Data provided a basis for setting goals for change ("I'll eat a low calorie snack instead") and finding ways to reinforce new behaviors ("I'll tell myself how well I'm doing"). Keeping records served as a measure of commitment of the individual to change.[1] Weight loss graphs for the obese and records of physical exercise, blood sugar, and blood pressure are other self-monitoring techniques.

SELF-MANAGEMENT

In most behavior modification programs for weight control, the client and counselor are together only for brief durations at specified intervals. Consequently it is not possible for the counselor to be continually in control of the dispensing of rewards and punishments, or withholding of rewards, for appropriate and inappropriate behavior, which is the basis of behavior modification. Therefore, self-regulation or self-man-

Table 5-3. Self-monitoring Food Record

Time	Food/Amount/ Method Prep	Room Place	Others Present	How You Felt Before Eating	Activities Same Time
Example: 9:30 p.m.	8 cookies, 10 oz milk	family room	husband	bored, tired	watching TV

Examine the above information and answer: What cues your eating? What reinforces your eating? How did you feel after eating?

agement techniques are taught to clients so that they can regulate and control their own behavior. In this way progress may be achieved in the interval between meetings of the client and counselor.

Research has shown the importance of developing behavioral self-management techniques. Skinner explained that self-management or "self-control" occurs when the individual manipulates the variables on which the behavior depends.[17] Self-management programs have been "designed to help persons become aware of and modify the social and physical antecedents of eating, to self-administer rewarding consequences for habit change," (or appropriate behavior), "or to self-administer aversive stimulation for inappropriate eating (behavior)".[10] As self-management programs have evolved, more emphasis has been placed on cognitive change. People have been helped to modify thoughts and beliefs which interfered with adherence to specific dietary regimens and to utilize self-reinforcing thoughts when appropriate behaviors occur.

For individuals in a weight reduction program, for example, it would be important to get in touch with their hunger. A simple exercise would be to rate hunger on a scale of 1 to 10, with 1 being ravenously hungry, 10 being filled to capacity verging on excess, and 5 being just comfortable. The individual should be encouraged to try not to eat unless hunger is at a 1, 2, or 3 level, and to try to stop eating when hunger is at a 4, 5, or 6 level. Becoming aware of one's inner state can be of assistance in achieving the desired self-management.

SOCIAL SUPPORT

The environment of clients includes a number of people they contact daily. It is important to include the person's family and significant others when planning lifestyle and dietary changes. The dietitian should include family members in counseling for change whenever possible, since the changes in food plans at home may affect them as well. Social factors may be contributing factors to obesity. If the family system supports an obese lifestyle with high calorie foods and little physical activity, change will be difficult for the client unless the whole family participates in the challenge.[11] There have also been suggestions that the involvement and support of spouse and family play an important role in weight loss.[18]

Ideally, family and friends are supportive of the efforts of the client in changing eating behaviors. The dietitian may need to discuss with clients the important role of support in achieving permanent change. In nonsupportive environments, the dietitian may suggest that clients request help from family or friends by seeking their agreements not to eat forbidden foods in front of them, or not to purchase or prepare the wrong foods. In addition, clients might ask their spouses, families, and friends to offer positive reinforcement for their efforts. Role-playing some of these situations with clients may be helpful.

When family members are present at the counseling session, they should be asked to discuss ways that they can contribute to the client's lifestyle change. Reinforcing proper behavior by the use of praise is an example. Controlling antecedents by having proper foods available is of great assistance. Family and friends should avoid acting the role of judge. "You shouldn't eat that," "It's bad for you," and "I told you so" are not helpful remarks. Jealous and envious reactions may also be expected. "You've lost enough weight," "Just this once won't hurt your diet," and "Your skin is getting to look awful" are remarks that the client may need to tolerate or confront.

APPLICATIONS

Obesity

The most frequent application of behavioral principles and methods to the treatment of nutritional problems has been in the management of obesity. In 1959, Stunkard noted that traditional psychotherapeutic approaches to obesity, as well as medical and dietary approaches, had not produced positive results. He reported that "most obese persons will not stay in treatment for obesity. Of those who stay in treatment most will not lose weight and of those who do lose weight, most will regain it."[19]

There is some difference of opinion regarding the efficacy of behavior modification techniques developed for use in treating overweight clients. Brownell reports that behavior therapy is more effective than any other treatment with which it has been compared and is an essential part of any weight reduction program.[20] Coates, by contrast, noted that "behavior modification has prospered under the protective shield of an especially good press."[10] These two reports, while emphasizing differing evaluative statements regarding the outcomes of behavior modification, are not mutually exclusive and both could indeed be accurate. Obesity is a complex state and is not treated easily. The obese may be overweight for a variety of reasons, only one of which may be improper eating behaviors. The biology of weight control must be considered. Stunkard, for example, recognizes that "there must be a very powerful biological pressure against losing weight."[21] This does not mean, however, that it is futile to attempt to control one's weight.

The American College of Sports Medicine, in a position statement, stressed that lifelong weight control requires commitment, an understanding of one's eating habits, and a willingness to change them.[22] Realistic goal setting, combined with reduction of fat and caloric intake, combined with a sound exercise program is recommended. Behavioral methods have been used successfully in diet planning, nutrition education, and a strenuous physical education program in a residential summer camp for obese boys. This combined approach resulted in significant improvement in body weight for the group.[23]

A recent study was designed to include a 2-year follow-up to assess the effectiveness of a behavioral weight control program.[24] The researchers found that after 2 years, 65.3% of the subjects were still below their baseline weights, 36.6% of the entire study group had maintained or enhanced the weight loss achieved during treatment, and 16.1% weighed at least 10% less than their baseline weight. These results, the authors felt, indicate that the behavior weight control program had an important and long-term impact on the weight status of a large sample of obese men and women. However, long-term weight loss remains a difficult task, and although weight loss may be achieved during the treatment period, many clients regain a portion of that weight during follow-up. Clearly, improved methods to facilitate a higher level of success are needed. This search continues.

Motivation must be present for behavior change. This is particularly true for eating behaviors. There are several factors relevant to the prediction of success in weight control, one of which is motivation to reduce weight. Brownell has stressed the importance of screening patients adequately before the initiation of any weight control program. A behavioral test of motivation as a screening device has been suggested.[20] Requiring a fee for treatment is one approach, but a deposit-refund system has been used also. In the latter system patients are asked to deposit money which is later returned if the patient attends meetings faithfully and/or achieves a previously determined weight loss. This system appears to be effective in reducing the drop-out rate.

An added benefit of significant weight reduction based on cognitive-behavioral treatment in a long-term therapeutic setting has been the production of a reduction in psychosomatic symptoms, anxiety, and depression in treated clients. More adaptive behavioral alternatives in longer goal-oriented programs seemed effective in promoting continued weight loss.[25,26] Research results, therefore, emphasize the fact that there is no "quick-fix" in weight reduction and the outlook must be long-term.[27,28]

Eating Disorders

Anorexia and bulimia are common disorders among adolescent and young adult females, estimated to occur in up to 1 to 3% of these populations. Therapist errors in treating eating disorders have apparently contributed to patient resistance, treatment ineffectiveness, and premature treatment termination. A variety of medical and psychological approaches have been used in treatment. It is most important for the therapist to be aware of the alternatives for treatment. The behavior modification approach is one of these alternatives.[29-31]

A now classic report detailed the use of behavior modification techniques for the nutritional disorder, anorexia nervosa, a chronic failure to eat.[32] A female who was 5 foot, 4 inches tall weighed only 47 pounds at the start of her behavior therapy. Before therapy commenced, the hospital environment provided many amenities and privileges. Because she appeared to enjoy them, these privileges and amenities were removed so that they could be used to reinforce appropriate behaviors, in this case, eating. All of the attention and sympathy that the hospital staff had used to coax the patient to eat were withdrawn. The therapist ate one meal a day with the patient, and the staff was allowed only to greet the patient on entering the room.

The social reinforcement which had helped to maintain noneating behavior was withheld so that it could be used later to strengthen eating behaviors. The therapist talked to the patient to reinforce her behavior when she picked up her fork, lifted food toward her mouth, chewed food, or performed any other eating behavior. She was then allowed the use of radio or television, but only after meals at which she increased her food intake over previous meals. As she gained strength and weight, other reinforcers were introduced, such as the privilege of choosing her own menu or inviting other patients to dine with her. Later reinforcers included walks, visitors, and mail.

The treatment was successful, and after 8 weeks of therapy, she was discharged to a program of outpatient follow-up weighing 64 pounds. Five years later, she had maintained her weight between 78 and 80 pounds and was successfully employed.[33] Locating potential reinforcers or behavior strengtheners is an essential first step in any treatment program. What reinforces behavior for one person may not function as a reinforcer for another.

A later study reported the successful inpatient behavioral treatment of anorexia and bulimia.[34] The treatment program was associated with increases in body weight and caloric consumption, which were generally maintained at 2-year follow-up. Self-monitoring of eating behavior, including caloric intake, emesis, and bulimia, proved to be a useful maintenance strategy. Other studies have noted the importance of self-monitoring and daily logging of intake, weight, and details of binge/purge episodes on progress and successful treatment of anorexia and bulimia.[35-37] These reported successes of behavioral treatment of anorexia and bulimia have involved inpatient therapy and outpatient follow-up.

Another finding from the research on anorexia nervosa concerned the effect of size of food portions on eating behavior. The serving of larger portions was associated with increased food intake. Apparently the subjects had been eating a relatively fixed proportion of the amount of food presented, whether the portion was large or small. This pattern of eating has been noted to occur in obese people as well, but not in normal adults or in young children.[8]

Behavior modification has also been used successfully in the treatment of chronic food refusal in handicapped children. Records of conditions before treatment began indicated that all patients accepted little food, expelled food frequently, and engaged in disruptive behavior. Treatment methods used were social praise, access to preferred foods, brief periods of play with toys, and forced feeding. Marked behavioral improvement was noted for each patient as well as an increase in the amount of food consumed. Further improvements were noted at 7- to 30-month follow-up.[38]

Participation in a behavioral treatment program proved useful when multiple problems were attacked in the case of a 29-year-old married woman, hospitalized with anorexia following a diagnosis of multiple sclerosis at 21 years of age.[39]

Many drug and hormonal therapies have been tried as treatments for this serious eating disorder. The most common treatment is behavior modification, combined with individual and family counseling.[40] To this point, no one has developed a reliable therapy for anorexia nervosa using either hormones or psychotherapy focusing on the underlying conflicts. The most effective treatment seems to be behavior modification. Under any treatment, however, a full return to normalcy in less than 4 or 5 years is rare.[41,42]

Diabetes Mellitus

Behavior modification methods have proven to be a useful component in the management of diabetes mellitus. Historically, poor patient adherence to dietary regimens has been a problem. Behavioral interventions such as cuing, self-monitoring, and reinforcement for appropriate behavior have been effective in promoting dietary adherence in patients with Type I diabetes. Success has not been as great, however, with behavioral techniques used in weight loss programs for obese patients with Type II diabetes.[43] As previously noted, though, the problem of control of obesity from the standpoint of any particular treatment is complex.

Behavioral management techniques have also been used with young diabetic patients to improve adherence to prescribed medical regimens. Subjects were given training in behavioral self-management. In addition, they received training in negotiation and contracting, which allowed them to develop a contract to earn reinforcement from parents for using learned self-management skills. These behavioral procedures led to a large increase in adherence to the prescribed medical regimen.[44] Young adults with diabetes improved their ability to estimate their blood glucose levels after participating in a discrimination training program, in which they received feedback regarding the accuracy of their estimates. These resulting increases in accuracy of glucose level estimation have established the opportunity for better nutritional control of the disease.[45]

Behavioral interventions, when used in the management of diabetes mellitus, should be geared to the developmental stage of the individual

in treatment.[46] An understanding of life span changes (i.e. preadoles-
cence, adolescence, and adulthood) in relation to life role, peer conformity pressure, eating disorders, sexuality, and pregnancy need to be
taken into account. The strategy that is effective with a diabetic adolescent struggling with peer conformity pressures may well be markedly
different from that which will be of assistance to a pregnant woman
with diabetes. There is a definite need to individualize interventions
directed toward behavior change.[47,48]

Cardiovascular Diseases

In the Multiple Risk Factor Intervention Trial (MRFIT), behavioral
scientists and nutritionists worked cooperatively with the aim of changing behaviors related to diet and smoking on a long-term basis to reduce
the risk of cardiovascular disease. A self-evaluation system for monitoring food intake was developed so that the counselor could estimate the
subject's progress in making appropriate dietary changes. A scoring
system was used for classifying foods according to their fat and cholesterol content as well as their predicted effect on blood cholesterol.
Subjects could use the system and select alternative food choices to meet
appropriate eating goals. The self-monitoring records were employed as
a method of measuring compliance, and also served to reinforce change
and provide positive feedback for appropriate behavior.[49]

In a study concerning the dietary management of hypertension, Tillotson and co-workers identified steps in patients' behavior that were
critical for the success of permanent dietary management.[50] These steps
are as follows:

1. The person acknowledges that he has high blood pressure.
2. The person considers diet as a sole or adjunctive method of
helping to control high blood pressure.
3. The person participates in assessing his current dietary pattern,
social environment, thoughts, beliefs, feelings.
4. The person acknowledges that successful dietary change will
require an extended period of time.
5. The person participates in developing an overall strategy and in
setting long-term goals for blood pressure and diet.
6. The person participates in the planning of each step in dietary
change.
7. The person makes each dietary change.
8. The person participates in assessing whether he has succeeded
in making each change.
9. The person participates in assessing his attainment of blood pressure control.
10. The person participates in devising a plan for maintaining dietary
changes as goals are approached.

Studies of healthy populations, of those at increased risk, and of
patients with cardiovascular disease have shown that risk-related be-

havior can be altered and in some cases, the incidence of cardiovascular disease reduced.[51-53] Since it is generally recognized that cardiovascular disease may result from voluntary behaviors such as smoking, inappropriate eating behaviors, and the pursuit of stress-prone lifestyles, it is most encouraging that we can emphasize the voluntariness of the behaviors and hence the possibility of modification of these self-defeating behaviors. Because these risk factors are behavioral in nature, it is particularly appropriate to attempt to alter them using psychological methods based on behavior modification.

Human Resource Management

The behavior of employees is of major concern to supervisors interested in productivity and good human relations. Blanchard and Johnson's book, *The One Minute Manager,* provides examples of behavioral modification strategies.[2] Goals begin new behaviors and in the "one minute goal," the manager uses observable, measurable behavioral terms to describe the discrepancy between the actual and desired performance. Supervisors need to convert ambiguous affective goal statements into a format that is useful for producing improved performance. For example. it is useless to encourage employees "to do better," if "better" is not defined and stated in behavioral terms.[54] Because behaviors are believed to be maintained by their consequences, the "one minute praise" and the "one minute reprimand," examples of rewards and punishments, are recommended. While most supervisors attempt to catch subordinates doing things wrong, Blanchard and Johnson suggest that they notice employees doing something right or approximately right and then gradually move them toward the desired behavior. The one minute praise is used immediately to reinforce proper behavior. Eventually some employees begin to praise themselves for the proper behavior, which provides additional reinforcement. Table 5-4 lists positive reinforcers for employees. The one-minute reprimand is also used immediately and concentrates on the improper behavior, not on the person.

Table 5-4. Positive Reinforcers

Praise
Positive feedback
Recognition (employee of the week, month)
Added responsibility
Compliments
Special assignments
Social events
Knowledge of results
Thank you letter
Salary increase
Bonus
Promotion

An important aspect of job satisfaction and performance is the employee's sense of personal control, so it is imperative that supervisors do not use behavior modification in ways that are seen as manipulative and degrading to employees.[55] Intrinsic motivation should be encouraged to emphasize the importance of a self-reinforcing loop.

IMPLICATIONS FOR THERAPY

Brownell has pointed out two major advantages of behavior therapy. Attrition from treatment programs is low, and patients in behavior therapy programs seem to show improved psychological functioning. Brownell asserts that such improvement has important implications for compliance and motivation, ingredients ultimately important for any type of treatment regimen.[20]

While eating behavior patterns are not altered easily, behavior modification therapy offers promising techniques that may be helpful to both the client and the counselor. Analysis of the ABCs—the Antecedents of eating, the eating Behavior itself, and the Consequences of eating—by the counselor and client leads to understanding of the problems, the setting of goals, and the development of strategies for change. Efforts should be made to arrange consequences that reinforce and maintain desirable changes, with an ultimate goal being independent client self-management. Behavior modification may be used in conjunction with other counseling and education strategies.

REFERENCES

1. Stunkard, A., and Berthold, H.: What is behavior therapy? Am. J. Clin. Nutr., *41*:821, 1985.
2. Blanchard, K. and Johnson, S.: The One Minute Manager. New York, Berkley Books, 1981.
3. Hill, W.F.: Principles of Learning. Palo Alto, CA, Mayfield Pub. Co., 1981.
4. Schwartz, B., and Lacey, H.: Behaviorism, Science and Human Nature. New York, W.W. Norton, 1982.
5. Bandura, A.: Social Learning Theory. Englewood Cliffs, NJ, Prentice-Hall, 1977.
6. Sims, H.P., and Manz, C.C.: Modeling influences on employee behavior. Personnel J. *61*:58, 1982.
7. Craighead, W.E., Kazdin, A.E., and Mahoney, M.J.: Behavior Modification. Boston, Houghton Mifflin, 1976.
8. Barlow, D.H., and Tillotson, J.L.: Behavioral science and nutrition: A new perspective. J. Am. Diet. Assoc., *72*:368, 1978.
9. Mahoney, M.J., and Caggiula, A.W.: Applying behavioral methods to nutritional counseling. J. Am. Diet. Assoc., *72*:372, 1978.
10. Coates, T.J.: Eating-A Psychological Dilemma. J. Nutr. Ed., *13*:S34, 1981.
11. Rabb, C., and Tillotson, J.L. (eds): Heart to Heart. Washington, DC, U.S. Dept. of Health and Human Services, 1983.
12. Fensterheim, H., and Baer, J.: Don't Say Yes When You Want to Say No. New York, Dell, 1975.
13. Building Nutrition Counseling Skills. Vol. II. Washington, DC, U.S. Dept. of Health and Human Services, 1984.

14. Storlie, J., and Jordan, H.A.: Behavioral Management of Obesity. New York, Spectrum Pub., 1984.
15. Martin, G., and Pear, J.: Behavior Modification. Englewood Cliffs, NJ, Prentice-Hall, 1978.
16. Holli, B.B.: Using behavior modification in nutrition counseling. J. Am. Diet. Assoc., *88*:1530, 1988.
17. Skinner, B.F.: Science and Human Behavior. New York, Macmillan, 1953.
18. Abrahamson, E.: Behavioral treatment of obesity. Behav. Therapist, *6*:103, 1983.
19. Stunkard, A., and McLaren-Hume, M.: The results of treatment for obesity. Arch. Intern. Med., *103*:79, 1959.
20. Brownell, K.: The psychology and physiology of obesity. J. Am. Diet. Assoc., *84*:406, 1984.
21. Gurin, J.: Leaner, not lighter. Psychol. Today, *22*:32, 1989.
22. American College of Sports Medicine: Position statement on proper and improper weight loss programs. Med. Sci. in Sports and Exercise, *15*:IX, 1983.
23. McKenzie, T.L.: A behaviorally oriented residential camping program for obese children and adolescents. Educ. and Treatment Children, *9*:67, 1986.
24. Lavery, M.A., Loewy, J.W., Kapadia, A.S., Nichaman, M.Z., Foreyt, J.P., and Gee, M.: Long-term follow-up of weight status of subjects in a behavioral weight control program. J. Am. Diet. Assoc., *89*:1259, 1989.
25. Goldwurm, G.F., Jerich, D., Colombo, F., and Nol, D.: Cognitive behavioral treatment for obesity: Methods, results and consideration after one year's work. Act. Nerv. Super. *30*:114, 1988.
26. Wade, J.B., Hart, R.P., Kirby, D.F., and Mills, P.T.: An evaluation of the Garren-Edwards diet and behavior modification program. Group, *12*:172, 1988.
27. Bennett, G.A.: Cognitive behavioral treatments for obesity. J. Psychosom. Res., *32*:661, 1988.
28. Perri, M.G., Nezu, A.M., Patti, E.T., and McCann, K.L.: Effect of length of treatment on weight loss. J. Consult. Clin. Psych., *57*:450, 1989.
29. Yager, J.: The treatment of eating disorders. J. Clin. Psychiatry, *49*:18, 1988.
30. Thompson, R.A., and Sherman, R.T.: Therapist errors in treating eating disorders: Relationship and process. Psychother. *26*:62, 1989.
31. Cox, G.L., and Merkel, W.T.: A qualitative review of psychosocial treatments for bulimia. J. Nerv. Ment. Dis., *177*:77, 1989.
32. Bachrach, A., Erwin, W., and Mohr, J.: The control of eating behavior in an anorexic by operant conditioning techniques. In Case Studies in Behavior Modification. Edited by L. Ullman and L.P. Krasner. New York, Holt, Rinehart, and Winston, 1965.
33. Reese, E.: The Analysis of Human Operant Behavior. Dubuque, IA., William C. Brown Co., 1966.
34. Cinciripini, P., Kornblith, S., Turner, S., and Hersen, M.: A behavioral program for the management of anorexia and bulimia. J. Nerv. Ment. Dis., *171*:186, 1983.
35. Leitenberg, H., Gross, J., Peterson, J., and Rosen, J.: Analysis of an anxiety model and the process of change during exposure plus response prevention treatment of bulimia nervosa. Behav. Therapy, *15*:3, 1984.
36. Cullari, S., and Redmon, W.: Treatment of bulimorexia through behavior therapy and diet modification. Behav. Therapist, *6*:165, 1983.
37. Smith, G., and Medlik, L.: Modification of binge eating in anorexia nervosa. Behav. Psychotherapy, *11*:249, 1983.
38. Riordan, M.M., et al.: Behavioral assessment and treatment of chronic food refusal in handicapped children. J. Appl. Behav. Anal., *17*:327, 1984.
39. Touyz, S.W., Gertler, R., Brigham, S., and Somerville, B.: Anorexia nervosa in a patient with multiple sclerosis: A case report. Internat. J. Eating Disorders, *8*:231, 1989.
40. Hsu, L.K.G.: The treatment of anorexia nervosa. Am. J. Psychiatry, *143*:573, 1986.

41. Crisp, A.H., Hsu, L.K.G., Harding, B., and Hartshorn, J. Clinical features of anorexia nervosa. J. Psychosom. Res., *24*:179, 1980.
42. Schwartz, D.M., and Thompson, M.G.: Do anorectics get well? Current research and future needs. Am. J. Psychiatry, *138*:319, 1981.
43. Wing, R., Epstein, L., and Norwalk, M.: Dietary adherence in patients with diabetes. Behav. Med. Update, *6*:17, 1984.
44. Gross, A.: Self-management training and medication compliance in children with diabetes. Child Fam. Behav. Ther., *4*:47, 1982.
45. Gross, A.: Discrimination of blood glucose levels in insulin-dependent diabetics. Behav. Modification, *7*:369, 1983.
46. Hartman-Stein, P., and Reuter, J.M.: Developmental issues in the treatment of diabetic women. Psych. Women Q., *12*:417, 1988.
47. Morgan, B.S., and Littell, D.H.: A closer look at teaching and contingency contracting with type II diabetes. Patient Educ. Counsel., *12*:145, 1988.
48. Peveler, R.B., and Fairburn, C.G.: Anorexia nervosa in association with diabetes mellitus: A cognitive-behavioral approach to treatment. Behav. Res. Ther., *27*:95, 1989.
49. Remmell, P.S., Gorder, D.D., Hall, Y., and Tillotson, J.L.: Assessing dietary adherence in the Multiple Risk Factor Intervention Trial (MRFIT). J. Am. Diet. Assoc., *76*:351, 1980.
50. Tillotson, J.L., Winston, M.C., and Hall, Y.: Critical behaviors in the dietary management of hypertension. J. Am. Diet. Assoc., *84*:290, 1984.
51. Patterson, T.L., Sallis, J.F., Nader, P.R., and Rupp, J.: Direct observation of physical activity and dietary behaviors in a structured environment: Effects of family-based health promotion program. J. Behav. Med., *11*:447, 1988.
52. Dressler, W.W.: Type A behavior and the social production of cardiovascular disease. J. Nerv. Ment. Dis., *177*:181, 1989.
53. Johnston, D.W.: Prevention of cardiovascular disease by psychological methods. Br. J. Psychiatry, *154*:183, 1989.
54. Stuart, J.A., and Wallace, S.G.: Analyzing "affective" goal statements. Performance and Instruction, *27*:10, 1988.
55. Greenberger, D.B., Strasser, S., Cummings, L.L., and Dunham, R.B.: The impact of personal control on performance and satisfaction. Organ. Behav. Human Decision Processes, *43*:29, 1989.

SUGGESTED ACTIVITIES

1. Complete a food diary for 3 days following the format in Table 5-3. Identify your cues for eating. Identify your reinforcers. Set one goal for change with identified reinforcers.

2. Record and identify your own ABCs (antecedents, behaviors, and consequences) related to an activity other than eating, such as studying, exercising, smoking, and the like. How can these behaviors be made to occur more or less often by rearranging the antecedents and/or consequences?

3. Ask a friend or family member to keep a food record. Work with him or her to identify one goal for change and reinforcers. Follow up in 1 week.

4. Arrange to watch an adult interact with a child or children for half an hour. Tally the number of times the adult attends to desirable behaviors,

which reinforces them, versus the number of times desirable behaviors are ignored, which may lead to their extinction. Note whether the adult responds to undesirable behaviors, which reinforces them.

5. Make a list of leisure time activities which you enjoy, people you like to be with, and things you would purchase with extra money, to identify your own reinforcers following the format in Table 5-2.

6. You have been assigned two chapters to read (or a paper to write) during the next few days. Select an appropriate reinforcer for yourself, and identify a time schedule for dispensing the reinforcer.

7. Select an excessive behavior of your own that you would like to diminish. Record those situations in which it occurs for 3 days. Identify the controlling stimulus conditions just prior to the behavior and the reinforcement.

8. Identify situations where modeling occurs.

9. In a social situation with friends, tally the number of times in one-half hour that you dispense social approval (smiles, nods, appreciative words) versus disapproval (frowns, disparaging words).

10. List 10 phrases of social approval that you are comfortable using with others.

11. Discuss your personal experiences at work and compare them with those of others. Does your supervisor praise or punish? What are the consequences of the supervisors' actions on your behavior and that of other employees?

6

Counseling and Cognitions

Based on learning principles, behavior modification examines external environmental influences on an individual's behaviors as discussed in Chapter 5. A person's responses are linked to stimuli or cues in the environment, and behaviors are shaped by their immediate consequences or reinforcement without requiring the conscious involvement of responders.[1,2] A second approach by psychologists, which can be classified as internal, is exploring the relationship between cognitions or mental states and behaviors. Cognitions may be defined as thoughts or perceptions at a particular moment in time. Thinking patterns can profoundly influence how people behave and the way they feel.[3] While behavior may be influenced by its consequences, there is also a role that cognitions can and do play in explaining people's behaviors. In addition to examining external environmental cues and reinforcement, the dietetic professional may need to assess the client's internal cognitions when teaching clients to implement coping strategies for promoting better dietary adherence. Combining several approaches to treatment holds the promise of better results. Some weight control programs, for example, include components of behavior modification, cognitive change, exercise, social support, and nutrition.[4]

This chapter explores three interrelated areas—cognitions and cognitive restructuring, self-efficacy, and relapse prevention. Assessing a client's cognitions can provide valuable information about the maintenance of adaptive and maladaptive behaviors, because negative thoughts inhibit behavioral change. The dietary counselor and client need to identify distorted thoughts, their effect on behavior, and to modify them into more positive, coping cognitions. Self-efficacy, another cognitive process, deals with people's judgments about their competence to perform specific behaviors. These perceptions, not necessarily one's true capabilities, influence the initiation and maintenance of health and other behavior changes. Relapse prevention is a self-management program with both cognitive and behavioral components. To prevent relapse from a dietary regimen, the counselor works with the client to anticipate and prevent dietary lapses that may occur during high-risk situations, and to help the individual recover from minor slips before they become a full relapse or total breakdown in self-control.

Negative cognitions and low self-efficacy ratings are predictive of relapse. Individuals with positive cognitions and perceived self-efficacy tend to call upon their coping skills and regulate their behavior better. Albert Bandura does not believe that appropriate behavior is achieved by a feat of willpower. When people do not behave optimally even though they know what they should do, thoughts or cognitions may be mediating the relationship between what one knows and what one does.[1,5]

COGNITIONS

Cognitive events are conscious thoughts that occur in one's stream of consciousness. Beck refers to them as "automatic thoughts," since they run through the mind automatically, and Meichenbaum, as "internal dialogue."[6,7] An individual's thoughts, also referred to as "self-talk," can influence how one behaves, feels, and appraises the outcomes of a behavior. Although one's actions are not governed solely by thought, thought does enter into the determination of many actions.[5]

While people do not engage in self-talk all of the time, on some occasions they do. Times at which individuals are more likely to engage in self-talk include when they are integrating new thoughts and actions, such as making lifestyle and dietary changes or performing a new job, exercising choices and judgments as in novel situations, and anticipating and/or experiencing intense emotional experiences.[8] According to Bandura, cognitive processes "play a prominent role in the acquisition and retention of new behavior patterns."[2]

The client's internal dialogue is viewed as a learned response that, in turn, may be a cue for succeeding responses.[7] This self-talk may be positive, negative, or neutral. Positive cognitions support behaviors, while negative cognitions inhibit them. An example of a positive cognition supporting appropriate behavior is: "This diet isn't so bad," and a negative one inhibiting behavior is, "This diet looks difficult." Cognitive variables are important in modifying dietary habits and in maintaining eating disorders, such as anorexia nervosa and bulimia.[9] Dysfunctional thoughts and beliefs about "fattening" foods, fear of weight gain, and body image require examination and restructuring.[10] An employee may be thinking: "I like my new job," or "This job is boring."

Since cognitions are learned responses, the counselor may view the client's cognitions as behaviors to be modified or restructured. Counselors want to achieve desired changes in the client's behavior by altering thought patterns, beliefs, attitudes, and opinions. The approach is to help the client by getting rid of unproductive, debilitating thoughts or beliefs and adopting more constructive ones.

Cognitive Distortions

Since negative thoughts inhibit behavioral change, it is necessary for individuals to first become aware of distortions in their thought patterns. Faulty thinking almost always contains gross distortions. Burns identified 10 common cognitive distortions:[3]

1. All-or-Nothing Thinking. This refers to the tendency to evaluate personal qualities in black and white, and is the basis of perfectionism. Performance is either perfect, or one is a failure. For example: "I ate this piece of pie and I shouldn't have. I'm a failure."

2. Overgeneralization. One concludes that if one negative event happens, it will happen over and over again. For example: "I shouldn't have eaten that. It's no use. I can't follow the diet ever."

3. Mental Filter. A negative detail in a situation is dwelt upon, and the whole situation is perceived as negative. For example: "If I can't eat whatever I want at the party, the party won't be any fun."

4. Disqualifying the Positive. Some individuals transform neutral and even positive experiences into negative ones. For example: "I am following the diet now, but this is a fluke. I probably won't be able to do it later."

5. Jumping to Conclusions. A negative interpretation is made even though there are no facts to support it. (A) Mind Reading. People assume that other people are looking down upon them. For example: "People don't want to be my friend because I am so fat." (B) Fortune Teller Error. One imagines that things will turn out badly, and assumes that this is a fact. For example: "I don't think I can follow the diet."

6. Magnification and Minimization. One either blows things up out of proportion, called "catastrophizing," or shrinks them into the small and unimportant. For example: "I goofed up. Everyone will hear about it. I'm ruined." Or, "I did it this time, but that is such a small gain that it doesn't amount to anything." The anorexic client, for example, overinterprets small increases in weight.[11]

7. Emotional Reasoning. Negative emotions are taken as evidence of the truth. For example: "I feel inadequate. Therefore, I must be inadequate."

8. Should Statements. Individuals try to motivate themselves with "should," "must," and "shouldn't" statements. For example: "I should eat fruit," and "I shouldn't eat cake." When behavior falls short of the personal standards, guilt results.

9. Labeling and Mislabeling. Instead of describing an error, individuals attach a label to themselves. Instead of thinking that a lapse occurred on the diet, for example, the person thinks "I'm a pig."

10. Personalization. One sees oneself as the cause of some negative external event when one is not. For example: "What happened was my fault because I am inadequate."

Cognitive distortions are faulty thinking habits that have been learned. These negative thoughts create feelings which may lead to a negative self-image or sense of worthlessness. In addition, they can become a self-fulfilling prophecy.[7] Because they have been learned, they can be changed or relearned with practice. However, since some people have had these thoughts for years, change may require extended effort and counseling.[12]

To improve dietary adherence and outcomes, the dietetic practitioner should ask clients to keep records of their thoughts, should reinforce positive and coping thoughts, and should help them recognize and restructure the negative ones. Cognitive assessment allows one to examine the role of thoughts and thinking processes in the development of adaptive and maladaptive behaviors. An example of a client log of cognitions is found in Table 6-1.

Cognitive Restructuring

Cognitive restructuring techniques refer to a variety of approaches involved with modifying the clients' thinking and the assumptions and attitudes underlying their cognitions.[7] The focus is on the false thoughts, inferences, and premises. Thus the counselor attempts to become familiar with the client's thought content, feelings, and behaviors and to understand their interrelationships. One needs to help the client identify specific misconceptions and distortions and to test their validity and reasonableness.[7]

Cognitive behavior modification consists of three phases, not necessarily in progression.[7] The first step is concerned with helping the client understand the nature of the problem. A basic principle is that one cannot change a behavior without increasing one's awareness, raising one's consciousness, or noticing a pattern in how one thinks, feels, behaves, and the impact on others in various situations. The client's recognition is a necessary first step, although not a sufficient condition to bring about change.[7] Rarely does the client recognize that thinking processes are a source of the dietary problems. The counselor should enlist clients in a collaborative, investigative effort to understand. The client needs self-observations to heighten the awareness of the relationship between dysfunctional thoughts, feelings, and maladaptive behaviors.

Burns suggests having the client keep written, self-monitoring records with three columns, including first the false thought or self-criticism, then the type of cognitive distortion or thinking error it represents, and finally a self-defense response or the substitution of a more objec-

Table 6-1. Log of Cognitions

Date	Time	Place	Food eaten	Thoughts about eating before/during eating.	Thoughts about eating after eating.
1/10	2:15	Home	6 cookies coke	"I feel hungry and tired." "The cookies taste great."	"I'm not hungry any more. I feel better."

Table 6-2. Assessing and Altering False Thoughts

Daily Record	Date	
False thought or belief	Type of Distortion	Self-defense, coping thought
"I shouldn't have eaten those cookies. I'm a failure."	All-or-none thinking	"Eating 3 cookies does not make me a failure. I can improve."
"I ate the pie. I'm a pig."	Mislabeling	"Pigs are animals and I am human. I don't have to be perfect."
"I don't have time to eat right."	Fortune teller error	"I have just as much time as anyone else."

tive thought.[3] (See Table 6-2 for an example) In addition to written records, the dietitian can discuss in an interview the range of eating situations, past and present, during which the client has false thoughts, such as thoughts about previous attempts to lose weight or follow a specific diet. The dietitian should ask clients to verbalize their thoughts and feelings concerning food, eating, and the dietary goal or change during the counseling session by asking: "How do you feel about . . . ;" "What do you think about . . ." to determine what individuals are thinking to themselves, about the eating behavior to be changed, about their ability to change it, and at follow-up appointments, about their progress. In group counseling, cognitions can be discussed as, for example, the negative self-talk of the obese. Clients need to realize the false, self-defeating, and self-fulfilling aspects of their self-statements.

During the second phase, the counselor helps the client to explore and consolidate the conceptualization of the cognitive problem. As the client reports negative, self-defeating, and self-fulfilling prophecy aspects of thoughts, the counselor can ask how these affect overt behavior. The client needs to interrupt the automatic nature of negative self-talk and appraise the situation. The negative cognitions are viewed as hypotheses worthy of testing rather than as facts. The client should be encouraged to ask the following questions:[3]

What good does it do to focus on negative thoughts?
What is the worst that could happen versus the likeliest?
What is the factual evidence for thinking this thought?
What can I say about myself in self-defense?

Asking clients questions about their thoughts, rather than providing answers, promotes self-discovery.[13]

In the third phase, actual change takes place. The counselor helps clients to modify their internal dialogue or self-statements and accompanying feelings and to produce new, more adaptive thoughts and behaviors. Clients are encouraged to control negative self-destructive statements, to offer positive self-statements as a coping strategy, and to reinforce themselves for having coped. An obese woman who is following a dietary change, for example, can tell herself how well she is doing and to keep it up. The "power of positive thinking" is great.[14]

Besides these techniques, it may be necessary to teach the person other coping skills, such as problem solving skills, mental rehearsal, and "thought stopping." Problem solving approaches will help to teach a client to stand back and systematically analyze a problem situation.[7] A problem solving method called STOP requires the individual to: (1) Specify the problem; (2) Think of options; (3) Opt for the best solution; and (4) Put the solution into practice.[15] Cognitive rehearsal permits attention to the important details of a future, desired behavior. If individuals think about or imagine themselves overcoming barriers and performing adequately, actual performance is likely to improve. Another behavior therapy procedure is "thought-stopping." Clients are trained to self-instruct themselves by saying "stop" whenever they are having false thoughts or negative self-talk.[7] In addition, some of the same behavioral techniques used to modify overt behaviors discussed in Chapter 5, such as modeling and operant conditioning, can be used for covert thoughts. A cognitive behavioral therapy package for obesity including six lesson plans offers suggestions.[16]

Besides the role of cognitions in acquiring and regulating behavior, motivation, which is concerned with activation of and the continuation of behavior, is partly rooted in cognition. The ability to represent future consequences or outcomes in positive thoughts provides a source of motivation.[1,2] For example, positive thoughts that one will feel better, look better, or be in better health may contribute to motivation.

SELF-EFFICACY

In addition to correcting faulty ways of thinking, the actual mastery of new ways of behaving may disconfirm faulty thought patterns and lead to heightened self-percepts of efficacy. Bandura recognized that learning and behavior change are influenced not only by external environmental influences, including rewards and punishments, but also by the interaction of environmental demands and one's coping capabilities. In his view, successful therapies work by increasing an individual's sense of personal mastery or self-efficacy.[1,2] This, in turn, allows individuals to exercise greater control over their own behavior, motivation, and environment.[17] Although it has received limited attention in the literature of health education research and practice, self-efficacy appears to play a critical role in the initiation and maintenance of health behavior change.[18]

Self-efficacy is a cognitive process dealing with people's judgments or beliefs about their capabilities to perform a behavior or set of behaviors adequately in specific situations and how their self-percepts of efficacy affect motivation and actual behavior.[5,19] Competent functioning requires both a set of skills and self-beliefs of efficacy to use them effectively.[20] Self-percepts of efficacy can affect people's choices of activities, how much effort they expend, and how long they will persist in the face of difficulties. The line, "I think I can" from the children's story *The Little Engine that Could,* for example, provides a vision of succeeding in performing a difficult task through sustained effort.

Bandura distinguishes between outcome expectancies and efficacy expectancies.[2,5,18] An outcome expectancy is a person's estimate or belief that a given behavior will or will not lead to a certain outcome. For example, reducing dietary sodium will lead to an outcome of lower blood pressure and better health; following a dietary regimen will lead to an outcome of weight loss; or successfully completing a project for one's superior will lead to a salary increase or promotion.

A self-efficacy expectation is the belief that one is or is not capable of performing the behavior required to lead to the desired outcome. A male client may or may not believe, for example, that he can reduce his dietary sodium intake sufficiently to attain the outcome. With staff, an employee may believe that performing work optimally will lead to the desired outcome of a promotion, but may or may not believe that he is capable of optimum performance on a continuous basis. The two are differentiated because people may believe that certain actions can produce the outcomes, but they may have serious doubts about whether they can cope with the necessary changes in their behavior.

Choice Behaviors

Self-percepts of efficacy are generally good predictors of how people are likely to behave on specific tasks.[1,2,5,19,21] Survey studies of self-efficacy by Strecher suggest a strong association between self-efficacy and progress in health behavior change and maintenance.[18] Where the health practice is believed to lead to desired outcomes, but the change is difficult to make, self-efficacy considerations are probably paramount. In addition, goal setting influences motivation to perform a task in part through self-evaluative reactions to one's behaviors and self-efficacy mechanism.

People commonly have a higher sense of self-efficacy about one type of activity than another. For example, a woman may feel confident in performing in a theatrical production, but doubt that she can sustain the effort to maintain the dietary changes necessary to lose weight and/ or increase exercise. A male employee may feel confident of his ability in one job, but not another. People's judgments about their self-efficacy affect their behavior in a wide variety of situations, ranging from solving problems to making dietary and lifestyle changes.

Efficacy expectations are a major determinant of people's choice of activities.[1,2] The client involved in a change of behavior must make decisions about whether or not to attempt a dietary regimen, how long to continue, how much effort to make, and in the face of difficulties or aversive experiences, whether or not to persist. Bandura believes that these decisions are partly governed by judgments of self-efficacy. People tend to avoid situations which they believe exceed their coping capabilities, but are willing to undertake activities they judge themselves capable of executing. The stronger the perceived self-efficacy, the more persistent are the efforts, even in the presence of obstacles. When difficulties arise, those with lower perceptions of self-efficacy make less effort or may give up entirely.[5]

Dimensions of Efficacy Expectations

The dietetic practitioner needs to assess the clients' thoughts about their abilities to make changes in eating behaviors or employees' thoughts about work behaviors. Different dimensions of thoughts may be examined, such as level and strength. When tasks have different levels of difficulty, efficacy expectations may limit some individuals to the simple tasks, while others may feel comfortable with the moderately difficult or difficult ones. Self-efficacy differs also in strength. Weak self-beliefs are easily extinguished by disconfirming experiences, whereas those with strong efficacy expectations will persevere in their coping efforts even through difficulties.[5]

A two-step approach to measuring self-efficacy is suggested. First, given a group of tasks of varying levels of difficulty, ask clients which dietary goals or behaviors they can undertake. Second, for each designated task in the behavior change, ask the individuals to rate the strength of their expectancy of success.[2] Self-appraisals of efficacy are reasonably accurate, and the individual's verbalized intentions provide a basis for predicting behavior.[5] People successfully execute tasks within their perceived capabilities, but shun those that exceed their perceived coping abilities. According to Bandura: "Unless people believe they can master and adhere to health-promoting habits, they are unlikely to devote the effort necessary to succeed."[5] Efficacy expectations and performance should be assessed periodically during the dietary change process, as the stronger the perceived efficacy, the more likely people are to persist in their efforts until they succeed.

Sources of Efficacy Information

One's expectations of personal efficacy are based on four major sources of information: (1) actual performance accomplishments, (2) vicarious experiences (modeling) by observing the performance of others, (3) verbal persuasion, and (4) physiological states.[1,2,5] While verbal persuasion is used commonly by counselors, it is among the least effective approaches in influencing another's capability for coping with change.

The most influential source of efficacy information is based on performance accomplishments or personal mastery experiences. "Nothing succeeds like success" reinforces this idea. Personal successes raise mastery expectations while failures lower them, especially early in the course of a change. Repeated successes strengthen expectations as does overcoming obstacles through sustained effort. People also perfect their coping skills and lessen their vulnerability to stress. Success begets success; failure begets failure.

A second source of efficacy information comes from modeling followed by guided performance. Clients can learn how to handle situations by observing a model demonstrating the appropriate behavior, such as ordering the proper food from a restaurant menu. The vicarious experience of seeing another perform, which relies on inferences from social comparison, can generate expectations that if another can do it, "so can I." To enhance self-efficacy, clients should then be given an opportunity to perform the modeled behavior successfully. Employees also learn by observing and modeling after other employees. Stronger efficacy expectations, however, are produced by personal performance accomplishments than by only observing a model.

A third approach, verbal persuasion, is widely used in attempts to influence behavior. Telling people what to do, that they possess the ability to do it, and informing them of the benefits, is not as effective, however, especially if the individual has had a previous disconfirming experience, such as a failure to follow dietary changes or perform a task at work. The impact of verbal persuasion may vary greatly depending on the perceived credibility of the persuaders, their prestige, trustworthiness, and other factors.[5]

Finally, people partly judge their capabilities from physiological states or emotional arousal. Situations in which the individual has to cope may produce anxiety, stress, hunger, and tension which elicits emotional arousal. Whether or not one can perform in the face of negative physiological signals provides personal information concerning one's competency. Individuals susceptible to anxiety may become self-preoccupied with their perceived inadequacies in the face of difficulties rather than with the task at hand. Relaxation exercises may be of help when these problems arise.

The dietetic practitioner may use one or more of the four sources of efficacy information to raise or strengthen self-perceptions of clients and employees. Personal mastery of a dietary change or accomplishment of a goal is compelling. Small "wins" build confidence for additional changes.[22] Models, such as former clients may be enlisted to explain how they overcame difficulties by determined effort. Persuasive information is given by informing people what they are capable of doing. The meaning of physiological information, such as anxiety, hunger, and stress, should be explained to make sure that the individual does not misread body signals and abandon efforts. With employees, personal accomplishments give better efficacy information than telling people that they are capable of performing a job. Modeling after the performance of others, such as seeing that hard work leads to a promotion, is another source of efficacy information. Behaviors are adopted from seeing what others are doing.

Cognitive Appraisal of Efficacy Information

Many factors affect successful performance. The extent to which success raises self-efficacy depends in part on the amount of effort expended. Laborious effort connotes less self-efficacy than success achieved through minimal effort. A performance suggests higher self-efficacy if attained through continuous progress rather than through discouraging reversals and plateaus.

In addition, a number of factors enter into personal appraisals. Some individuals underestimate their self-efficacy. If people are not fully convinced of their personal efficacy, they abandon the skills they have been taught when they fail to get quick results or when they experience obstacles to success. Those with negative self-beliefs do not discard them readily. Even when actual performance attainments are beyond their previous expectations, they may discount their importance through faulty appraisal or credit their achievements to extreme factors rather than to their own capabilities.

One may guide individuals to self-efficacy by guiding them through small, manageable steps or goals that gradually lead them to do more than they ever thought they could. Attainment of proximal subgoals indicates personal mastery, which can enhance self-efficacy and motivation, while distant future goals are not as good, as they are too far removed to have an effect.[5,20,23] For example, attaining the subgoal of following the dietary regimen today is an immediate commitment rather than a future goal of never eating desserts again. With employees, improving performance today is better than a distant goal for the month.

In a study of dropouts from obesity treatment, it was found that self-efficacy at the beginning of treatment was an important predictor of the decision to drop out.[24] Dropouts had lower expectations of success and were more likely to have doubts about whether they would ever reach their goal weights, while stayers felt confident that they would.

In the obesity study, perceptions of success proved more important than actual success in predicting who would drop out. Although it might seem that actual success in weight loss would have an important relationship to dropout, little relationship was found. Success results in greater increases in self-efficacy only when the subjects' successful experience is appropriately evaluated. "People are influenced more by how they read their performance successes than by the successes per se," according to Bandura, and this determines the course of cognitive and behavioral change.[1] Thus efficacy expectations reflect a person's perceived rather than actual capabilities, and it is these perceptions and not one's true abilities that often influence behavior.[18] Effective weight control as well as other regimens may need to include program elements aimed at higher participant perceptions of success.[24]

If one ascribes success to one's ability or one's effort, self-efficacy is reinforced. Cognitive appraisal of the difficulty of the task accomplished further affects self-efficacy. Even in the face of setback, if relative progress is perceived, efficacy may be raised.

Thus, in their daily lives, people will approach, explore, and try to deal with situations within their self-perceived capabilities, but will avoid situations with stressful aspects in their environment they perceive as exceeding their ability. Bandura's theory posits a central processor of efficacy information. People "process, weigh, and integrate diverse sources of information concerning their capability, and they regulate their choice behavior and effort expenditure accordingly."[2] Efficacy expectations are presumed to influence the level of performance by enhancing intensity and persistence of effort. Thus the dietitian needs to inquire of clients and employees about their judgment of their capabilities to perform a variety of tasks and the strength of that belief.

RELAPSE PREVENTION

The problem of relapse is a challenge for clients engaging in dietary changes and for the practitioners who counsel them. Relapse rates on dietary regimens are high, varying from 50 to 100%, as noted in Chapter 1. The likelihood of relapse may be increased by social and psychological provocations, emotional reactions to initial slips, and problems in reestablishing control.[25] Dietary counselors need to advise clients of the possibility of lapses and relapse and how to handle them. Failure to do so deprives the client of the opportunity for developing skills for coping with these situations and/or minimizing damage if one occurs.[26] Using the term "lapse" avoids the value judgment association with a term like "cheating."[27]

Marlatt and Gordon define relapse prevention as a self-management program designed to enhance the "habit-change process."[28] The change process is one in which old habits are unlearned and new adaptive behaviors are gradually learned and acquired to replace previous eating responses. Errors may occur, but each mistake is viewed as an opportunity for new learning. The goal is to teach the individual involved in a behavior change program how to anticipate and cope with the possibility of lapses and relapse.

Relapse prevention is based on the principles of social learning theory and includes both behavioral and cognitive components.[28] In the social learning view, behaviors may be viewed as overlearned, maladaptive habits which can be analyzed and modified. The eating behavior of individuals with anorexia nervosa, bulimia, and obesity, for example, may be viewed as overlearned, maladaptive habit patterns with maladaptive coping mechanisms.[9] These maladaptive behaviors are generally followed by some sort of immediate gratification, such as feelings of pleasure or the reduction of anxiety, tension, boredom, or loneliness. When eating takes place during or prior to stressful or unpleasant situations, it represents a maladaptive coping mechanism.

Habits or behaviors are assumed to be shaped by prior learning experiences. Changing these habits involves the active participation and responsibility of the client involved, who eventually becomes the agent of change. In a self-management program, the individual acquires new skills and cognitive strategies so that behaviors are under the regulation of higher mental processes and responsible decision making. As applied to a program to prevent relapse, the goals are (1) "to anticipate and prevent the occurrence of a relapse after the initiation of a habit change" and (2) "to help the individual recover from a 'slip' or lapse before it escalates into a full-blown relapse."[28]

Marlatt does not view relapse as an all-or-none phenomenon in which there is either absolute control and total restraint or in the other extreme, loss of control and total indulgence. He makes a useful distinction between a "lapse" and a "relapse."[28] A "lapse" is a single act, a slight error, a temporary fall, a reemergence of a previous habit or behavior, or a slip, not a total failure. Control is not lost and corrective action can be taken. A lapse may provide a learning experience if one examines the immediate precipitating circumstances and how to correct them in the future. After a lapse, one may continue with positive change or proceed to total relapse. A "relapse" may be defined as the individual's response to a series of lapses or a "perceived loss of control."[25] A lapse does not necessarily become a relapse.

A Relapse Model

Marlatt and Gordon have defined a cognitive-behavioral model of relapse based on the coping response process in high-risk situations. They believe that an individual's control continues until the person encounters a high-risk situation, defined as "any situation that poses a threat to the individual's sense of control and increases the risk of potential relapse."[28] Examples of high-risk situations for a person on a dietary regimen are attendance at a social gathering, feelings of anxiety, boredom, fatigue, or hunger, and the like.[26] There are two possibilities when a person is in a high-risk situation—a coping response or lack of a coping response (see Fig. 6-1). If the individual copes, self-efficacy is increased and there is less probability of a lapse or relapse. On the other hand, if there is no coping response and the person feels unable to exert control, the person experiences a decrease in self-efficacy, sometimes coupled with a sense of helplessness and passive giving in to the situa-

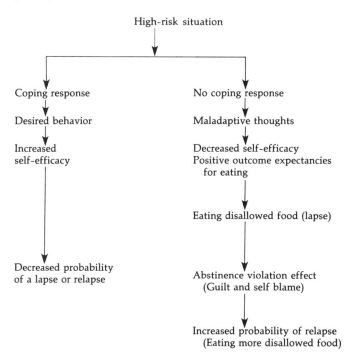

High-risk situation

Coping response	No coping response
Desired behavior	Maladaptive thoughts
Increased self-efficacy	Decreased self-efficacy Positive outcome expectancies for eating
	Eating disallowed food (lapse)
Decreased probability of a lapse or relapse	Abstinence violation effect (Guilt and self blame)
	Increased probability of relapse (Eating more disallowed food)

Figure 6-1 Cognitive-behavioral model of the relapse process. (Modified from Marlatt and Gordon.)

tion. ("It's no use. I can't stop myself.") If the person has positive outcome expectancies from eating, ("It will taste delicious. I will feel better if I eat this.") and ignores the delayed negative health consequences, the probability of lapse or relapse is enhanced. The individual experiences a conflict of motives between a desire to maintain control and the temptation to give in.[29,30] The person consumes disallowed foods, and a slip or lapse has occurred.

Abstinence from disallowed foods is frequently viewed by individuals from an all-or-nothing perspective. Marlatt postulates a cognitive "abstinence violation effect" when a person moves from control or restraint and eats a disallowed food.[28] This brings elements of guilt, and blaming oneself for the loss of control or indulgence. ("I shouldn't have, but I did. I'm guilty.") The obese individual may continue to eat to relieve the guilt ("I ate one cookie and I blew it. I might as well eat the whole bag") or alter his cognition from being a restrainer to an indulger. ("I never could follow the diet anyway.") The reward of instant gratification may far outweigh negative health effects in a distant future. People may even justify the action by rationalizing, "I deserve a break today. I owe myself this food," or change their commitment to save face, as "I changed my mind about following this dietary regimen and decided to eat whatever I want."[29] Thus, a single lapse, or series of lapses, may snowball into a full-blown relapse from which it is more difficult to recover.

Determinants and Predictors of Lapse and Relapse

High-risk situations may be classified as individual, situational (environmental), and physiological.[25,26] Individual factors are within the individual or reactions to environmental events. They include negative or unpleasant as well as positive emotional states, moods or feelings, inadequate motivation, responses to treatment, and coping skills.

Negative emotional states, such as depression, anxiety, stress, frustration, anger, boredom, and the like prior to or at the time of the lapse are related to relapse. They increase the chance that a slip will occur and become a relapse.[25] Positive emotional states in which one desires to increase pleasure and/or celebration are also a problem. A study of dieters found that negative emotional states occurring when the individual was alone and positive emotional states involving other people, such as social gatherings, were both difficult high-risk situations to handle, suggesting that emphasis on managing these situations should be incorporated into counseling programs.[26] Another study found that almost all "relapsers" in a weight control program reported problems with eating in response to day-to-day emotions and stress, while "maintainers" did not report these problems. "Relapsers" appeared to deal with emotions by eating.[31]

Clients initiate dietary changes with varying degrees of motivation. In addition, some who appear to be highly motivated initially may discover that long-term change is more difficult than first imagined. Initial response to treatment may predict later success. Patients on weight reduction diets who lose some weight, for example, and those who struggle but adhere to their dietary regimens, may be able to cope with temporary setbacks.[25] Coping skills include cognitive responses, such as positive self-talk ("I can do it."), behavioral responses, such as calling a friend instead of eating disallowed foods, and beliefs about self-efficacy, or whether or not one can respond effectively in a situation.

Besides individual factors, situational or environmental factors also play a role in relapse. These include social support and environmental stimuli. The support of family, friends, or self-help groups is associated with better success, while the opposite situation, interpersonal conflicts with family, friends, or the employer are a sign for relapse.[25] In addition, events in the environment may provoke a relapse. Cues in the environment, for example, may include parties or social pressures from others. Social pressures from verbal interactions with others ("Eat it. Just this once won't hurt you.") and seeing others as models when they are consuming disallowed foods ("Everyone else is eating it. Why shouldn't I?") are problems.

Finally, negative physiological factors may contribute to relapse. Genetic factors, urges and cravings for foods, feelings of hunger, fatigue, or headache, changes in metabolic rate during weight loss, and metabolic tendencies toward weight regain when lapsing from a diet may increase the likelihood of relapse.

Identification and Assessment of High-Risk Situations

Assessment of high-risk situations may be viewed as a two stage process.[32] In the first an attempt is made to identify specific situations that may pose a problem for a client in terms of lapse or relapse. The use of self-monitoring records is helpful in identifying high-risk situations as well as in raising the individual's level of awareness of choice points. Eating may be an automatic response which cannot be dealt with until there is a conscious awareness that one is eating without any conscious decision to do so. Self-efficacy ratings in which the client is given a series of descriptions of specific situations and asked to rate how difficult it would be to cope, autobiographical statements about the history and development of the dietary problem, and descriptions of past relapses are other techniques which may be used.[32] The second stage is an assessment of the client's coping skills or capacity to respond in a high-risk situation. One can evaluate these in simulated situations with role playing or in written form. The individual can role play responses to high-risk situations with the counselor or fellow group members. Videotapes of these sessions may be helpful if they are available.

Treatment Strategies

The counselor needs to prepare the client for the possibility of a lapse and of relapse. Marlatt and Gordon use the metaphor of a fire drill. A person practices to escape a fire even though fires are rare.[28] Brownell prefers the metaphor of a forest ranger whose responsibilities include both preventing fires, but also containing fires that start.[25]

Relapse prevention strategies are important both in initial treatment and in maintenance phases. The cornerstone of the relapse prevention approach is to teach the client coping strategies with skill-training procedures.[32] Skill training implies the actual acquisition of a new behavior through overt practice and rehearsal. One does not acquire a new skill, such as playing tennis, by verbal instruction alone. Actual practice of coping skills is essential.[32] Both cognitive and behavioral coping strategies may be needed. "Practice makes perfect," as an old saying goes.

Modeling, behavioral rehearsal, direct instruction, and coaching and feedback from the counselor are useful. Role reversal with the client teaching the dietary counselor how to cope with a high-risk situation and how to handle a lapse will give the client more convincing arguments than any counselor could provide. Increasing self-efficacy and modeling of positive self-statements are recommended, such as "I can do it."[32]

Relapse rehearsal through imagined scenarios in which the client engages in coping responses, which is called covert modeling, may be used to cope with reactions to a slip or lapse.[32] Relaxation training, meditation, exercise, and stress management procedures may be needed as an antidote to stress. Adopting a problem solving orientation to stressful situations is helpful or modeling problem solving by thinking out loud with clients. When lapses are discussed, it is preferable to discuss how the individual might have succeeded in preference to focusing on the failures.

Cognitive restructuring teaches people to interpret events, attitudes, and feelings rationally, and to respond in high-risk situations. Cognitive restructuring may be used also to counter the cognitive and affective components of the "abstinence violation effect."[28] Instead of seeing the first lapse as a sign of failure characterized by conflict, guilt, and personal attribution, the client is taught to see it as a single event or small mistake rather than a total disaster, and that it is possible to resume the dietary regimen right away and learn from mistakes.

When the individual's high-risk situations are identified, one can teach the person to look for cues, such as an upcoming party, vacation, or stressful time at work. The client can take preventive action and make advance decisions about how to cope.

Chronic problems may require long-term treatment even in the maintenance stage of change.[9,25,33] Just as Rome was not built in a day, neither is successful dietary change established in a short period of time. It may not be sufficient to teach new ways of eating and turn people loose and unaccountable on a maintenance program. They need to learn strategies to cope with the normal urge to lapse into old habits. They should be more successful when they keep in contact with a counselor, at least by phone for a year or more. In a study of treatment for obesity, the group that maintained its weight loss best was one that received behavior therapy plus relapse prevention training and post-treatment contact by mail and telephone.[34] The model of life-long treatment is used by several groups, such as Alcoholics Anonymous, Overeaters Anonymous, and the lifetime membership offered in Weight Watchers.[25]

Counselors should give clients a summary or overview of the relapse prevention model. Together they should identify the individual's high-risk situations and coping skills. If clients have a level of awareness in high-risk situations, they are better prepared to utilize their coping skills and take remedial action. People need to see themselves as capable agents of control rather than as helpless victims in situations beyond their control.

REFERENCES

1. Bandura, A.: Self-efficacy mechanism in human agency. Am. Psychol. *37*:122, 1982.
2. Bandura, A.: Self-efficacy: Toward a unifying theory of behavioral change. Psychol. Rev. *84*:191, 1977.
3. Burns, D.D.: Feeling Good. New York, New American Library, 1980.
4. Brownell, K.D., and Wadden, T.A.: Behavior therapy for obesity: Modern approaches and better results. In Brownell, K.D., and Foreyt, J.P.: Handbook of Eating Disorders. New York, Basic Books, 1986.
5. Bandura, A.: Social Foundations of Thought and Action: A Social Cognitive Theory. Englewood Cliffs, NJ, Prentice-Hall, 1986.
6. Beck, A.: Cognitive Therapy and Emotional Disorders. New York, International Universities Press, 1976.
7. Meichenbaum, D.: Cognitive-Behavior Modification: An Integrative Approach. New York, Plenum Press, 1977.
8. Meichenbaum, D.: Cognitive-behavior modification. In Kanfer, F.H. and Goldstein, A.P.: Helping People Change. 3rd ed., New York, Pergamon Press, 1986.
9. Mines, R.A., and Merrill, C.A.: Bulimia: Cognitive-behavioral treatment and relapse prevention. J. Counsel. Dev.: *65*:562, 1987.
10. Wilson, G.T.: Cognitive-behavioral and pharmacological therapies for bulimia. In Brownell, K.D., and Foreyt, J.P.: Handbook of Eating Disorders. New York, Basic Books, 1986.
11. Garner, D.M. Cognitive therapy for anorexia nervosa. In Brownell, K.D., and Foreyt, J.P.: Handbook of Eating Disorders. New York, Basic Books, 1986.
12. McMullin, R.E., and Giles, T.R.: Cognitive-Behavior Therapy: A Restructuring Approach. New York, Grune & Stratton, 1981.
13. Holli, B.B.: Using behavior modification in nutrition counseling. J. Am. Diet. Assoc.: *88*:1530, 1988.
14. Mahoney, M.J., and Mahoney, K.: Permanent Weight Control. New York, W.W. Norton, 1976.
15. Glasgow, R.E., Tooberi, D.J., Mitchell, D.L., Donnelly, J.E., and Calder, D.: Nutrition education and social learning interventions for type II diabetes. Diabetes Care *12*:150, 1989.
16. Fremouw, W.J., and Heyneman, N.E.: Obesity. In Hersen, M.: Outpatient behavior therapy. New York, Grune & Stratton, 1983.
17. McLeod, B.: Rx for health: A dose of self-confidence. Psychol. Today *20*:46, 1986.
18. Strecher, V.J., DeVellis, B.M., Becker, M.H., and Rosenstock, I.M.: The role of self-efficacy in achieving health behavior change. Health Educ. Q. *13*:73, 1986.
19. Maddux, J.E., Norton, L.W., and Stoltenberg, C.D.: Self-efficacy expectancy, outcome expectancy, and outcome value: relative effects on behavioral intentions. J. Pers. Soc. Psychol. *51*:783, 1986.
20. Bandura, A., and Schank, D.H.: Cultivating competence, self-efficacy, and intrinsic interest through proximal self-motivation. J. Pers. Soc. Psychol. *41*:586, 1981.
21. Bandura, A., Reese, L., and Adams, N.E.: Microanalysis of action and fear arousal as a function of differential levels of perceived self-efficacy. J. Pers. Soc. Psychol. *43*:5, 1982.
22. Kayman, S.: Applying theory from social psychology and cognitive behavioral psychology to dietary behavior change and assessment. J. Am. Diet. Assoc. *89*:191, 1989.
23. Bandura, A., and Cervone, D.: Self-evaluative and self-efficacy mechanisms governing the motivational effects of goal systems. J. Pers. Soc. Psychol. *45*:1017, 1983.
24. Mitchell, C., and Stuart, R.B.: Effect of self-efficacy on dropout from obesity treatment. J. Consult. Clin. Psychol. *52*:1100, 1984.
25. Brownell, K.D., Marlatt, G.A., Lichtenstein, E., and Wilson, G.T.: Understanding and preventing relapse. Am. Psychol. *41*:765, 1986.

26. Sternberg, B.: Relapse in weight control: definitions, processes, and prevention strategies. In Marlatt, G.A., and Gordon, J.R.: Relapse Prevention. New York, Guilford Press, 1985.
27. Wylie-Rosett, J., Swencionis, C., and Stern, J.: Nutritional and behavioral strategies for the obese individual with diabetes. Top. Clin. Nutr. *3*:9, 1988.
28. Marlatt, G.A.: Relapse prevention: theoretical rationale and overview of the model. In Marlatt, G.A., and Gordon, J.R.: Relapse Prevention. New York, Guilford Press, 1985.
29. Marlatt, G.A.: Cognitive factors in the relapse process. In Marlatt, G.A., and Gordon, J.R.: Relapse Prevention. New York, Guilford Press, 1985.
30. Marlatt, G.A.: Cognitive assessment and intervention procedures in relapse prevention. In Marlatt, G.A., and Gordon, J.R.: Relapse Prevention. New York, Guilford Press, 1985.
31. Gormally, J., and Rardin, D.: Weight loss and maintenance and changes in diet and exercise for behavioral counseling and nutrition education. J. Counsel. Psychol. *28*:295, 1981.
32. Marlatt, G.A.: Situational determinants of relapse and skill-training interventions. In Marlatt, G.A., and Gordon, J.R.: Relapse Prevention. New York, Guilford Press, 1985.
33. Marlatt, G.A.: Lifestyle modification. In Marlatt, G.A., and Gordon, J.R.: Relapse Prevention. New York, Guilford Press, 1985.
34. Perri, M.G., Shapiro, R.M., Ludwig, W.W., and Twentyman, C.T.: Maintenance strategies for the treatment of obesity: An evaluation of relapse prevention training and posttreatment contact by mail and telephone. J. Consult. Clin. Psychol. *52*:404, 1984.

SUGGESTED ACTIVITIES

1. Keep a log of what you eat during one day noting your thoughts about food before eating, during eating, and after eating.

2. Identify your own high-risk situations for eating and how you respond.

3. For each of the following client cognitions, forecast how the client will behave. Then develop a more positive, coping thought.

A. "I've never been able to stick to any low calorie diet for more than a week."

B. "The food doesn't taste any good without salt."

C. "There are chocolate chip cookies in the cupboard, and I sure could use a few after the day I've had. I deserve a treat."

D. "This television show is boring. Here is a commercial break—a good time to see what's interesting in the kitchen."

E. "That leftover pie looks good, but I don't need it."

F. "I've blown my whole diet eating that apple pie with ice cream. What's the use?"

G. "I don't have time to prepare all of that special food today."

4. For 2 days, keep a tally of the number of times people use the terms "should," "shouldn't," "must," "have to," or "ought to" in statements about themselves.

5. Place yourself on a modified diet for 2 or more days (low fat, low calorie, restricted sodium, high fiber etc.). Keep a log of your thoughts. Identify any high-risk situations.

7

Group Process

When people gather together in groups, they do not act in the same way as when they are alone or with one other person. The "behavior" that is observed when people come together is often discussed under the topic of "Group Dynamics." Each group develops its own pattern of interaction as it goes through various phases, and as members become comfortable in the group, learning to know and trust one another. Individuals promoted into management are often expected to convert their behavior from performing a task to managing a staff without being given the necessary training to exercise the required new skills. Activities such as conducting performance appraisals, counseling, disciplining staff, facilitating group meetings, enhancing morale through the building of group cohesiveness among staff, initiating change and managing any accompanying resistance all require well-honed communication skills.

When people are advanced into management without adequate training in these areas, the chances of their succeeding are hindered. During the 1990s and beyond, dietitians who manage need not only an extensive understanding of the applications of computer science and technology to assist them in decision making, but also the knowledge and ability of how to harness the power of their work and client groups.[1,2]

This chapter provides the dietitian with a general overview of the dynamics inherent in groups, and the variables that influence their direction, growth, and development. These process variables refer to how the group functions internally, how the members relate to one another, how they communicate among themselves, and how they do their work as a group.[3] The following topics are discussed: change in groups, cohesiveness in groups, the relationship of cohesiveness to change in groups, informal work groups, facilitator preparation, group facilitation skills, facilitator/participant functions, synergy, the guidelines for managing meetings effectively, and groups as a supplement to individual nutrition counseling.

Much of this chapter is devoted to exploring skills required of the group leader and participants. The reader is cautioned, however, that one cannot develop these skills simply from reading a chapter, or even from reading it again and again. To develop these skills, individuals must make a personal commitment to risk feeling unsure and awkward as they attempt to practice them. Individuals need not wait until they are in management positions. In fact, the time to develop group skills is while one is still a student or a subordinate. The skills can be practiced with friends, with family, and in the community. In that way, when one advances to a position of authority, the skills will have become refined from the earlier practice and experience.

Although interpersonal and group interaction skills can be taught, the most effective way for individuals to learn them is through experiencing and observing others whom they admire and view as effective communicators. Communication skills can be effectively "caught" as well as taught, and dietitians have an opportunity to develop these skills among staff and clients through their own "modeling" of them. Whether or not one intends it, and whether one's behavior is good or bad, the dietitian is a role model for staff and clients. By learning interpersonal and group skills and then consciously applying them, the dietitian constructively and proactively enhances their development among staff and clients.

CHANGE IN GROUPS

Group skills help the dietitian to manage change with both staff and client groups. Ongoing change in organizations is inevitable. When changes are minor, the administrator can simply announce the changes and expect others to follow without resistance; however, other changes may be perceived as threatening by the staff. When changes arouse a sense of fear, ambiguity, and uncertainty, they are resisted. One of the first steps in overcoming this resistance is to facilitate the overt expression of concerns, even when the disclosures may provoke conflict. The administrative dietitian needs to learn how to process the conflict that arises in the group in order that it can be managed constructively.[3,4]

There is a direct correlation between the amount of time, consideration, and participation in the proposed change allotted to those affected by the change and the amount of resistance likely to occur. When people are given consideration and an opportunity to voice their anxieties and questions, with their recommendations being incorporated whenever possible, they are less likely to resist the changes and more likely to assist in upholding them among others who may resist. When an entire work group is involved in discussion of problems and potential changes, with their supervisor acting as facilitator, agreement can be reached to employ new methods, procedures, or solutions. Those members of the group who later object are reminded by the others that they had adequate opportunity to make suggestions and express their concerns, and that objecting now is inappropriate.[5-8] Subsequent discussion will examine the group phenomena of change and cohesiveness and their effect upon one another.

Communication among work groups is affected by a constellation of variables, each of which is related to every other. Currently no theoretical model exists which takes into account all of the elaborate networks of sender, receiver, and message variables in small groups. In this section the two most salient variables, "change" and "cohesiveness" are explored. It is to the advantage of dietitians not only to understand the power and influence of the two phenomena on organizational life, but also to understand and apply appropriate strategies to use the "change" and "cohesiveness" variables for the good of the organization, department, and staff.

COHESIVENESS IN GROUPS

Because employee turnover is constant in most organizations, intense cohesiveness in work groups is rare; however, a knowledgeable manager can enhance the group's level of attraction and support toward one another through an understanding and application of what behavioral scientists have learned regarding group cohesiveness.

"Cohesiveness" is an elusive concept; there is no single definition which completely defines it. An eclectic definition is perhaps the best way to discuss the concept. A cohesive group is one which has strong feelings of "we-ness," members talking more in terms of "we" than "I"; one which displays loyalty and congeniality to fellow members; one in which members work together for a common goal with everyone ready to take responsibility for group tasks; one which may endure pain and frustration for the group; and one which defends against criticism and attack. A summary of factors influencing group cohesiveness is found in Table 7-1.

Table 7-1. Factors Increasing Group Cohesiveness

1. All members perform worthwhile tasks and feel they are appreciated by the group.
2. Members clearly perceive the group's goals and consider them to be realistic.
3. Members perceive the group as an entity in its own right and refer to it as such, calling it "the group" or "our group."
4. The group develops a history and tradition. All cohesive groups, church, state, family, work, etc. perform traditional rites and rituals, passing on to new members the "secrets" of the past and strengthening the existing ties among the group's veterans.
5. The group has prestige.
6. Members possess knowledge or material needed by the group.
7. There is full and direct member participation in the determination of the group's standards.
8. Members perceive the issues at hand to be of importance.
9. Personal interaction among members is based on equality, with no one exercising much authority over anyone else.
10. There are shared ideals and interests among members, or a common enemy outside the group, or a common satisfaction of individual needs for protection, security, and affection.
11. Members are not jealous and competitive with one another.
12. Group size is small rather than large.
13. The group is more homogeneous than heterogeneous.

The specific reasons cohesion thrives in some groups, dissipates in others, and fails to emerge at all in still others are as elusive as its definition. The most fundamental reason for groups tending to gravitate toward cohesive units stems from a basic tenet of human nature: people like to be liked. This desire to be accepted and liked leads people to engage in actions that will maintain or increase the esteem they receive from those around them. There is, therefore, always a tendency to go along with the group. Once a group feels itself to be cohesive, it attempts to preserve the state. Cohesiveness, however, is not static. Even highly cohesive organizations change membership, altering the nature of the internal structure and the interaction patterns of members. Over a period of time, therefore, a group may lose its cohesiveness.

In addition to the increase in self esteem which generally accompanies members' participation in a cohesive group, other benefits emerge as well: members or individuals can be honest in their dialogue with other members, and they can relax and not be continuously on their guard. Because members feel a stake in the group, they are more likely to disagree and argue about decisions affecting it. When a decision is made, each member feels committed to it and will take responsibility for it. Even if meetings are uninhibited and unruly, the topic is more likely to be fully explored, errors are more likely to be pointed out, and poor reasoning or attempts at manipulation on the part of various individuals are more likely to be exposed in the cohesive group than in the more self-conscious and cautious non-cohesive group. From the dietitian's perspective, maintaining high cohesiveness provides a highly desirable work climate, especially when the manager employs participative decision making and group problem solving strategies.

Individuals in non-cohesive groups are likely to argue less, be more polite, and more easily bored. When members disagree, they feel less secure in expressing themselves and often give no overt signs; instead, they may frown, look away, or plead ignorance. Members worried about their own security hesitate to challenge others; therefore, non-cohesive groups frequently stick to irrelevancies, safe topics, or procedures rather than become involved in discussing the real issues. Unlike the members of cohesive groups, they generally do not fully explore the topic, expose manipulation or poor reasoning, argue for what they believe, or take full responsibility for the group's decision. Agreement may be only external for the sake of apparent cohesion, in which case the individual does not feel bound to the group's goals or decisions. Clearly the quality of any group decisions or solutions to work-related problems made in these groups is poorer than that made in more cohesive work groups. It is the manager's responsibility to create a climate where individuals will dare to differ from the group without fear of expulsion.

It is the newer members who generally are the most easily intimidated because they are more likely to feel inferior to the established members of the work group. The individual's sense of acceptance in the work group is a highly prized possession, and anything which produces disharmony or conflict of views is likely to disturb it. New members are the most likely to accept and adopt the group's norms because of the pressures of being in a group where everyone else is acting, talking, or thinking in a certain way. This can occur even without any overt or conscious pressure by group veterans.

In summary, the major advantage of the cohesive group is its tendency toward a greater quality of communication, with the interaction more equally distributed than in the non-cohesive group. Members feel freer to disagree and challenge one another, providing that they do not perceive the message as a threat to their own status or security. Messages are usually more fully explored in the cohesive group, and the communicator has a better chance of achieving a shared understanding of the message, which could lead to a favorable attitude change in the entire group. If, however, the group interprets a message as a threat to its cohesiveness, it will reject it more hastily than will the non-cohesive group.

Conforming to norms may stifle the individual's identity and creativity and may restrict, inhibit, and change the values of individual members. It is paradoxical that cohesive groups also provide individuals with opportunities for need fulfillment, personal growth through work satisfaction and camaraderie, and are the most likely to achieve synergy. Developing cohesiveness within the group and then using it to produce superior problem-solving and decision-making can only be achieved consistently through the enlightened facilitator's careful monitoring and "fine-tuning" of the group's dynamics. The manager needs to maintain authentic reactions from individuals within the group while at the same time safeguarding the sense of unconditional acceptance among the other group members.[9]

The Relationship of Cohesiveness to Change in Groups

A spate of data concerning group influences has been accumulated in recent years, and the evidence of its power and potential force is convincing. The discussion below reviews the relationship of cohesiveness to change in groups.

While group change can be fostered through coercion and intimidation, permanent change promoted in this way is rare. Group change is most easily and optimally developed in meetings and workshops where trust, team building, and open communication are facilitated among members. Change has the best chance for acceptance and permanence when the need for and value of the change arises from within the group. Change occurring under these conditions receives mutual support and reinforcement from the entire group. After all channels of communication are opened and the needs for change explored, the members may experience a short-lived increase in hostility, but eventually, after all have shared perceptions and arrived at mutual agreement or compromise, the new norms are enforced.

Although there may be some who disagree with the change and revert to the old behavior, frequently the group pressures and the individuals' perceptions of their own dissonance cause them to abide by the group-accepted behavior. Suggestions for promoting group change are summarized in Table 7-2.

In summary, people's attitudes, beliefs, and values are all rooted in the various groups to which they belong. The more genuinely attached individuals are to their groups and the more attractive these groups become in fulfilling the various needs of group members, the more likely for these members to be in close and continuous contact with their group. Under these conditions group-anchored behaviors and beliefs are extremely resistant to change, with the group being able to exercise firm control over its members. The more attractive a group is to its members, moreover, the greater its power to change them. For the group itself to be used most effectively as an agent of change, it must first be cohesive with a strong sense of oneness existing between those who are to be changed and those who desire change. Attempts at changing individuals

Table 7-2. Suggestions for Promoting Group Change

1. If attitude change is desired, small open-ended, off-the-record discussion groups where the person feels secure are most effective.
2. When people need to change behaviors, participation in group discussions is 2 to 10 times more effective than a lecture that presents the reasons for and pleas for change.
3. Active discussion by a small group to determine its goals, methods, work, new operations, or to solve other problems is more effective in changing group practices than are separate instructions, supervisor's requests, or the imposition of new practices by an authority. Group involvement brings about better motivation and support for the change and better implementation and productivity of the new practice.
4. Group change is easier to bring about and more permanent than change in the separate individual members of the group. The supposed greater permanence stems from the individual's assumed desire to live up to group norms. It follows that the stronger the group bonds, the more deeply based are the individual's attitudes. Another explanation suggests that the public commitment to carry through the behavior decided upon by the group members creates an awareness of the expectations that the members have for each other, thus creating forces on each member to comply.
5. The best way for a teacher or manager to initiate change is to create an atmosphere that will lead to a shared perception by the entire group of the need for change. Then they will call for the change themselves and enforce it.[6] After all facts have been shared with all members and all channels of communication have been opened, there is frequently a sudden but short-lived increase in hostility; however, without this complete sharing among all group members, there can be no real change, only mistrust and subtle hostility.
7. High-status persons have more freedom from group control than do other members, and the group allows for more tolerance of eccentricity among high-status members. The greater the prestige of individual group members, the greater the influence for change they can exert on the others.
8. The "big brother" or "buddy system" of change, where the change is suggested by a peer, is better than having it demanded by an authority figure.[10]

must be aimed at either countering the influence of the group or encompassing it in the change. Either way, all attempts at changing individuals must also consider the dynamics of their groups.[5,6]

INFORMAL WORK GROUPS

Dietitians need to be aware of the inherent power and influence of the informal work group. Since the 1920s, when the Hawthorne studies were carried out at the Western Electric plant near Chicago, social scientists have been studying the "Hawthorne Effect," which refers to the theory, and its corollaries, that employees perform more efficiently when they believe that they are being given special attention. The theory suggests that the major influences affecting efficiency and production are group social structures, group norms, and group pressures.

Dietitians need to be sensitive to the dynamics and influences of the informal work group. They must learn ways to provide a forum where social, task-related, and organizational concerns can be expressed, responses can be offered, and any resistance to change can be overcome. To become conscious of the influence inherent in the informal work group, and to tap into the grapevine of informal communication, the administrative dietitian needs to be aware of the networks of communication that exist within the department as well as those within the organization.

Communication networks are the patterns of message flow, or linkages of who actually speaks to whom.[11] In all organizations, there are distinctions between the "permissible" and the actual channels of communication and network linkages. The permissible channels are the linkages dictated by the organization's structure, which determines the hierarchy of power and influence; the actual channels are the patterns that do, in fact, occur. Often, secretaries are ultimately more influential, because of their connections within the network, than others who are considerably higher on the organization flow chart. A later section in the chapter discusses "process meetings" as a way of tapping into the informal group and airing common group concerns.

Although they constitute a minority in the 1990s, some people perform best when under the direction of an authoritarian leader. When persons come from backgrounds where they have not been encouraged to think and have been punished for initiating ideas, it is predictable that in a work situation they will lack the self-confidence to offer suggestions within a group. If treated with patience, however, and given continued positive reinforcement each time they risk contributing an idea, they may gradually gain the confidence to become valuable group members. In general, however, members of today's work force, many of whom are "baby boomers" and have grown up with a preference for egalitarian treatment, perform best in groups with a leader who can act as a facilitator, involving employees rather than prescribing to them.

"Facilitators" are those who understand the value of group decision-making, and see their function as being to help the group get started, to establish a climate of work, to give support to others, and to keep the group on track so that its objectives are achieved. The group's activities and the facilitator's attitude toward the group are based on respect for what can be accomplished through group discussion and on the fostering of a group climate where people feel comfortable and secure enough to contribute their ideas.[12]

FACILITATOR PREPARATION

Facilitators' responsibilities begin prior to the discussion, in their preparation of the appropriate meeting environment. They must make sure that the room itself is comfortable, with adequate ventilation and lighting, and with a consciously arranged seating pattern. Sitting in a circle, for example, allows group members to see one another's faces, which tends to increase interaction among them. When people are arranged at long rectangular tables, persons tend to interact most with those in direct view and little with those on either side of them.[13]

When meetings involve individuals who do not know one another, the facilitator should supply name tags or cards for everyone in the group. A sense of group spirit develops more quickly when people use one another's names as they interact.[10] Allowing members time to introduce themselves is time well spent toward developing a comfortable climate. "Small talk" in groups is not a small matter. Just hearing one another allows the members to make some assumptions that help them to reduce anxiety. The individuals' tone of voice, dress, diction, and manner provide valuable clues to their character. Often, negative inferences disappear after the other's voice is heard and some information regarding the person's background is gathered.

GROUP FACILITATION SKILLS

The dietetic literature emphasizes the needs of nutrition counselors and educators to assist in group problem solving by further developing their roles as expert information disseminators, diagnosticians, team members, empathizers, and group facilitators.[15,16] Most dietitians will eventually need to direct others in groups and facilitate interaction among them. Effective facilitation requires training and discipline to stay in the role of guide and not become a participant. Described in the following paragraphs are specific skills that need to be practiced as one trains to develop group facilitation skills.[11,13,16,17]

Relieving Social Concerns. A tenet of group dynamics suggests that social concerns take precedence over "task" or work-related concerns. In other words, an individual's first concern is with being accepted and acknowledged as worthy. If individuals feel anxiety about being with unknown others, or others who may bear them ill will, they generally will not participate. One way a facilitator can attend to social concerns is to spend a few minutes at the beginning of each meeting, allowing people to interact socially and to reestablish positive regard for one another. If ill will does exist among some of the participants, and the facilitator is aware of it, he can attempt to have the members resolve their conflict prior to the meeting, or if they are willing, the conflict can be resolved at the meeting. Only after the members have had their social concerns met can they wholeheartedly participate in "task" concerns.

Tolerating Silence. After facilitators have made opening remarks, have made sure that everyone knows everyone else, have articulated the desire for everyone's participation, and have stated the reasons or purpose for the meeting, they might rephrase the topic in the form of a question and then invite someone to comment. Because members are frequently hesitant to express opinions with which their superior may disagree, they often wait to hear the supervisor's opinion first. There may be times when no one wants to initiate discussion and reduce the tension. Silence is likely to occur most during the early stages of an ongoing group. Once the group comes to understand that the facilitator truly does not intend to dominate, lead, or force opinions, members will begin to use the meeting time to interact with one another. For those first few meetings, however, the facilitator should repeat the intention not to participate, should encourage others to participate, and then should just sit patiently. If the silence is tolerated long enough, someone will eventually take the responsibility for directing the discussion.

Guiding Unobtrusively and Encouraging Interaction. The facilitator guides indirectly, helping the members to relate better to one another and to complete the task. Facilitators ought not allow themselves to become the focus. The facilitator can encourage interaction among the group members by looking away from speakers in the group as they attempt to harness his eyes. Although this behavior may seem rude, the speaker will quickly get the idea and look to the other group members for feedback and response as the talk continues. The facilitator should resist the temptation to make a reply after others talk, but needs to wait for someone else to reply. If no one else makes a comment, however, the facilitator can ask for reactions. A question such as "Any reaction to that, Mary?" is preferred to "my reaction is . . . ."

Because facilitators wish to keep the focus on the group, they should remind group members during the first few minutes of the meeting that their purpose primarily is to get things started and then simply to serve as a guide. This assertion will eventually be tested. Most people have heard the same sentiment expressed by teachers and others, and have learned that while some do mean it, the majority are paying it lip service only, want things done their way, and expect ultimately to be followed.

Knowing When and How to Resume Control. Just as a facilitator who rules and dominates in an authoritarian manner can stifle the group's creativity, facilitators who are too timid, uncertain, or frightened, and who let the group wander, can hinder the group's potential for synergy, i.e., for finding superior solutions. Facilitators need to determine if the group is capable of facilitating for itself. When it is, the facilitator's function is to remain on the sidelines. Only when there are no competent participants available to perform the necessary functions does the facilitator become an active member of the group.

Reinforcing Multi-Sided Nature of Discussion. The facilitator can reinforce the nondogmatic, multi-sided nature of discussion by phrasing questions so that they are open-ended. Examples include questions such as "How do you feel about that, Helen?" "Who in your opinion. . . ?" and "What would be some way to. . . ?" Facilitators need to think before asking questions in order to avoid closed and leading questions, questions that can be answered by only one or two words, or questions suggesting a limited number of alternative responses.

Exercising Control Over Loquacious Participants. The most common problem facilitators have is knowing what to say to someone who is overly talkative. There are, of course, many appropriate ways of handling this participant, and individual facilitators need to decide which techniques they personally feel most comfortable using, keeping in mind that when they interact with any single member of the group, all other participants experience the interaction vicariously. If the facilitator treats individual participants without respect, or humiliates or embarrasses them, all members will be affected by the experience.

Several techniques can be effective in dealing with the loquacious participant. The facilitator might interrupt the participant, commenting that the point has been understood, and begin immediately to paraphrase concisely so that the participant knows that he has been understood. While it is true that some group members talk excessively because they enjoy talking and because they believe that they are raising their status within the group through the quantity of their interaction, other talkative members often repeat themselves because of insecurity. They are not convinced that they have been understood. Usually, this kind of participant stops talking after being paraphrased. Of course, this process may need to be repeated several times during the course of the discussion.

A second problem arises with the participants who simply enjoy talking and do perceive increased status from it. These people do not stop talking after being paraphrased. They may need to be told that short concise statements are easier to follow and that the group is losing the point from their extensive commentary. If that does not work, the facilitator may need to talk with the participant privately. Often, talkative group members are unaware that others are offended by their domination. The facilitator can point out to them that he has noticed others stirring and wanting to enter the discussion. It needs to be stressed to these participants that long-windedness cuts down on the time allowed for others to contribute to the discussion.

Recent studies are suggesting that "time-wasters" can also be controlled by establishing additional meeting guidelines on an *ad hoc* basis. The facilitator, for example, may say, "Because of the brief time remaining, we will no longer be able to permit interruptions."[18]

Encouraging Silent Members. For various reasons, including boredom, indifference, felt superiority, timidity, and insecurity, there are usually some members who refuse to participate. The facilitator's action toward them depends on what is causing them to be silent. The facilitator can arouse interest by asking for their opinions of what a colleague has said. If the silence stems from insecurity, the best method is to reinforce positively each attempt at interjection. A smile, a nod, or a comment of appreciation for any expressed opinion is sufficient. Sometimes silent members "shout out" nonverbal signals. An overt frown, nod, and/or pounding fingers are all signals that should be interpreted as the silent member's willingness to be called upon to elaborate; however, if silent members have their heads down and blank facial expressions, it would be a mistake to force them into the discussion.

Halting Side Conversations. Generally, the facilitator should not embarrass members who are engaged in private conversations by drawing attention to them in the presence of the group. Their conversation may be related to the subject, or it may be personal. If the side conversation becomes distracting to other members of the group, those engaged in the conversation might be called by name and asked an easy question.

Discouraging Wisecracks. If someone in the group disrupts with too much humor or too many wisecracks, the facilitator needs to determine at what point the humor stops being a device to relieve tension in the group and starts to interfere with the group's interests. When facilitators believe that the humor is taking the focus off group issues and onto the joker, they need to interrupt, smiling, with a comment such as "Now let's get down to business." If the comment needs to be made a second time, intense eye contact with the joker and no smile as the same remark is repeated usually halts the disruption.

Helping the Group to Stay on the Topic. When the group itself seems unable to stick to the agenda and wanders, a device under used by facilitators is a flip chart to jot down points that have been agreed upon as a way to chart the group's progress. With a minimum of interaction, the facilitator can prod the group on by simply summarizing and writing down the points. Generally, the group's reaction is to go on to the next item on the agenda.

Avoiding Acknowledgment of the Facilitator's Preferences. Facilitators hinder the group when they praise the ideas they like and belittle those they dislike. It is particularly important that they avoid making comments that may be taken as disapproval, condescension, sarcasm, personal cross-examination, or self-approval. Once the group members know the facilitator's preferences, they will tend to incorporate these preferences in their own comments. Because the dietitians are in a position to reward or punish subordinates, the group members quickly learn that if what the supervisors want is to be followed and not disagreed with, that is how they will behave toward them.

FACILITATOR/PARTICIPANT FUNCTIONS

In addition to the specific skills required of facilitators, there are numerous group skills that both participants and facilitators should possess. There is a mistaken notion that it is the facilitator's responsibility alone to see to it that the group's tasks are accomplished and that a healthy group spirit is maintained. In reality, these responsibilities belong to anyone who has the training and insight to diagnose the group's weaknesses and who has the skills to correct them. Because most people are used to being "led" in groups, the facilitator may need to reinforce verbally the functions that all participants are expected to perform. The following paragraphs describe some of these skills and functions that both facilitators and participants have a mutual obligation to develop in themselves:

1. Groups need members to propose new ideas, goals, and procedures. Individual members are expected to accept the responsibility of *initiating.* Any member who has the insight into what should be initiated and waits for someone else to do it is ignoring an obligation. The facilitator might also remind participants of the spate of behavioral literature that verifies the correlations between employee/participant involvement and superior decisions.[11,19,20]

2. Everyone shares the responsibility of *seeking information and opinions.* One does not have to have vast knowledge of the topic being discussed to be a valuable member. Asking the right questions and seeking information from others in the group who have knowledge are valuable functions.

3. *Clarifying* what others have said by adding examples, illustrations, or explanations is a major contribution. People are not all on the same "wave length." Because of background, life experiences, education, natural intelligence, or environment, some people tend to understand one another more easily than do others. Two people who have grown up under similar conditions, for example, have an easier time communicating than two people from different backgrounds. People who understand what someone else in the group is struggling to make clear and add examples and explanations to clarify the thoughts for the others, have made significant contributions. Simply nodding in agreement and saying nothing is a disservice to the others.

4. Another function related to clarifying is *coordinating* relationships among facts, ideas, and suggestions. If one has the insight to understand how the ideas and activities of two or more group members are related and how they can be coordinated, the member serves a valuable function in expressing this relationship to the others.

5. *Orienting* is a name given to the function of processing for the group the pattern of its interaction and progress. The orienter clarifies the group's purpose or goal, defines the position of the group, and summarizes or suggests the direction of the discussion. Orienting by providing frequent internal summaries, for example, allows the group an opportunity to verify whether everyone is understanding the direction in which the group is going, and provides those who disagree or who have misunderstood with the opportunity to speak.

6. Perhaps the least understood and most valuable function one can perform for a group is being a *supporter.* Supporters are those who praise, agree, indicate warmth and solidarity, and verbally indicate to the others that they are in agreement with what is being proposed. It is a valuable function because without verbal support from others, good ideas and suggestions are often disregarded. If one person expresses an idea that the majority dislike and that no one supports, the idea is quickly dismissed. Generally, if only one person supports the idea, the group will seriously consider the proposal. Frequently, a minority opinion can gain majority support because a single supporter agrees, causing the group to consider seriously the possible merits of the proposal. Support can be given by briefly remarking, "I agree," "Well said," "I wish I had said that," or "Those are my sentiments, too." Generally, one person alone cannot influence a group: one person with a supporter, however, has an excellent chance of doing so.[21] This topic is developed further in the final section of this chapter.

7. *Harmonizing* is also a valuable contribution to the group. It includes mediating differences between others, reconciling disagreement, and bringing about collaboration from conflict. It is common for individuals to sit silently as they hear the valid arguments on both sides of an issue. One of the ways in which discussion differs from debate, however, is that discussion assumes that most issues are multi-sided, while debate tends to lend itself to two-sided issues only. The group member who verbally reinforces the positive aspects of the various factions and helps to suggest new and alternative solutions that include the best points of all sides is harmonizing.

8. Conflict, stress, and tension in groups are inevitable. When the stress or the tension mounts, it can enhance the conflict and the disagreement. Individuals who can find humor in the situation, reduce the formality or status differences among group members, and relax the others are called "tension relievers." A problem can occur when the tension reliever seeks recognition for himself and continues to joke, drawing the attention away from the issues. *Relieving tension* is valuable up to a point, after which it can be disruptive.

9. The final function in this discussion is *gatekeeping.* In gatekeeping, one notices which members have been sending out signals that they want to speak but have not had the courage or opportunity to enter the discussion. Gatekeeping ensures that all have an equal chance to be

heard. As pointed out in the discussion of the facilitator's functions, there is a difference between people who are nonverbally signaling that they have strong feelings—by raising their eyebrows, tapping loudly, or grunting—and people who are silent. Group members become uncomfortable when they sense that other members might force them to talk. All members share the responsibility to protect others from being coerced into sharing opinions. Gatekeepers tend to say things such as "You look like you have strong feelings," or "I can tell by your face that you disapprove." Such comments are generally all the prodding the silent participant needs to enter the discussion.

Too often individuals believe that in the ideal group, a single leader is responsible for each of the functions just discussed. In fact, all members—participants as well as facilitators—are responsible, and they need to be alert to perform as many of the functions as they see a need for. Some people may be natural "harmonizers" or natural "orienters," or may be able to perform effortlessly some other valuable function; however, if the group needs a gatekeeper and none is present, the natural harmonizer who sees the need must exercise the gatekeeping function. One of the ways people familiar with group dynamics and with the skills needed to enhance the working of groups can detect members who have had training in the same area is by their willingness to act on their insight to correct a weakness in the group. As pointed out in a previous chapter, the mind operates several times as fast as the speed of human speech. While members of the group are talking, other sophisticated group members need to be reflecting on the dynamics of the group and on the needs at the moment. This process leads to an understanding of which functions need to be performed to help the group accomplish its task and maintain its healthy spirit.

Paradox of Group Dynamics. There is a paradox inherent in groups: they possess the potential, on the one hand, to stimulate creative thinking and to promote a decision or solution that is superior to what any individual working alone could accomplish. On the other hand, groups possess the potential to stifle creative thinking and thus promote a quality of outcome inferior to what individuals working alone might accomplish. Ordinarily, no one person is solely responsible for what happens in any given session; however, whether a group becomes a force to promote creative thinking and problem solving or a force that inhibits these functions depends primarily on the skills of its leader, and to a lesser degree, on the skills of the participants. There are specific behavior patterns that help a group to function effectively, and others that hinder the progress. Knowing how to facilitate positive behavior in groups and how to inhibit the negative behavior is an asset to dietitians.

SYNERGY

Dietitians need to appreciate "group process" and to discover what can be done to stimulate their staff and/or client group so that they become a creative force that promotes "synergy." Synergy refers to the phenomenon that the group's product (i.e., conclusion, solution, or decision) is qualitatively and/or quantitatively superior to what the most resourceful individual within the group could have produced by working alone.[22] Today, much is understood about the phenomenon; however, it has not yet filtered into management practice. Although greatly influenced by the style of their facilitators, all groups possess the potential to be either a force for creative innovative thinking or a force that works to preserve the status quo and stifle new ideas. The purpose of this section is to offer suggestions on how to promote the former. The major variables that affect the group's potential for synergy are whether a single expert is available within the group, whether the group is heterogeneous or homogeneous, and whether the group and its facilitator are trained in the consensus-seeking process.

Facilitators should begin each meeting by stating their desire to promote a climate of acceptance and freedom of expression. Hearing the facilitator express this desire helps to set a group "norm" whereby everyone has a responsibility to participate. A norm is an unwritten rule to which the group adheres. Members "pick up" the code of appropriate behavior by noticing what the facilitator reinforces positively, ignores, tolerates, or rejects. Eventually, the facilitators' expressions of their desire for everyone to participate and the rights of each member to express subjective opinions without being abused by others will be tested. It is not enough to articulate these norms; they must be enforced. If individuals are abused by others, told to be silent, embarrassed, humiliated, or insulted, for example, and the facilitator does not intervene to protect them, his articulated norm will be discounted and the actual behavior that has been tolerated will be considered the "real" norm. For that reason, it is critical that group facilitators realize the importance of their function to stimulate group interaction while protecting group members from being verbally abused or stifled. Realizing that synergy is most likely to occur in groups where people can react authentically and are free to challenge the facilitator and the other participants, the dietitian needs to convince the group that they need to listen and respond honestly to one another's ideas.

As a rule, if a single expert is available and the rest of the group members are relatively ignorant of the matter being discussed, the expert should make the decision. In practice, however, there is usually no single expert available, and some group members are more informed than others, with a wide range of opinions being represented in the group. Under those conditions, the potential for synergy exists.

The variable of a heterogeneous versus homogeneous group of participants is more complicated. When group members are untrained in the consensus-seeking process and form a homogeneous group, they have less conflict and generally produce superior decisions to those produced by an untrained heterogeneous group. It is understandable that people who are similar in age, background, culture, life experiences, values, and the like have an easier time agreeing than with those with whom they have little in common.

The heterogeneous group that is untrained is likely to respond in one of the following ways. If individuals in the group do not know one another, they will probably remain silent. Most people become anxious in the presence of strangers, whose response to them is unpredictable. Rather than risk sharing a contrary opinion and being insulted, humiliated, or embarrassed, they tend to go along with the opinions expressed by other members of the group. Decisions in such groups may appear to be produced by consensus, because there is no apparent disagreement, but in fact, consensus may not be present. Because there is no group commitment and cohesion, conflict presents a threat to the group's interpersonal structure. Members try to smooth conflicts rather than resolve them. When disagreement arises, the members make quick compromises to get along. They resort to conflict-reducing techniques, such as majority rule and trade-offs. The quality of decisions made in these groups tends to be low.

The other possibility is that a great deal of verbal conflict will occur among the untrained members in a heterogeneous group, with each member insisting on his own point of view, so that the group never arrives at a decision with which everyone can be satisfied. This tends to occur most often in ad hoc groups with high-power personalities.

The variable of training in the consensus-seeking process is the most critical of all for producing synergy. In studies conducted by Dr. Jay Hall, a social scientist, trained and untrained groups were measured; both types of groups produced synergy. In the trained groups, however, synergy occurred 75% of the time, while in the untrained groups, it occurred only 25% of the time.[22] The implications are obvious: group leaders, facilitators, managers, supervisors, and all those who try to work with others in a participative manner need to understand the principles of training and instruct their groups in the process. A second finding was that under conditions of training, the heterogeneous groups performed better than homogeneous groups. In fact, the broader the range of opinions presented, the better the group's chances of arriving at superior decisions. The implication here is that a group of "lemons," group members who fight and cannot agree, can be turned into "lemonade" if the facilitator trains them in the consensus-seeking process.

GUIDELINES FOR SEEKING CONSENSUS

The training required to move a group from 25 to 75% efficiency in achieving consensus is based on a set of guidelines for group behavior; it is simple and not time-consuming. Dietitians who decide to use this method with staff need to understand, however, that it may take several weeks of regularly reminding the group of the guidelines, and interrupting each time the guidelines are not followed, before the process becomes natural to the group. These guidelines for achieving consensus in groups are as follows:

1. All group members have the responsibility and obligation to share opinions.

2. After group members have expressed opinions on a particular issue, they have the right to ask others to paraphrase these comments to their satisfaction.

3. After being paraphrased, they may not bring up their perspective again unless asked to do so by another group member. Insisting on one's own point of view or blocking discussion is not allowed.

4. Everyone has the responsibility to understand the arguments and opinions of the other members, and may ask questions for clarification.

5. After all perspectives are understood, the group needs to arrive at a solution or decision with which everyone can be satisfied. In accomplishing this task, the group may not immediately resort to the stress-reducing techniques of majority rule, trade-offs, averaging, coin-flipping, and bargaining.

6. Differences of opinion should be viewed as natural and expected. Members need to be encouraged to seek them out so that everyone is involved in the decision process. Disagreements can help the group's decision because with a wider range of information and opinions, there is a greater chance that the group will develop superior solutions. Frequently, when the group members suspend their own judgment, new solutions emerge that no single individual would have been able to develop alone. These solutions tend to incorporate the best points of all views—of both the majority and the minority. Such solutions tend to be synergistic. At times, however, after considerable discussion, no new solution emerges. In those instances, alternative problem-solving techniques can be applied.[21,22,23]

Alternative Problem-Solving Techniques. When a group is unable to agree on a solution, several other methods, each with its advantages and disadvantages, can be used. One method is for the leader to make the decision. The advantage is that the decision is arrived at quickly; the disadvantage is that those who dislike it may not support it. While leaders may feel that they have "won," others who feel that they have "lost" may attempt to subvert the decision or solution. Another possibility is for some members to accommodate others by no longer insisting on their preferred solution. This method will immediately relieve the group of conflict, but those who accommodated may later resent having done so and may not feel obliged to uphold the solution. Perhaps the most common method is compromise, each side giving in a little until both can agree. The problem with compromise is that often what is given up is sought back eventually. Compromise solutions tend to be short-lived. Other conflict-reducing techniques such as majority rule, trade-offs, and coin-flipping also tend to be short-lived because the members who gave up something to satisfy the immediate need for a solution feel no obligation to support the solution.

Group Participation in Decision-Making. There are both advantages and disadvantages to participative decision-making. The dietitian needs to be aware of them in order to decide, on a contingency basis, when this method is appropriate.

Advantages. 1. When managers meet their team members one at a time, problems of communication and perceptual distortion may occur. Each time the manager discusses the issues on a one-to-one basis, the superior's manner and language vary, with each subordinate asking questions from a different perspective. Meeting together to discuss such matters as operational activities and politics provides an opportunity for everyone to hear the same descriptions at the same time, and to ask questions, which may clarify perceptions, so that everyone shares a common understanding.

2. Interpersonal relationship problems can be resolved, particularly when the staff is aware of the need for teamwork.

3. Motivation can be enhanced since the individuals involved in the decision may become more committed to it and may better understand how it is to be carried out. Resistance to change is lessened when individuals consider the alternative actions together and decide together on the goals and objectives for achieving change. They experience a greater commitment to changes that they themselves have either initiated or participated in developing.

4. The synergy of problem-solving can occur, allowing the group to arrive at solutions that are qualitatively superior to any that a single individual could arrive at alone.

Disadvantages. 1. Group participation in decision-making can be time consuming; however, the time spent in goal setting, problem definition, and planning can result in more rapid implementation of the solution and less resistance to change.

2. Cohesive groups can become autonomous and work against management's preferences.

3. Groups can sometimes become a way for everyone to escape the responsibility for taking action, since each person may assume that someone else is ultimately responsible.

4. The goals and interests of employees and those of management may not be compatible.

5. Employees may not be qualified to participate. Participation requires not only a desire to be involved, but also an ability to communicate insights, reactions, and desires. Not everyone possesses these skills to the same degree, and some who have the desire, but not the ability, may need to be trained.

6. Individuals whose ideas are continuously rejected can become alienated.

7. Managers may use groups as a way to manipulate employees into making the decision that they, the managers, have already decided upon.

8. Work group involvement may raise employees' expectations that cannot always be met or that the manager did not intend, and once started, employees may want to be included in all decision-making, whether or not their participation is appropriate.

9. The hazards of "groupthink" refer to the phenomenon of a group stifling individual creativity to preserve the status quo. It is the mode of thinking that persons engage in when seeking concurrences becomes more important in a cohesive group than a realistic appraisal of the alternative courses of action. The symptoms of groupthink arise when group members avoid being too harsh in their judgments of their leaders' or their colleagues' ideas for the sake of preserving harmony. All members are amiable and seek complete concurrence on every important issue to avoid conflict that might spoil the cozy, group atmosphere.[23,24]

Dr. Irving Janis, social psychologist, is the leading expert on the groupthink phenomenon. Below are some of the remedies he suggests to prevent its occurrence. Dietitians need to consider ways of adapting these practices to their own style of group facilitation with staff.[23,25]

1. At each meeting, the facilitator should verbalize the desire that all participants assume the role of "critical evaluator." Members need to be encouraged to look for the weaknesses in one another's arguments. The facilitators' acceptance of criticism from others is critical if the others are to continue the practice with them and with one another.

2. The facilitator should adopt an impartial stance instead of stating preferences and expectations at the beginning. Such a stance encourages open inquiry and impartial probing of a wide range of policy alternatives.

3. The organization should routinely set up several alternative policy planning and evaluation groups to work on the same policy question, with each group deliberating under a different leader. This practice can prevent the insulation of an in-group.

4. Before reaching a final consensus, the group members should discuss the issues with qualified associates who are not part of the decision-making group, and should then report back to the others the results of their informal surveys.

5. The group should invite one or more outside experts to each meeting on a staggered basis and encourage the experts to challenge the views of the dominant group members.

6. At every meeting of the group, whenever the agenda calls for an evaluation or policy alternatives, at least one member should be assigned to play the "devil's advocate," challenging the testimony of those who advocate the majority position

7. After reaching a preliminary consensus about what seems to be the best policy, the group should hold a "second-chance" meeting,

during which time members express as vividly as they can all their residual doubts. This meeting gives everyone a last opportunity to rethink the entire issue before making a definitive choice.[11]

MEETING MANAGEMENT

This section offers the dietitian several concise suggestions for exploring the "process variables" that affect staff as they work together in groups. There will be times when the dietitian senses tension among the staff but is uncertain of its cause. At these times, a department meeting can be called for the specific purpose of resolving and exposing work-related problems. Knowing how to assist the group in solving problems is a major responsibility of the dietitian. Enlightened supervisors recognize the value in calling the group together occasionally for "process meetings."

A process meeting is one called for the specific purpose of discussing the group as a group. The items discussed include the process variables mentioned at the beginning of this chapter: how the group functions internally, how the members relate to one another, which procedures the group follows, how members communicate among themselves, how they do their work as a group, and how they react to proposed changes. Dietitians should initiate such meetings whenever they see a need; however, anyone in the department who sees a need for such a meeting should be encouraged to suggest it.

When supervisors decide to call the entire group together to share concerns about the dynamics in the work group, they should be sincere and candid in asking for assistance, and they should schedule the meeting at an appropriate time and place. The right time is when the staff is not preoccupied with other urgent problems and when they are being paid for their time. A group should never be given too brief a time limit when the task is to discuss the dynamics of their work group.

Until the staff becomes comfortable with them, the first process meetings may be slow in starting, with people asking, "Why are we here?" After the facilitator describes the reasons for inferring tension in the group, he should remain quiet until group members begin to offer their own subjective explanations for the tension. While "process meetings" are not yet common, supervisors who do hold them regularly find that they are able to short-circuit departmental problems by giving the staff members time to vent their feelings and to resolve conflicts with one another. An underlying assumption here is that the supervisor is already skilled in the techniques of conflict resolution and counseling.

A trend likely to continue through the nineties is the practice of taking an entire staff to an off site planning retreat, process meeting, or problem-solving discussion. The alternative relaxed and casual environment with the extended open-ended time periods allows for optimal authentic interaction among the group and an ideal setting for extended process meetings.[24,26,27]

A serious problem among administrators, department heads, and others who regularly need to depend on a staff for participative decision making is keeping group members motivated to participate, to follow through on assignments and tasks, and to be fully prepared prior to the meeting so that they can offer informed opinions. If there is a general problem with the group's not being prepared at meetings and the dietitian is not sure what the underlying causes are, the practitioner might consider distributing a survey. The survey could be passed out prior to the meeting, with members asked to remain anonymous. The facilitator could then tabulate the results and use the data as the basis for a process meeting. Usually, the facilitator manages process meetings; however, from time to time he may wish to appoint another to moderate the meetings, especially if he observes himself talking too much or becoming defensive.

No two work groups are exactly alike or have identical problems and concerns. For that reason, facilitators should be creative in designing surveys that are tailored for their specific groups. The survey might be used to point out discrepancies between how people think the group feels about a particular work issue versus how it actually feels. The survey could also ask for opinions regarding the members' perceptions of the clarity of group goals, the degree of trust and openness within the group, the level of sensitivity and perceptiveness among group members, the amount of attention to group process, the ways in which group leadership needs are met, the ways in which decisions are made, how well the group's resources are used, and the amount of loyalty and sense of belonging in the group. As pointed out in Chapter 2, selective perception often leads individuals to motives and opinions that do not correspond with fact. Group discussion of survey results exposes the different perspectives existing subjectively within the group.

It may be that the group is satisfied with the status quo, and the supervisor is dissatisfied. Perhaps he objects to the fact that the staff members insist on deviating from the agenda, or that they ignore responsibilities they had agreed to at previous meetings, or that they are not prepared to discuss the issues on the agenda that had been sent to them to consider. When it is the facilitators who are dissatisfied, they should facilitate the process meeting, albeit very carefully. They need to reaffirm the norms they want, making sure that everyone understands the norms, and then the facilitators need to stop people any time a norm is violated.

Even among a group of individuals who see one another regularly and do not feel any need for a formal "process meeting,"there is still value in providing a time for them to relieve social concerns when they are called together for group meetings. It is a good idea for the supervisor to plan on giving the work group 5 to 8 minutes to settle in socially before they get down to business. Providing extra time requires that the business agenda be tailored accordingly. If 45 minutes of business have to be conducted, the facilitator needs to allow 55 minutes for the total meeting time. The group should be reminded regularly that those first minutes are intended to be social and not used as "grace time" for latecomers. Everyone is expected to arrive on time so that the social time is used for that purpose. The supervisor's arriving early to greet people provides an opportunity for individuals to discuss any special problems or concerns.

A common inference among work groups is that the "boss" is looking for a "rubber stamp" group and is not truly interested in what the members believe. Unfortunately, the "boss" or dietitian is usually the last to discover this inference. This phenomenon is called the "good news barrier to communication." An archetype common in the classic Greek tragedies of Aeschylus, Euripides, and Sophocles is that the messenger who brought the news to the king that his son had been killed in battle was then killed himself. The ancient Greek dramatists were tapping into a universal fear, which is alive and well today in the workplace. This unconscious fear causes negative situations to be described more positively to the supervisor and causes groups to fail to expose the "real" problems. It is to the dietitian's advantage to be informed of the most "truthful" and objective data available. A way to foster openness in groups of staff members is to be consistently supportive, relieving the anxiety that might accompany being candid in group discussions. The staff needs to be asked for input on how the meetings could be improved. Once their suggestions are understood, as many as possible should be implemented.

Often, a common complaint among administrators regarding staff meetings is that no one seems to have anything to say. The groups seem noncreative or unwilling to generate new ideas. Suggestions on how to solve this problem might include assigning members the task of writing brief reports prior to the meeting. Including their names on the agenda next to the report topic is usually enough to inspire them to gather their thoughts beforehand. Of course, group leaders can stop the meeting at any time and dictate discussion questions to the group. After the group has been given 10 minutes to jot down some response, even in a personal shorthand, the meeting can be resumed. (Members should be reassured that no one else will read their answers.) In this way, everyone can have something to contribute. Another technique is to divide the group into small subgroups and allow each subgroup time to discuss various issues or problems. Often, individuals who are hesitant to speak up in a large group will converse with one or two others. When the large group is reconvened, the subgroup, not the hesitant individual, can give a report on its conclusions. In that way, minority opinions that might not otherwise surface often obtain recognition within the group.

At the end of a meeting, assignments for the following meetings can be distributed. The supervisor can increase the likelihood of the group following through with their assignments by asking all members to paraphrase their responsibilities for the next meeting. The act of acknowledging responsibility in the presence of the others adds pressure on the participant to complete the assigned tasks. If members do come unprepared regularly, the supervisor should consider adjourning the meeting until they are ready. Usually, this needs to be done only once for members to get the point.

Several days prior to the meeting, the facilitator should have notes sent out with the agenda to remind participants of their obligations to report, read documents, have subgroup meetings, and the like. Placing names next to agenda items acts as stimulus for members to be prepared to report at meetings.

Often, dietitians assume that they must know how to handle all problems that may occur in the work groups and at staff meetings, mistakenly believing that they are expected to have the insight, expertise, and competence to correct all problems. What they actually need to have is the humility and courage to ask for help. Supervisors need to be conscious of the various resources in their work groups and be willing to utilize the talents of group members whenever possible. Allowing individuals who may be especially competent in a particular area to share their knowledge with the others, to manage individual group meetings, or to train subordinates involves more than just delegation. It involves showing respect for and raising the self-esteem of the individual subordinate. Supervisors must lead, but not always by leading. They can perform just as efficiently simply by seeing that the leadership takes place.

Supervisors must consider the possibility that they themselves are the cause of the group members' underlying tensions or of their being unable to "gel" at meetings. Some common pitfalls among supervisors include not allowing time at the end of meetings for people to comment on how meetings might be improved, making sarcastic remarks to participants during meetings, or becoming defensive when comments about the supervisor do emerge. Group members may be unable to participate optimally and may feel frustrated with the facilitator if he neglects to do the following:

1. send out agendas
2. inform the group of the core topic for the meeting
3. give assignments to individuals
4. provide essential information to participants prior to the meeting
5. inform especially resourceful individuals of how they can participate
6. provide adequate time at meetings to discuss the topic fully

GROUPS AS SUPPLEMENT TO INDIVIDUAL COUNSELING

Group and individualized counseling may be used together. Even
those persons who require intensive individual counseling can benefit
by the examples, support, and ideas available in groups. When special-
ized and intense one-on-one dietary counseling does not produce the
desired results, group counseling may be advantageous. When problems
are mutual, the group can provide support, reinforcement, and all the
advantages of synergy in solving problems. Groups also provide the
resources for conducting role plays and rehearsing actions for the real
world.

As used in nutrition counseling, groups differ from group therapy.
Group counseling is intended to be not a form of therapy, but a format
to help people find solutions to dietary problems. These solutions can
then be demonstrated, attempted, and evaluated with group support.[28]

A primary goal in nutrition counseling is to promote self-sufficiency
in clients. In groups where people learn basic change strategies by helping other group members design personal dietary change programs,
and by encouraging mutual follow-through, this self-sufficiency goal is
enhanced. Once the group understands the basic strategies, the dietitian
can facilitate nondirectively, allowing the members to consult with one
another.

Some consider group counseling impractical when it is limited to a
single session. One-on-one counseling, however, is time consuming.
With the cutbacks in staff at some hospitals, any time saver, such as
the use of groups, is helpful. Behavior change requires more than one
session, but a single group session may be an efficient and time saving
way to give information to a group of patients or clients with similar
problems. The dietitian is saved from having to explain basic concepts
over and over. Being with others who share similar problems often
encourages participants to change more than if they were counseled
individually.

When the group is designed primarily for the dietitian to convey
nutrition and dietary information, to teach principles of dietary change,
and to encourage group members to use them, several principles should
be incorporated into the teaching aspects of group sessions.[28]

1. The number of major points covered per meeting should be limited. The dietitian should focus all efforts toward motivating the group
to understand and use these main principles.

2. Since learning is a gradual process, teaching time in groups should
be devoted to essential and necessary information. The intricate techni-
calities can be taught later.

3. The principles of education covered in other places in this book
should be used: the goal of the session should be stated, examples
should be given, and group discussion and problem solving should be

stimulated. Participants should be encouraged to summarize the points learned and their intended applications of them.

4. The content should be presented and reinforced through a variety of means: written presentations, audiovisual media, role-playing, and demonstrations.

5. Group members should be required to write down or publicly verbalize short-term goals that are specific and "doable," so that they can be reviewed in the group the following week.

This chapter has stressed the necessity for dietitians to study group process and internalize the behaviors needed to participate in, facilitate, and model group interaction skills. Under proper leadership, groups can stimulate solutions and insights the individuals might not experience otherwise. Once they develop the skills needed to diagnose group needs and the ability to correct them by focusing on the group's resources, dietitians can function as change agents and as communication models for the other group members, while at the same time becoming more effective administrators.

REFERENCES

1. McLaughlin, M.: The executive of the 21st century: a change of mind. N. Engl. Business, *11*:42, 1989.
2. Goddard, R.W.: Work force 2000. Personnel J., *68*:64, 1989.
3. Conlin, J.: Conflict at meetings: come out fighting. Successful Meetings, *38*:30, 1989.
4. Sinetar, M.: The informal discussion group—a powerful agent for change. Sloan Mgmt Review, *29*:61, 1989.
5. Koehler, K.: Managing Change. Small Business Reports, *14*:15, 1989.
6. Breuer, J.: Orchestrating culture shock: what happens when companies must change. Inform., *3*:11,46, 1989.
7. Carron, A., Widmeyer, N., and Brawley, L.: Group cohesion and individual adherence to physical activity. J. Sport and Exercise Psychology, *10*:127, 1988.
8. Anonymous., Group decision making. Small Business Report, *13*:30, 1988.
9. Dobbins, G.H., and Zaccaro, S.J.: The effects of group cohesion and leader behavior on subordinate satisfaction. Group and Organization Studies, *11*:203, 1986.
10. Fisher, A.B. and Ellis, D.G.: Small Group Decision Making. New York, McGraw-Hill Book Co., 1989.
11. Brilhart, J.K. and Galanes, G.J.: Effective Group Discussion. 6th ed., Dubuque, IA. William C. Brown, 1989.
12. Schultz, B.G.: Communicating in the Small Group. New York, Harper and Row, 1989.
13. Mill, C.R.: Activities for Trainers: 50 Useful Designs. San Diego, University Associates Press, 1980.
14. Owen, A.L.: Challenges for dietitians in a high tech/ high touch society. J. Am. Diet. Assoc., *84*:285, 1984.
15. Franz, M.: The dietitian: A key member of the diabetes team. J. Am. Diet. Assoc., *79*:302, 1981.
16. Baird, L.S., Schneier, C.E., and Laird, D.: Training aid for dealing with special students. In The Training and Development Sourcebook. Edited by L.S. Baird et al. Amherst, MA, Human Resource Development Press, 1983.
17. Patton, B.R., Giffin, K., and Patton, E.N.: Decision-Making Group Interaction. New York, Harper and Row, 1989.
18. Anonymous: How to control time eaters (without being rude). Working Woman, *14*:110, 1989.

19. Bernard, P., and Hill, N.: Improving organization effectiveness through employee involvement., Business Qtrly (Canada), *53*:58-61, 1989.
20. Watson, W.E., and Michaelsen, L.K.: Group interaction behaviors that affect group performance on an intellective task. Group and Organization Studies, *13*:495, 1988.
21. Watson, R.T., DeSanctis, G.P., and Marschall, S.: Using a GDSS to facilitate group consensus. MIS Qtrly, *12*:463, 1988.
22. Hall, J.: Decisions, decisions, decisions. Psychology Today. *6*:61, 1971.
23. Janis, I.: Groupthink. Psychology Today. *6*:43, 1971.
24. Hargreaves, J.: How to make a workshop work. Industrial Marketing Digest (UK). *13*:57, 1988.
25. Moorhead, G. and Montanari, J.R.: An empirical investigation of the groupthink phenomenon. Human Relations. *39*:399, 1986.
26. Cronin, F., and Goodspeed, S.W.: The planning retreat with the one-track mind. Healthcare Forum. *32*:30, 1989.
27. Sipos, A.: Organizational Climate and Employee Involvement. J. for Quality and Participation. *11*:62, 1988.
28. Rabb, C., and Tillotson, J. (eds.): Heart to Heart. Washington, DC. U.S. Dept. of Health and Human Services. 1983.

SUGGESTED ACTIVITIES

1. In groups of three, discuss the "best" small group experiences you have ever had. What occurred that qualifies them as superior? Describe specific behaviors of both the group's leader/facilitator and the participants that seem to have made a difference. Time should be allotted for each group to share its insights with the others.

2. In groups of three, plan to meet in three different settings over the next 2 days, with different seating, room size, lighting, etc. Report your observations on the effects of the environment to the entire class. Notice whether different groups had similar reactions and were influenced by the same factors. A simpler variation on this activity would be to hold a discussion for 10 minutes with the group arranged in a circle and then to continue the discussion with the group sitting in a straight row.

3. Make a list of at least three small groups in which you have been active, and describe the functions you performed in each. Compare your perceptions of yourself as a contributing group member with the perceptions that your friends or classmates had of you. Do you notice that you performed different functions in different groups? Do some functions overlap from group to group? Are your classmates in agreement with you regarding your functions within their group?

4. Thinking back to some recent experiences in group discussions, complete each of the following statements:
    A. My strengths as a group participant are. . . .
    B. My strengths as a group facilitator are. . . .
    C. What is keeping me from being more effective both as a participant and facilitator is. . . .
    D. What I plan to improve is. . . .

5. How do you determine if needed leadership and facilitative services are being provided during a discussion? Compare your observations with those of your classmates.

6. Write a question or description of a problem or issue, preferably from your own personal or professional experience, for which you do not have a solution. Present it to a small group and facilitate their discussion. Possible questions might include "Do people need to take vitamin supplements?" "What are the best food choices when eating at a fast food outlet?" and "What recommendations should one give to someone who desires to lose weight or exercise more?"

7. Group together 4 to 5 people who have a common problem such as needing to lose weight, needing to start eating breakfast, wanting to control excess consumption of snacks, needing to select nutritious meals, wanting to increase the fiber content of their diets, or wanting to exercise more often. State the problem, and have the group attempt to solve it.

8

Delivering Oral Presentations and Workshops

A significant responsibility included in the day-to-day professional life of many dietitians includes making oral presentations and/or conducting workshops for groups of patients, for other professionals, for the general public and for various other groups and organizations which wish to be educated in the areas of the dietitian's expertise. Like so many of the other skills discussed in this book, the skills needed to deliver a message orally and articulately cannot be learned by reading alone; one must be prepared to digest the information and then have the courage to R-I-S-K.

While entire books are written on the broad and general subject of giving oral presentations, the purpose of this chapter is to develop and to discuss concisely the most salient principles occurring in the process of preparing and delivering oral presentations and workshops.

Following are suggestions for advance planning and organizing of a presentation, advance physical arrangements of the room, delivering the presentation, and post-presentation actions.

ADVANCE PLANNING AND ORGANIZATION FOR THE PRESENTATION

The key to holding an audience, particularly one with limited time to absorb the speaker's ideas, is to be coherent and to communicate simply; otherwise their minds will wander. The secret of conciseness and simplicity is for speakers to know their objectives prior to planning their talk. What do they want to accomplish? What changes do they want to take place in the attitude or behavior of the audience? Do they want them to perform a task or recall some information? A common mistake made among untrained presenters is to attempt to cover too much in the time allotted. Inexperienced speakers often feel the need to parade their expertise and overload the audience with information.

Unlike reading where one can go back and reconsider an idea, listening requires ongoing concentration. When the brain begins to feel overloaded and saturation sets in, it protects itself by shutting down.

Has not everyone had the experience of pretending to be listening to an overly meticulous speaker as the imagination went elsewhere on holiday? Oral presentations need to be limited to a few major points that can be clearly explained and reinforced through details, examples, and a variety of media. Too much information and too many different points defeat the purpose. When listeners know where the presentation is going and are able to follow the presenter's reasoning, grasping examples with ease, they are much more likely to give their full attention.

Although presentations are often as brief as 10 minutes or as long as 90, presenters would do well to remember when adapting their goals to their group what the Reverend William Sloane Coffin said about the length of an effective sermon, "No souls are saved after 20 minutes." Once presenters have their general and specific goals tailored to their group, the next task is to organize them.

Introduction Critical to Speaker Credibility. Each of the three generally accepted divisions of a presentation, (Introduction, Body, and Conclusion) requires its own internal organization and serves a specific function. The "introduction" serves speakers by providing them the opportunity to establish credibility, to link themselves in some way to their audience, to let them know in what ways they will be better off as a result of having attended, and to describe for the audience in some serial fashion what they intend to cover.

Often when individuals are introduced to speak, their credentials are presented in advance; however, there will be times when no one is present to introduce the speaker or, when an "introducer" is available, she may neglect to mention important items related to enhancing the speaker's credibility. While self-serving comments delivered in a braggadocious manner may have a negative effect on audiences, audiences do, nevertheless, want to know that the person talking to them is worthy and knowledgeable. Dietitians, therefore, should subtly let them know during the introduction that they are qualified. For example, one might say, "in an article I wrote last year for the Journal of the American Dietetic Association . . .," or "while I was completing my graduate work at . . .," or "of the several hundred patients I have worked with in the past. . . ."

Audiences tend to be more attentive when they believe that the person speaking to them is able to relate to their circumstances. During the introduction, whenever it is possible, speakers would do well to underscore any connection they may have with a particular group. For example, one might say, "I have lived in this community for 15 years . . .," or "I was once 25 pounds overweight myself . . .," or "I see we are all baby boomers and share many of the same sentiments about wellness." If one gives it some thought, almost all audiences have some traits with which the speaker can identify.

During the introduction speakers need to let the audience know how the topic relates to their needs; in other words, presenters should answer the unasked question in everyone's mind, "What is in this for me?" Abraham Maslow has synthesized the basic human needs into five areas: physiological; safety and security; belonging and social activity; esteem and status; self-realization and fulfillment. When the dietitian announces that after listening to the speech, the listeners will in some way be better able to control their health, be more secure, be in a position where others think better of them or respect them more, think more of themselves, or feel they have the knowledge to develop latent potential in themselves, the audience "perks-up" and prepares itself to attend to the forthcoming message. Not every human need can be related to every topic, but as many as possible and as appropriate should be suggested during the introduction. During the "body" and "conclusions" of the speech as well, the speaker should remind the audience how what is being discussed can be related to fulfilling their own needs.

Finally, the last critical component to be included in the introduction is a list of the topics that will be discussed. It might be presented something like this: "Today I intend to discuss three specific points. Number one, I will discuss the relationship of diet to heart disease; number two, I will illustrate the fat and cholesterol content of foods; and thirdly, I will model how to order at a restaurant." As mentioned above, not only does this help the audience to listen to the talk with an expectation of what is to come, but the organization itself, adds to the "halo effect" and increases the audience's perceptions of the speaker's credibility.

Three Key Objectives of the "Body" of the Presentation. The "body" of the presentation is the second major division and the place where the points mentioned in the introduction are actually developed. Presenters need to have a rationale for the way they decide to organize this major section. The overall objectives generally are threefold: that the audience fully understand the message, that the audience believe, and that they be comfortable enough with the speaker to share their objections in the event that they are confused or wish to challenge the presenter.

To safeguard the first objective, understanding, speakers need not only to construct the message clearly and concisely, but also to design visual aids, handouts, and/or participative experiences to enhance the audience's understanding. The second objective, audience belief, needs continuously to be reinforced throughout the presentation. Credibility or lack of credibility continues to be inferred from the presenter's style and the quality of all aids associated with the presentation. The third objective, to develop a rapport with the audience to the extent that they dare challenge or question, is critical. When objections are unexpressed, presenters may infer falsely that the audience agrees and understands, causing the speaker to move too quickly from one point to another, leaving confused members behind.

A Presentation can be Concluded in More Ways than One. Like the first two, the third division of the presentation, the "conclusion", may be handled successfully in many different ways. The key is that all the ingredients be included somewhere. Ingredient one is for the audience to "feel" that the presentation is "winding down" and about to end. This needs to be done gradually and smoothly. It sounds nonprofessional and haphazard to end with remarks like "any questions," "that's all folks," "thank you for your attention." Remember the presenter's credibility is influenced by the audience's perceptions of how well he is organized. Clues such as "In conclusion . . .", "To summarize," "Before concluding, I want to leave you with one more thought," are helpful in letting the audience know that the presentation is about to terminate. If a summary is warranted, it should be given; if a final plea or pitch is warranted, that should be given; if a final quote, anecdote, or joke makes the point one more time, then that is appropriate.

One last word about conclusions is to be proactive in anticipating asking if there are any questions. Of course there are, but people are often hesitant to ask. The speaker should prepare a few for the audience, and then call on a participant who has been paying attention for a reaction. One might say, for example, "I noticed that you looked confused when I was discussing the fatty acid content of foods. What is it you would like further discussion of?" After responding to that first question generated by the presenter, it is often much simpler to get others to respond when the question is asked, "Are there any *other* questions or comments?"

Correlation Exists between "Form" and Speaker Credibility. Although the discussion of the presentation's design is generally divided into the three areas of introduction, body, and conclusion, there is no one perfect way to organize. Speakers, each with varied styles, can be successful. There are, however, several points to consider when deciding upon a presentation's format. A fact that most people are not aware of is that the presentation's organization is critical, primarily because it relates to the presenter's credibility.

For example, if a speaker were to deliver a talk to two different audiences, giving one audience ten slices of information in an organized way and giving the second audience the same ten slices of information in a disorganized way, both audiences would retain about the same amount of information after hearing the talk, but only one audience would consider it seriously or possibly change their attitude toward the subject matter.

When an audience hears an organized speaker, one who gives the audience a sense of his knowing exactly where he is going, with a defined beginning, middle, and end, they are more likely to infer that he is competent in the area he is talking about. On the other hand, many brilliant and qualified professionals are not taken seriously when giving presentations because they sound too "loose", too unprepared, too disorganized.

Media Credibility is Related to Inferences Regarding Presenter's Credibility. All media, the way they are designed, presented, and utilized, are an extension of the speaker and, consequently, reflect directly on the speaker's credibility. Media include such things as handouts, blackboard, flip chart, pad/easel, overhead projector, 35mm slides, motion pictures, sound recordings, video cassettes, samples of food products, food models/mock-ups, and so forth. "Excellence" tends to be inferred from those that are obviously carefully put together. For example, a presenter whose overhead transparencies are executed with large print that can easily be read, as opposed to ordinary typewriter print, which cannot be easily read from a transparency, allows for the inference of an experienced and considerate presenter. Other signs include using stenciled letters in bold colors on posters, rather than sloppy printing or cursive writing. The condition of the poster itself leads either to positive or negative impressions of the speaker. Those that are discolored, bent, and old looking suggest that the presenter does not care enough to add fresh aids for this group. Even the quality and color of the paper used in handouts can add or detract from the overall impression. If it is possible, the presenter is wise to try to coordinate all aids in colors that may be symbolic or meaningful. For example, a presenter giving a talk to a group on Saint Patrick's Day could make use of green; a talk to an Italian-American Club could be done in red, white, and green. This may sound superfluous but audiences do respond on an unconscious level to the extra care and preparation the speaker has made in tailoring a presentation on their behalf.

An unfortunate judgment often occurs to presenters who do not carefully proofread all their materials, including handouts, overhead transparencies, flip charts, posters, and the like, prior to the audience's exposure to them. While it is not rational, audience members do tend to make negative inferences about how credible presenters are in their area of expertise if they can't spell, count, or interpret statistics. **Proofread carefully!**

Whenever presenters are going to be using audio/visual equipment with which they are unfamiliar, it is critical that they arrive early enough to study it beforehand. The most competent presenters may lose their credibility entirely by not knowing how to turn on a machine or advance a slide.

Language and Style of Oral Presentations Differ from Those of Written Presentations. The written text and the oral presentation are entirely different. There is no objection to a presenter writing out the entire talk, carefully organizing it according to topics, causes and effects, chronology, or whatever else seems appropriate. Once the talk is written, however, the speaker needs to recognize that the written manuscript represents the "science" of a presentation; the actual delivery represents the "art". Each time it is delivered, it should be somewhat different, using different words, different examples, different anecdotes, and so forth to suit each particular audience and situation. The word choice too in the spoken language tends to be different from the word choice used in the written language. Sentences in oral speech tend to be simpler, shorter, and sound more conversational, including common words and contractions, while the written manuscript may be more erudite and academic. The only way for speakers to develop this "art" is to rehearse from a simple outline and not a manuscript, and to rehearse in front of real people who will react and comment, not mirrors, walls, or car windshields.

Oral Presentations Ought Never to be Read or Memorized. There are other good reasons for not rehearsing from a manuscript. The speech tends eventually to become memorized, and that can be deadly. Once a speech is memorized, speakers tend to become more "speaker-centered" than "audience-centered," which means that they tend to become more concerned about whether or not they can remember each line exactly as it is written on the manuscript and less concerned about whether or not the audience is enjoying, learning, listening, and understanding. Another problem that arises from manuscript speaking is that it is DULL! Because the facial expressions and vocal intonations are not spontaneous, the monologue tends to sound memorized and can easily become boring to listeners.

Advance Arrangements Need to be Carefully Considered. Take control of seating the listeners before everyone settles down. It may be their boardroom, gymnasium, or meeting hall, but it is the presenter's "show." Conscious decisions should be made about whether or not to pull the group into a circle, half circle, rows, around tables, and so forth. When it is possible to know beforehand which persons are the most influential, their seats should be reserved and placed in the best position to see, hear, and appreciate any visual aids as well as the speaker. A final checklist for presentations is found in Table 8-1.

Creating Positive Impressions Begins the Moment the Presenter Enters the Room. Presenters are being "sized-up" and adding to the presentation's ambiance from the moment they enter the room. They should, whenever possible, arrive early and make an effort to meet people. Their own self-confidence, whether real or feigned, will relax the audience and increase their perceptions of the speaker's desire to share information. Presenters should never volunteer any negative information regarding their own stress or fear of speaking. The audience wants to learn and enjoy, and when they are aware of the speaker's fragility or stage fright, they tend to become nervous themselves in sympathy.

If the presenters are waiting to be introduced and are seated among the audience or on a stage, they should be aware that those people who know they are the guest speakers, will be watching their every move.

Table 8-1. Final Checklist

Attend to details and prepare a final checklist. Listed below are a few questions that the presenter might consider in order to avoid last minute problems.

Do I have my presentation notes?
Do I have all my supporting materials?
Have I enough copies for each of the attendees?
Will the facility be unlocked and open?
Are the tables and chairs arranged to suit my design?
Do I understand how to operate the lighting system?
Do I understand how to operate the ventilation system?
Do I know the location and operating condition of the electrical circuits?
Do I know how to work the projector?
Do I have an extra bulb, cassette, video, extension cords, etc.?
Will the projection screen be in place and adequate for this size group?
Do I have the type of sound system I require? Is it working?
Have arrangements been made to handle messages during the presentation?
Are there arrangements for hats and coats?
Will there be a sign to announce the place of the presentation?
Will some one be introducing me, and have I given her all the information I want
   shared with the group?

That means that even before beginning the presentation, speakers must be careful to smile, look confident, and extend themselves to others. Once introduced, the way the speaker walks up to the podium is critical. During those first moments an initial impression is being created. The speaker should consciously walk confidently, looking and smiling toward the audience. Prior to uttering the first words to the audience, it is a good technique to spend a long 3 seconds just looking out at the audience, smiling and establishing eye contact with several individuals. This allows them to infer poise, confidence, and the speaker's desire to "connect" with them.

DELIVERING THE PRESENTATION

Never Share Internal Feelings of Fright or Anxiety. Speakers experience themselves in the situation from the inside out; the audience experiences them from the outside in. Simply, that means if asked if they are nervous, anxious, etc., speakers should always answer "NO!" The audience is picking up the "tip of the iceberg" from their observations of the "outside" of the speaker; they do not actually feel the intensity of the speaker's anxiety and will probably be totally unaware of it, unless it is brought to their attention through one's own confession. One must act confident, even when one may not feel it internally.

One of the worst things presenters can do is to admit to an audience that they are scared, ill prepared, missing material, or have done the presentation better in the past for other groups. The audience does not know what it might be missing, and is generally much less critical of speakers than the speakers are of themselves.

"Stage Fright" is a Vestige from Our Ancient Past. The feelings commonly referred to as "stage fright" may date back to the dawn of the human race, a time when our prehistoric ancestors had to survive by living in caves and sharing the food supply with other beasts. Faced by a predator, our ancestors had a genuine use for a sudden jolt of energy, which gave them the power to do battle or run, fight, or flight. The vestiges of this power, stemming from the secretions of the adrenal gland, still manifest themselves today when people sense danger. Who has not felt that ice block in the stomach while being reprimanded by the boss, or experienced the sweaty palms and racing heart while walking into a room full of strangers? Occasionally one still reads in the newspaper of accounts where individuals under conditions of fear or danger exhibit superhuman strength, the father, for example, who lifts the car off his child who has been pinned under the wheels. This is an example of the power that comes with the adrenaline jolt; however, when one is unable to fight, run, or in some other way utilize this surge, he may become overwhelmed by the internal feelings themselves. It is this feeling prior and during a presentation that is commonly labeled "stage fright."

The best safeguard against stage fright is adequate preparation and rehearsal. The more one practices in front of *live others,* the less nervousness one will have. Other ways of dealing with these feelings include being active during the presentation and "acting" calm and confident. If presenters know they are going to be full of extra energy because of their excess adrenaline secretions, they could plan on engaging in demonstrations during the presentation, passing handouts, using a pointer, or any other activity that involves motion. Motion is a release for the tension and anxiety and allows the audience to infer enthusiasm from the speaker's movement rather than fright, nervousness, or tension. It may not work for everyone, but many people can learn to control their public behavior if they visualize themselves as acting.

All movement should be meaningful. Do not pace. Presenters ought to look for opportunities to break the invisible barrier between themselves and their audience. Walking toward the audience, walking around the audience, walking in and out of the audience, walking among the audience are all acceptable ways of delivering a presentation. What is not acceptable is pacing back and forth, particularly with eyes down, as one pulls his thoughts together before uttering them. Movement into an audience is a communication vehicle in itself. When presenters penetrate that invisible barrier between themselves and the audience, they are nonverbally indicating their desire to connect, to be close, to better "sense" what it is the audience is feeling about the speakers and the content. In fact, as speakers walk among the audience, the audience can begin to be seen from a different perspective, and one may gain new insights into how better to clarify particular points and issues from this experience.

Unnecessary Barriers Between the Presenter and Audience Should be Omitted. Presenters do best when they omit all barriers between themselves and their audience. Avoid using a podium or lectern, even when one is provided by the sponsoring organization. Of course, there may be times when because of the quantity of material, a place to store things may be required. Even under this condition, using a table to set handouts and other materials on is preferred to a podium. A lectern should only be used when the speaker does not intend to move about; intends to lecture and needs a stand to rest against and place notes upon. Adults generally do not learn optimally through the lecture method and unless the speaker is extraordinarily good, straight lecture behind a podium should be avoided. When one delivers the message standing in front of the group, without a barrier, one is more disposed to stop the talk to respond to their verbal or nonverbal feedback. Gestures and movement too can be more expansive and visible without the lectern barrier.

Voice, Cadence, Pitch, Variation, and Rate are Communication Vehicles. Vocal inflection and variation add interest and add to the impression of speaker enthusiasm. For some people controlling this variation is simple and natural, but for others this is a challenge; nevertheless, the presenter needs to attend to voice modulation. The goal when speaking in front of a group is to sound natural and conversational; however, what sounds natural and conversational when one is standing in front of a large group of others is not the same as what sounds conversational in a small face-to-face group. "Natural and conversational" from the presenter's point of view is exaggerated. The highs need to be a bit higher and the lows need to be a bit lower. What may sound to the presenter's ear as "phony" and "theatrical" generally sounds far less so to the listener. The good news is that this trait can be fairly easily and quickly developed, even in those who recognize a problem in this area. It requires risking sounding foolish and exaggerated in front of trusting others, until adequate reinforcement has convinced the presenter that the increase in vocal variation is really to his advantage and allows him to be attended to more easily. In any case, a delivery that is of narrow range or monotone is difficult to attend to for more than a few minutes.

When talking in front of a group, generally the speaker should attempt to speak more slowly than in ordinary conversation. What is an appropriate rate in a small face-to-face discussion is probably too fast for a group presentation. For some reason, there seems to be a correlation between the speech rate of the speaker and the size of the audience. What might be easily grasped at a more rapid rate in face-to-face conversation, is not understood as quickly in large groups. Also the speaker's slower rate allows him to scan the audience better as he is speaking, to see if he is being understood, to see if some people need an opportunity to disagree, to see if he needs to talk louder, or increase his variation because some look bored.

Nonverbal Behavior, the Silent Language, can be Meaningful and Controlled. It is good practice to keep hands away from the body and from one another. Allow them to be free to gesture, and avoid holding anything in them while talking, unless it is a useful prop like a pointer or a visual aid. After 25 years of teaching presentational speaking to college undergraduates, this writer (R.J.C.) knows empirically that once speakers allow their hands to mesh together or to grasp one another behind the back, there is only a slight chance of their being released to gesture. Often people feel awkward with their hands hanging loosely at their sides. Perhaps if they could see themselves on videotape in this posture, they would realize that it is natural looking, but even more importantly, they would probably see that one tends not to stay in that position. As one talks with hands hanging loosely at the sides, eventually they begin to rise and gesture spontaneously to emphasize points the speaker feels important.

It is dangerous to begin a presentation holding a pen, paperclip, rubber band, or other instrument not directly related to the presentation. Unconsciously, the fingers begin to play with the instrument, and the audience becomes fascinated with watching to see what the speaker will do. A former student actually straightened out a paper clip and began to stab herself while talking. Needless to say, for the remainder of her presentation the class could not take their eyes off the mutilation scene, and missed the speaker's concluding points.

As One Speaks so Will One be Judged. Professional speakers attend to their diction, particularly when pronouncing words like "for," "can," "with," "picture," "going to," and "want to." In ordinary conversation one is not likely to judge negatively a speaker who mispronounces common words and engages in sloppy diction saying, for example, words like "fer," "ken," "wit," "pitcher," "gunna," and "wanna," for the words listed above; however, when that speaker is in front of an audience, these mispronounced words often stand out and lead to negative inferences regarding the speaker. If one thinks of well-known television anchor men and women, one will be unable to recall any who have faulty diction. Professionals who present themselves in front of groups must attend to their diction because they risk losing credibility if it is poor. Logical? No! True? Yes!

When individuals have decided to become conscious of their diction and decide to improve it, several steps are required. Step number one is to inform trusted others who are often around them to listen critically, and to stop them each time a diction error occurs. Only after individuals are made aware of their common errors, can they begin to train themselves to hear the errors. That is step two. Because the human mind operates generally at 5 times the rate of human speech, it is possible to listen critically to ourselves as we speak. Individuals attempting to rid themselves of poor diction or some other vocalized interference ("um," "ah," "and a", etc.) can train themselves to listen for the error and then to correct themselves. Like learning to ride a bicycle or to use a computer, this learning and training task is uncomfortable at first, but improvement comes quickly. Working on one's diction is an ongoing task. Professional speakers never stop listening to the way their words are coming out and planning ahead to pronounce them correctly.

The Visage Itself is a Communication Vehicle. Presenters need to train themselves to keep their faces animated, using a variety of facial expressions. For many of the same reasons expressed above, it is important that speakers use all the communication vehicles available to them in order to maintain the audience's attention. One's facial expression is itself a communication vehicle. When it is lively, animated, expressive, and changing regularly while the speaker reacts to the feedback coming toward him from the audience, it enhances the verbal message and allows the audience to go on unconsciously inferring the speaker's audience-centeredness. Because of their natural dispositional personality, ethnic background, life experience, and so forth, this is easier for some people to do than for others; however, everyone can improve! Because it is not easy for one to "act" expressive does not mean that one cannot grow considerably in the ability to look expressive. Indeed one can.

Eye contact is a vehicle of communication. It should be used to see everyone and respond to the nonverbal feedback. It is surprising how many people seem to remember having learned some rule about being able to fool the audience into thinking that the speaker is seeing them while actually looking over the heads of the people in the last row. The point is that when speakers have the opportunity to present themselves and their ideas to an audience, they want the audience to understand them, to believe them, to follow their recommendations. One has the best chance of being successful in achieving those goals when one is able to interpret the audience's ongoing reactions to what is being said. Even though presentational speaking is generally considered a one way communication situation, with the speaker talking at the audience as they listen, it is, in fact, a two way situation with audience and speaker communicating with one another constantly and simultaneously. Trained speakers see almost everything from their position in front of the room. If they are alert, they may see people who are beginning to fidget, and they can interpret this feedback. They might decide consequently to give the audience a short break; they might liven their own movements to regain attention; they might engage in a new activity, one perhaps that involves audience participation, and so forth. They might see some people coming in late, looking awkwardly for a seat. This gives them the opportunity to publicly welcome them and ask others to move over to provide seating. They might see people who look angry. This gives them the opportunity to say, "You look angry. What has been said to offend you?" In other words speakers who use their eyes to "connect" with the audience make them a part of the presentation. The audience knows it, and will begin to send signals when they realize the speaker is sensitive to them.

Facial expressions are important. Presenters must remember to smile, and look like they are enjoying the experience of sharing information. Smiling can be rehearsed and may feel phoney, but it needs to be built into the design of the presentation. Speakers do not need to be constantly grinning, but they do need to maintain an expression of gentleness, approachableness, and nondefensiveness. The easiest way to convey these impressions is smiling often. Unfortunately, it is not easy to smile when one is unsure of the material. All the principles above can only be heeded after the speaker has sufficiently mastered the content and consciously, through rehearsal, developed skills.

Although individual situations may make this difficult, a general rule to remember is that when speaking for an hour or less, always plan on at least 10 minutes for some audience interaction. In talks of more than 45 minutes, actual audience participation activities should be planned whenever possible and appropriate.

POST PRESENTATION

Remember to bring business cards and to remain afterwards for people who may want to talk. Speakers who have done a good job with eye contact, smiling, and have prompted the inference of warmth will almost always have some audience members who wish to engage them in some consultation afterwards. This is frequently a source of repeat talks to other groups, and it is an opportunity for the best kind of public relations, face-to-face. When there is a long line of persons waiting to talk and time is limited, pass out business cards and tell everyone they are entitled to one call for free consultation. It is amazing how many people follow up on the offer.

WORKSHOPS

There are significant differences between a presentation and a workshop or training session. The differences are in the amount of time needed, the amount of audience participation recommended, and the goals of the leader. Presentations generally run no more than 90 minutes, while workshops may run from 90 minutes to several days. Audience participation and training are an integral part of workshop design, and the goals of workshops are generally to teach and train, while a presentation's goal often is to persuade the audience to accept a specific proposal. The following suggestions are particularly appropriate when designing workshops.

Workshop leaders should plan on using techniques that involve all participants and encourage open communication between themselves and the participants and among the participants. Ways to encourage participation include dividing the larger group into smaller groups, always giving them time in their small group to get to know one another, and then giving the small group activities related to the workshop topic. These small group activities may include such things as case studies, either real or hypothetical, role playing, and questionnaire completion and discussion. Occasionally a group may be given a pre-workshop assignment to complete a questionnaire, read material related to the workshop, or some other task. Reactions to these tasks can be processed among the participants in small groups.

Frequently, the most important point in determining the climate and direction of the workshop occurs during the first 20 minutes. Some suggestions for using the opening minutes to establish an open climate include using a group introductory activity to promote a relaxed and open atmosphere. When the group is small enough, generally twenty or less, spending time allowing participants to express themselves by identifying their major concerns and questions tends to promote this involvement. Workshop leaders can relieve participant anxiety by introducing themselves, sharing both personal and professional information, giving a brief overview of their objectives for the workshop, the main topics to be covered, their sequence and approximate time span. They should also reinforce that they do have expectations in terms of participants' cooperation and participation. Even when such introductory activities take as long as an hour, they are justifiable, because of the importance in establishing a common frame of reference with shared goals in a relaxed and receptive setting.

The leader should be aware of signals of fatigue or boredom from participants. Some of the techniques to foster this include identifying two or three participants whose behavior provides some type of clue to group climate, providing a variety of activities to break-up the routine, and providing a change of pace. Most successful workshops are a blend of information presenting activities with "hands-on" experiential type of activities. Another way to safeguard understanding and attention is regularly to summarize what has occurred, especially before moving on to a new topic. Continuity of training is promoted if there are purposeful and periodic reviews and summaries during the workshop. Leaders should note that it is not essential that they do the summarizing; in fact, having the participants do it for themselves provides feedback as to whether or not the group has grasped the important points.

Just as the introductory period to the workshop should not be rushed, so too should closure be carefully attended to. Depending upon how much time is available for the entire workshop, of course, but in a full day's workshop of from 6 to 8 hours, allowing a full hour at the end for closure is appropriate. During this time loose ends are tied; the group's original expectations are reviewed and assessed as to how well these expectations have been met. Requiring the group to complete an evaluation of the workshop during the time provided for the workshop is the method most likely to get the largest return. These evaluations are most helpful to leaders who want to continue growing. They will process the evaluations and make changes in subsequent workshops based on the responses. Sample evaluation forms are included in Appendix G. The emphasis in a workshop is always on quality, not quantity. It is not how much the audience has heard; it is how much they have learned, will remember, will utilize in the future that is the final measure of the workshop's success.

ADDITIONAL READING

1. Anderson, D.: How to prepare for presentations. Training, *20*:98, December, 1983.
2. Bertrand, K.: Speak now, or. . . . Business Marketing, *75*:68, January, 1990.
3. LeRoux, P.: Mastering the art of the winning presentation. Working Women, *10*:84, February, 1985.
4. Mandel, Steve: Effective Presentation Skills. Los Altos, CA, Crisp Publications, 1988.
5. Mandel, Steve: Technical Presentation Skills. Los Altos, CA, Crisp Publications, 1989.
6. Mambert, W.A.: Effective Presentations. New York, John Wiley and Sons, 1976.
7. Raines, R.: Visual Aids in Business. Los Altos, CA, Crisp Publications, 1989.

SUGGESTED ACTIVITIES

1. Presentation I: Design and deliver a 10-minute presentation on some issue related to foods, nutrition, or dietetics, such as safety of the food supply, a new food product, fiber in foods, reduced fat or calories in foods, snacks, restaurant meals, or sodium.

2. Presentation II: Design and deliver a presentation intended for a group of parents of obese children. A minimum of two visual aids are required, transparencies and posters. Included with the 20-minute presentation should be 5 full minutes of audience/speaker interaction. "Are there any questions" at the conclusion is not acceptable.

3. Presentation III: Design and deliver a 30-minute presentation intended for a group of people who have recently learned they have diabetes. A minimum of three visual aids are required, including flip chart and handout material. Plan on at least 8 minutes of interaction with audience; this should be prompted by the speaker's perceptions of the nonverbal feedback emanating from the audience.

4. Presentation IV: Design and deliver a 60-minute presentation intended for a group of people who have paid to be taught and/or trained by you in an area related to your specialty in the area of dietetics. Develop whatever aids seem appropriate.

If possible all presentations should be videotaped. Presenters should provide reaction sheets to the audience and later write a critique of the taped presentation, responding to their own subjective reactions, the critique sheets of the audience, and the instructor's comments.

9

Planning Learning

Teaching is one of the major job responsibilities of all dietitians, whether they specialize in clinical, community, or administrative practice. Dietitians must be skilled in providing appropriate learning opportunities to patients, clients, and employees to facilitate their acquisition of knowledge, attitudes, skills, and new behaviors. Most dietitians are experts in the content that they teach, but they also need preparation in the process of helping others to learn. Dietitians are expected to be effective teachers.

Dietitians in clinical and community practice educate clients and patients about normal nutrition, and about dietary modifications necessitated by such medical problems as cardiovascular disease and diabetes. The dietitian may one day be teaching a 50-year-old man about fatty acids and cholesterol in foods and the next day be teaching an 18-year-old pregnant woman about prenatal nutrition. A study of Army dietitians reported that the time dedicated to nutrition education varied from 13 hours weekly for chiefs of nutrition care divisions to 36 hours for chiefs of clinical dietetics.[1] A wide variety of group and individual interventions was offered including weight control, prenatal nutrition, well-baby clinic, basic nutrition, alcohol rehabilitation, diabetic, low sodium, fat controlled instructions, fitness, wellness, and drug, alcohol, and cardiac rehabilitation programs.

Nutrition education has been defined as:

... the teaching of validated, correct nutrition knowledge in ways that promote the development and maintenance of positive attitudes toward, and actual behavioral habits of, eating nutritious foods (within budgetary and cultural constraints) that contribute to the maintenance of personal health, well-being, and productivity.[2]

Nutrition education has also been defined as a process "that assists the public in applying knowledge from nutrition science and the relationship between diet and health to their food practices."[3] The practitioner wants the individual not only to know what to do, but also to change current dietary behaviors and adopt and practice new ones. The changes sound simple: to avoid or decrease consumption of certain foods, to increase consumption of others, to shop for different foods, to read food labels, to change cooking methods, to order different foods at a restaurant, and the like. But they are not simple to accomplish. The

172

internal and external forces that have shaped people's eating habits, however, are complex, are of long-standing, and create barriers to successful, long-term change. Nevertheless, the final criteria of health education effectiveness has been described as "the adoption of desirable nutritional practices and their sequelae, better health and reduced disease prevalence."[4] The dietitian must be a facilitator of positive behavioral change in an ongoing educational process.[5]

Many dietitians are responsible for the supervision of one or more employees. Orientation, training, and development programs (human resource development) are necessary for these subordinates. An employee's on-the-job performance must meet standards acceptable to the organization, and it is the responsibility of the superior to ensure that training needs are recognized and met. The goal of training is to have employees know their job responsibilities and when necessary, learn and substitute new practices for current ones. The fact that an employee knows proper procedures but may not always follow them is an indication of the difficulty involved in getting a person to change.

Frequently, the terms "teaching" and "learning" are confused. Some people have the mistaken notion that if they teach something, the audience or individual learns automatically and will transfer the learning to appropriate situations. One may teach a pregnant woman what the four food groups are, for example, tell her why it is important to use them in menu planning, and give her printed handouts. A passive learner who has not participated actively in the learning may not make any connection between what was taught and her own food selection or menu planning. To change behavior, education should endeavor to further the adoption of better practices. Although knowledge is a prerequisite for change, knowledge in itself does not necessarily lead to a different behavior. In a study of the consumption of foods high in fat, nutrition knowledge was not found to relate to attitudes or to food consumption behaviors.[6] Research has shown that knowledge accounts for "4% to 8% of the variance in eating behavior, leaving 92% to 96% of the behavior to be accounted for by other influences."[7] Motivation and intention are vital for change. A person may be knowledgeable about a healthy diet, but lack perseverance. For example, a client may be familiar with the sodium-restricted diet, but still may consume salted pretzels.

Teaching factual information should not be mistaken for education. Education can be defined as the process of imparting or acquiring knowledge or skills in the context of the person's total matrix of living. Education should assist people in coping with their problems as they adapt to circumstances. The term "teaching" suggests the educator's assessment of the need for knowledge and the utilization of techniques to transfer knowledge to another individual, while the term "learning" refers to the process through which the individual acquires and stores the knowledge or skill and changes his behavior due to an interaction with, or experiences in, an educational environment. The change in behavior may be related to knowledge, attitudes, values, or skills. Health teaching and health education have been differentiated by their goals. The objective of the former, health teaching, is the "effective transmission of knowledge and skills, and that of the latter is to help people cope more effectively with problems related to their present and future health."[4] Achterberg describes the nutrition educator as a person who "deliberately seeks to progressively empower learners to act on food and nutrition-related issues such that the learner is gradually freed from the intervention and the materials."[8] She suggests that there is a planned effort, that the effort is a step-by-step process, that people are enabled to act on their nutrition knowledge, and that eventually people can act on their own making positive changes in their behavior and practicing self-care.

This chapter examines theories and principles of learning and compares the characteristics of adult learners with those of children. A model or framework for planning, implementing, and evaluating learning is presented. The first three steps, which are preassessment of the learner, planning performance objectives, and determination of the content, are examined along with information on grouping people together for learning. Discussion of the additional steps in the learning process follows in Chapter 10. The question of motivation is examined in Chapter 11.

PRINCIPLES AND THEORIES OF LEARNING

The scientific study of learning is carried on primarily by psychologists. Research has provided two major families of theories: (1) behaviorist theories, and (2) cognitive theories. They are discussed briefly and applied to principles of learning.

Behaviorist Theories. Behaviorist psychologists have concentrated on how individuals learn new habits or behaviors. Research has dealt with the stimulus, the response to the stimulus, and the consequences. A strengthening or weakening of behaviors as a result of the consequences has been noted. Satisfying consequences strengthen the connections between a learning stimulus and the response behavior, and increase the probability of recurrence of a behavior, while annoying states or aversive consequences weaken this connection. Thus, positive reinforcement or reward can be used to condition responses, but punishment is considered less effective. Behaviorists believe that to solve novel problems, learners may depend on similar stimulus-response situations, and if that does not work, they use trial and error responses.[9] The research of Pavlov, Thorndike, and Skinner is discussed more fully in Chapter 5, which the reader may wish to review.

The following are some principles of learning derived from the behaviorist research:[10]

1. Arrange for the prospective learner to be successful at the activity that is to be learned, since positive consequences reinforce responses and tend to make them recur, while bad experiences decrease responses so that people avoid the learning activity. The old saying "Nothing succeeds like success" reflects this phenomenon.

2. Be sure that every time a correct response occurs, some kind of satisfier or reward follows. This reinforces the response, so that the behavior is more likely to persist.

3. When teachers want someone to learn something, they should wait until the person demonstrates the particular knowledge or behavior, and then reward it. Too often incorrect responses receive attention, while correct responses are ignored. Correct actions should be reinforced.

4. Reward of a desirable response should follow immediately and not be delayed, since the strength of the connection between the stimulus and response is greater with immediate reward.

5. In the early stages of learning, reinforce every desired response. Later, begin to omit some reinforcement and use an intermittent schedule of reward. When reward is overused, it loses its effect, so that after a learner has had some rewarded successes, rewards should be given less frequently.

6. For learning sequential activities, determine the relative need for practice at each step. Some learning requires a chain of responses. Schedule the practice, including reinforcement at each step.

7. Retention depends on repetition of learning. Stimulus-response connections are strengthened with repetition.

8. Generalization of learning to similar situations suggests the importance of practice in varied contexts. If the learner is expected to respond to a variety of stimuli, practice should be given with several of the variety.

9. Knowledge of results is an effective secondary reinforcer. Learners should know their stage of progress. If they know they are doing something properly, that knowledge reinforces the response.

10. Do not reinforce undesirable behaviors or responses. They should be ignored, which should lead to their extinction. Correct behavior should be reinforced instead.

11. Punishment is ineffective in fostering learning. It is an aversive consequence that will make the learner avoid the situation in the future.

12. Do not try to teach if the learner is tired, irritated, preoccupied, or avoiding the learning situation. The individual has to have

positive conditions and be ready to learn in order to find learning satisfying.

13. Conflicts, frustrations, and barriers to learning should be recognized and resolved so that the learner is ready for a positive experience.
14. In testing the learner, the teacher should not use "trick" questions unless the learner has been familiarized with the stimulus situation. The learner should first be taught the tricks.
15. Some novel behaviors can be enhanced through imitation of models. People learn by watching the experiences of others.

Cognitive Theories. Cognitive psychologists are concerned with cognitive structures and consider "insight" a possible factor in learning to solve problems. The learner perceives a relationship, which leads to the solution of problems. Learning is discontinuous and sudden, with behavior changing when insight occurs. Cognitive learning theorists view behavior as purposive and goal-directed, rather than a response to a stimulus, and the learner follows a sort of internal, cognitive map to a goal. The person is viewed as an active, organizing entity, rather than a passive respondent to stimuli in the environment.[9]

The principles of learning from cognitive theory differ from behaviorist theory:

1. The learner should be active rather than passive as a listener, viewer, or responder. "Learning by doing" is emphasized.
2. Setting goals is an important motivation for learning, and successes and failures at learning determine how the learner sets future goals. Behavior is purposive.
3. Attention should be paid to careful analysis of the tasks that confront learners. The way the problem is displayed is an important condition of learning. Problems should be structured so their features are clear to the learner.
4. The way in which knowledge is organized should be planned in advance.
5. Learning that is understood is more permanent and transferable than rote learning.
6. Cognitive feedback must be provided to confirm correct knowledge and correct faulty learning, so that the learner is always left with the correct answer.
7. Motivation and drive are important to purposive behavior.

ADULTS AS LEARNERS

When we accept responsibility for teaching a client, patient, or employee, it is natural to think back to our own past experiences, or how we were taught in school and college. Most educational experiences were the result of pedagogy, which may be defined as the art and science of teaching children.[11,12] The teacher was an authority figure, and students were dependents who complied with assignments.

Adult education has challenged some of the basic ideas and approaches of pedagogy. Knowles has focused attention on beliefs about educating adults and, instead of pedagogy, uses the term "andragogy." He maintains that the basic assumptions regarding adult learners differ from those regarding child learners. His five major assumptions for adult learners involve the following:[11-13]

1. changes in self-concept from being a dependent to being a self-directed learner
2. the role of expanding experiences as a resource for learning
3. readiness to learn based on developmental tasks of social roles or any change
4. orientation to learning shifting from subject matter to problem solving and from a future-oriented to a present-oriented focus
5. motivation to learn more from internal than external sources

Self-Concept. Childhood is a period of dependency. As a person matures, the self-concept changes, and the individual becomes increasingly independent and self-directed. People make their own decisions and manage their lives. Once individuals become self-directed adults, they prefer to be independent and self-directing in learning experiences. Any educational experience in which one is treated as a dependent child is a threat to the self-concept. Negative feelings may result, such as resentment or anxiety, and will interfere with learning.

Experience. As compared with children, adults have an increasing background of experiences, which they bring to new learning situations. This background is a resource for learning. Ignoring the adult's experience may be misinterpreted as a sign of rejection. A client who has had diabetes for 5 years, for example, has a wealth of experience that should be recognized when the dietitian discusses the diabetic diet. To ignore this prior experience and start from the beginning may annoy, bore, or possibly antagonize the client, and may place obstacles in the way of the learning process. Teaching methods such as lectures are deemphasized in adult education in favor of more participatory methods, such as discussion or projects that recognize the person's wealth of experience. Practical applications that apply learning to the individual's day-to-day life are appropriate.

Readiness. Readiness to learn differs from children and adults. Children are assumed to be ready to learn because there are subjects they ought to know about, and there are academic pressures to perform. Adults have no such pressures and are assumed to be ready to learn things required for performing their social roles in life—as spouses, employees, parents, and the like, or in order to perform more effectively in some aspect of their lives. Education of adults should be appropriate to the individual's readiness, and a timing of learning experiences needs to coincide with readiness. People seek information and are ready to learn when they are confronted by problems that they must solve. For example, new employees may be ready to learn about their job responsibilities, but not necessarily about the history of the company. Clients may not be ready to learn about their modified diets until they have accepted the fact that their medical conditions and future health require it.

Orientation. A child's learning is oriented toward subjects, while an adult's learning is oriented toward performing tasks and solving problems. These different approaches involve different time perspectives. Because children learn about things that they will use some time in the future, the subject matter approach may be appropriate. Adults approach learning when they have an immediate need to learn because of a problem to solve, or a task to perform. The implication is that learning should be oriented to problems or projects that the individual is currently dealing with. Adults learn what they want to learn when they want to learn it, regardless of what others want them to learn.

Motivation. Children are motivated primarily by external pressures from parents, teachers, competition for grades, and the like. The more potent motivators for adults are internal ones, such as recognition, self-esteem, the desire for a better quality of life, and the like.

From an examination of various educational theories, Knowles described the appropriate conditions for learning to take place.[11,12] He suggested that learners should feel the need to learn something, and should perceive the goals of any learning experience as their own personal goals. Adults should participate actively in planning, implementing, and evaluating learning experiences to increase their commitment to learning, and the process should make use of the person's life experiences. The physical and psychological environment needs to be comfortable. The relationship between the instructor and learner should be characterized by mutual trust, respect, and helpfulness, and the environment should encourage freedom of expression and the acceptance of differences.

The professional who accepts the assumptions of "andragogy" becomes a facilitator of learning or a change agent rather than a teacher. The educator involves the learner in the process of learning and provides resources for assisting learners to acquire knowledge, information, and skills, while maintaining a supportive climate for learning.

The helping relationship was described by Tough, who investigated the self-planned learning projects of adults.[14] Tough found that when individuals initiate a learning project, they often seek the assistance of others. As described in Tough's research, the ideal helper is warm, loving, accepting, supportive, encouraging, and friendly. The helper cares about the learner and the problem and takes the problem seriously. The helper regards the learner as an equal. In contrast to a person who wants to control, command, persuade, and influence, the ideal helper views his interaction with the learner as a dialogue with mutual interaction, listening, understanding, responding, and helping.

ENVIRONMENT

Psychological Environment. The psychological climate for learning is important, and it is determined by the approach of the educator. A supportive environment with a tolerance for mistakes and with a respect for individual and cultural differences makes people feel secure and welcome. Openness and encouragement of questions create an informal atmosphere. Individuals should be known by their names, and respect for their opinions should be demonstrated. In groups, participants should be encouraged to introduce themselves and to get to know one another. Collaboration and mutual assistance rather than competition should be promoted, and initial feelings of anxiety should be reduced so they do not inhibit learning. The professional who creates this informal, supportive, and caring environment for adult learners can obtain better results than one who creates a formal, authoritative environment. When learners have negative memories of their early experiences in school, for example, if clients or employees were dismissed from high school, a physical or psychological climate which reminds them of their past unpleasant experiences will create barriers to learning.

Physical Environment. One should consider not only the psychological climate, but also the physical environment. Comfort should be provided with appropriate temperature, lighting, ventilation, and comfortable chairs to create conditions which promote learning rather than inhibit it. Noise from a radio, television, telephone, or people talking may interfere with a client's or patient's attention. Individuals should be able both to see and to hear. Interaction is facilitated by seating groups of people in a circle or around a table where everyone has eye contact, as opposed to seating people in row upon row of chairs.

STEPS TO EDUCATION

Successful educational efforts that meet the needs of the adult learner include a number of interactive steps. The framework and components are as follows:

1. preassessment of the needs of the individual or group
2. planning of performance objectives that are measurable, feasible, and able to be accomplished in a stated period of time
3. determination of the content based on the preassessment and the objectives
4. selection of methods, techniques, materials, and resources appropriate to the objectives and the individual or group
5. implementation of the learning experiences to provide opportunities for the person to practice new information

6. evaluation of progress performed continuously and at stated intervals, including rediagnosis of learning needs
7. documentation of the results of education

PREASSESSMENT

The first step in education is to conduct a preassessment with the client or employee. Preassessment is a diagnostic evaluation performed prior to instruction for the purpose of placement, or for establishing a starting point, and it serves to classify people regarding their current knowledge, skills, abilities, aptitudes, interests, personality, educational backgrounds, and psychological readiness to learn.

A need for learning may be defined as a gap between what people should know and what they know now, or the difference between how employees should perform and their actual performance. If preassessment determines that an individual already has some prior knowledge and experience, such as a client with long-term diabetes who knows the exchange system, more advanced material is indicated. One determines in advance how much the individual already knows, since it would be a waste of everyone's time to repeat known information, which could lead to boredom or lack of attention on the part of the learner. Does the client have the intellectual capabilities to understand the instruction? Some people are unable to read, and such limitations require that the instruction be planned at the client's level. Educational planning should be based on the dietitian's preassessment of the client's or employee's knowledge and ability.

Psychological preassessment is also necessary since the dietitian must understand the attitudes that influence the client's or employee's behavior. Attitudes are thought to be predispositions for action. Problems in learning may not be cognitive, or caused by deficits in knowledge; the cause and solution may be found in the affective domain, or in attitudes, values, and beliefs. Nutrition behaviors are the result of many motivations, and having nutrition information does not necessarily mean that it will be applied.[2] For example, the hospitalized patient who has just learned of a confirmed diagnosis of chronic illness is unlikely to learn much about a prescribed dietary treatment at that moment. The patient may be thinking: "Why me?" "What did I do to deserve this?" "How will this affect my job? my lifestyle? my marriage?" A new employee may feel high levels of anxiety, which may interfere with learning for the first few days on the job. Anxiety may arise whenever a superior trains a subordinate. "What does the superior think about me?" "I will appear to be dumb if I don't understand, so I had better pretend I do understand." These feelings are barriers to learning that must be reduced or eliminated prior to teaching.

In some situations, preassessment may be handled by oral interviewing. One may inquire: "Have you been on a diet before?" "Can you tell me what foods are good sources of potassium?" "Can you explain the relationship between your diet and your health?" In general, the line of questioning should be based on what the person needs to know. The focus group interview technique was useful in developing a nutrition education intervention for rural seniors.[15] Interviewing may be used with employees as well. "Have you ever used a meat slicer before?" "Can you show me how you set tables at the restaurant where you worked previously?"

In more formal situations, a preassessment test may be developed and administered. The purpose of the test is to evaluate the individual's knowledge and capabilities before instruction begins and to identify what the individual already knows. Pretest results may be compared later with posttest results after instruction has been completed. Preassessment is most necessary when the dietitian is unfamiliar with the knowledge, ability, and values of the client, patient, or employee.

In business, training and development programs are planned to meet present and future goals and objectives. Training provides specific skills, often motor or manual in nature, under the guidance of established personnel so that employees meet standards acceptable to the organization. Training is needed by new employees and by current employees accepting new assignments, such as after a promotion or transfer. A need for training may be described as the difference between a person's actual and desired performance, or when the employee lacks the knowledge or skill to perform an assigned task satisfactorily. Training needs may be determined in a number of ways, for example, by discussing needs and problems with supervisors or subordinates; by directly observing the work; by structured interviewing of employees; by seeing what is done correctly and especially what is not; by examining reports of accidents, incidents, grievances, turnover, productivity, and quality control and assurance; and by administering employee attitude surveys.[16-19] One may ask: "What are the attitudes, skills, and knowledge employees need in order to perform their jobs effectively?"

PERFORMANCE OBJECTIVES

Developing precise statements of goals can help to organize one's thinking regarding the purpose of instruction, i.e., what is to be learned. The educator needs to decide what is to be learned prior to selecting the methods and techniques to accomplish it. References to goal statements are found in the literature under the terms "behavioral objectives," "performance objectives," and "measurable objectives." Because the term "behavioral objectives" may be erroneously confused with behaviorism, the term "performance objectives" is used in this chapter. Written performance objectives are helpful tools in planning, implementing, and evaluating learning.

A well-stated performance objective communicates the teacher's instructional intent for the learner. It specifies the learner's behavior or degree of competence after instruction is complete. Writing performance objectives has many advantages. It results in less ambiguity regarding what is to be learned. Also, clear performance objectives make it possible to assess the degree to which the objectives have been achieved. Both the teacher and the learner benefit from clearer instructions. When learners know what they are supposed to learn, it does not come as a surprise. Learners should not be kept guessing about what should be learned or about what is important. This is a waste of their time.

Thus, initial effort is devoted to delineating the intended results of instruction for the learner, rather than to the methods or processes of learning. One first defines the ends and then explores the means to the ends. Instruction must benefit the learner, not the teacher, so one must focus initially on the result in the learner. If clear objectives are not written, the instructor cannot select content or materials for instruction. One cannot select an educational filmstrip, for example, without knowing what it is to accomplish. As pointed out by Mager, "If you're not sure where you're going, you're liable to end up someplace else."[20]

Objectives should focus on the person learning, not on the teacher. The following objective is poorly stated: "The dietitian will teach the client about his diet." Note that this statement focuses on what the instructor will do, and not on what the client or learner will do. The following is preferred because it focuses on the client: "After instruction, the client will be able to plan appropriate menus using the sodium-restricted diet as a reference."

One of the most useful guides to writing performance objectives was written by Mager.[20] A key to writing measurable performance objectives is the selection of the verb that describes the desired outcome. Some verbs are vague and subject to misinterpretation, as in the following objectives:

To know (is able to know which foods contain potassium)
To understand (is able to understand that foods high in potassium should be consumed daily when certain medications are prescribed)
To appreciate (is able to appreciate the importance of following the dietitian's instructions)

In the written objective for "to know," it is not clear whether "knowing" means that the client will purchase foods high in potassium, consume foods high in potassium, be able to relate which foods are high in potassium, or recognize them on a list. "Understanding" could mean being able to recall reasons, being able to read an article about it, or being able to apply knowledge to one's own situation. The meanings of knowing, understanding, and appreciating are not clear.

Instead, one should select verbs that describe what the person is able to do after learning has taken place. Note that the phrase "after learning, the individual is able to" is understood, and not included completely in writing objectives since one is describing what the person will be capable of doing. Another method involves starting with the action verb.

The first two examples are rewritten from the unsatisfactory objectives in the previous list. Better verbs to use are summarized in Table 9-1 and include the following:

To recall (is able to recite five good food sources of potassium)
To explain (is able to explain why foods high in potassium should be consumed)
To write (is able to list the four food groups)
To compare (is able to compare the nutrient needs of an adult woman with those of a pregnant woman)
To identify (is able to identify on the menu those foods which are permitted)
To solve or use (is able to plan menus using a diet instruction sheet)
To demonstrate (is able to demonstrate the use of the mixer)
To operate (is able to slice meat on the meat slicer)

Mager noted that three characteristics improve written objectives: (1) performance, (2) conditions, and (3) criterion.[20] The "performance" tells what the learner will be able to do after instruction has been given. The second characteristic describes under what "conditions" the performance is to occur. Finally, a "criterion" tells how good the learner's performance must be to be acceptable. Conditions and criterion may not be included in all objectives. In general, the more that can be specified, the better the objective and the more likely that the patient, client, or employee will learn what the dietitian intends.

Performance. The performance component of an objective describes the activity in which the learner will be engaged. The performance may be visible or heard, such as listing, reciting, explaining, or operating equipment, or invisible, such as identifying or solving a problem. While overt or visible performance may be seen or heard directly, invisible or covert performance requires that the learner be asked to do something visible to determine whether or not the objective is satisfied and learning

Table 9-1. Verbs Describing Performance

analyze	discuss	prepare
apply	distinguish	produce
assemble	evaluate	recall
calculate	explain	recite
cite	identify	recognize
classify	illustrate	recommend
compare	interpret	repair
complete	list	select
construct	measure	solve
contrast	name	state
define	operate	summarize
demonstrate	plan	use
describe	practice	write

VERBS TO AVOID

appreciate	feel	learn
believe	grasp	like
comprehend	hope	realize
discern	know	understand

has taken place. In invisible performance, one adds an indicator behavior to the objective, for example:

Is able to identify the parts of the meat slicer (on a diagram or verbally)

Identifying is invisible until the learner is asked to identify the parts on a diagram or to recite them verbally, which is an indicator behavior. The major intent or performance should be stated using an active verb, and an indicator should be added if the performance cannot be seen or heard.

Conditions. Once the performance has been clearly stated, one may ask whether or not there are specific circumstances or conditions under which the performance will be observed. The conditions describe the setting, equipment, or cues associated with the behavior. With what resources will the learner be provided? What will be withheld? Conditions are in parentheses in the following examples:

(Given the disassembled parts of a meat slicer) is able to reassemble the parts in correct sequence
(Using the diabetic diet menu for tomorrow) is able to select the proper foods in the correct quantities
(Given a list of foods including both good and poor sources of potassium) is able to identify the good sources
(Given a copy of a sodium-restricted diet) is able to plan a menu for a complete day
(Without looking at the diet instruction form) is able to describe an appropriate dinner menu
(Without the assistance of the dietitian) is able to explain the foods a pregnant woman should eat on a daily basis

These objectives give a more accurate and complete picture of the exact performance expected of a learner. While every objective may not have conditions, there should be enough information to make clear exactly what performance is expected.

Criterion. Once the end performance has been described and the conditions, if any, under which it will be observed have been described, a criterion may or may not be added. The criterion describes a level of achievement, that is, how well the learner should be able to perform. It is a standard with which to measure performance. Possible standards include speed, accuracy, quality, and percentage of correct answers.[20]

A time limit can be used to describe the speed criterion. This is necessary only when speed is important, and if it is, it should be included in the objective. The following are examples:

Is able to type (50 words per minute)
Is able to reassemble the meat slicer (in 5 minutes or less)
Is able to complete a diet history (in 20 minutes)

For objectives that require the development of skill over a period of time, one must determine how much time is reasonable in the initial learning period as opposed to the time when the skill is well developed. A new employee cannot be expected to perform a task as rapidly as an experienced person.

While speed is one type of standard, a second is accuracy. Accuracy should communicate how well the learner needs to perform for his performance to be considered competent. Examples include:

Is able to type 50 words per minute (with 5 errors or less)
Is able to identify good sources of potassium (with 80% accuracy), when given a list of foods including both good and poor sources
Is able to plan a menu for a complete day (with no errors) when given a copy of a sodium-restricted diet
Is able to calculate the carbohydrate in the diabetic diet (within 5 grams)

If the learner is expected to perform with a degree of accuracy, this criterion should be included in the objective.

After considering whether speed and accuracy are important, one should examine the quality of the performance to assess what constitutes an acceptable performance. It is easier to communicate quality when objective standards are available to both the learner and the instructor. Any acceptable deviation from the standards can then be determined. Examples of such standards are as follows:

Is able to reassemble the meat slicer (according to the steps in the task analysis)
Is able to measure the amount of sanitizer (according to the directions on the label)
Is able to substitute foods on a diabetic menu (using the diabetic exchanges)

In these examples, the quality of performance has been stated according to a known standard.

Domains of Learning

After developing skill in writing measurable performance objectives, one should consider the range of objectives that may be written. Objectives have been organized into taxonomies or classification systems to focus on precision in writing, and one may examine the range of possible outcomes desired from instruction. There are three taxonomies: (1) the cognitive domain, (2) the affective domain, and (3) the psychomotor domain.

Cognitive Domain. A taxonomy of educational objectives in the cognitive domain was published by Bloom and others.[21] The cognitive domain involves the acquisition and utilization of knowledge or information and the development of intellectual skills and abilities. According to Bloom and co-authors, the cognitive domain has six major levels or categories and a number of subcategories as shown in the following:[21]

1.0 KNOWLEDGE
    1.10 Knowledge of specifics
    1.20 Knowledge of ways and means of dealing with specifics
    1.30 Knowledge of the universals and abstractions in a field
2.0 COMPREHENSION
    2.10 Translation
    2.20 Interpretation

2.30 Extrapolation
3.0 APPLICATION
4.0 ANALYSIS
    4.10 Analysis of elements
    4.20 Analysis of relationships
    4.30 Analysis of organizational principles
5.0 SYNTHESIS
    5.10 Production of a unique communication
    5.20 Production of a plan, or proposed set of operations
    5.30 Derivation of a set of abstract relations
6.0 EVALUATION
    6.10 Judgments in terms of internal evidence
    6.20 Judgments in terms of external criteria

The classes are arranged from simple to complex, from concrete to more abstract. The objectives in any one class are likely to be built on the behaviors in the previous class. The subcategories help to define the major headings further and make them more specific.

The educational planner needs to think beyond the simplest levels of knowledge and also to write objectives at higher, more complex levels. Without examining the possibility of writing higher-level objectives, one may tend to think only in terms of knowledge and comprehension, which are the easiest objectives to write. The learner may then be denied the opportunity of applying knowledge or using it in problem solving and will be reduced to memorizing facts. In nutrition education, for example, knowing facts is necessary, but the client also needs the ability to analyze food labels, to synthesize all information learned so that he may tell others about it, and to evaluate nutritional information in making wise food choices. In the following discussion of the six levels in the taxonomy, examples of objectives are given.

Knowledge. At the lowest level in the cognitive domain, knowledge involves the remembering and recall of information. This includes the recall of specific bits of information, terminology, and facts, such as dates, events, and places, chronological sequences, methods of inquiry, trends over time, processes, classification systems, criteria, principles, and theories.

Example: Is able to list foods high in sodium.

Comprehension. The second level, comprehension, is the lowest level of understanding. It involves knowing what is communicated by another person, and being able to use the information communicated. The use of information may include translation, restatement or paraphrase, interpretation, summarization or rearrangement of the information, and extrapolation or extension of the given information to determine implications or consequences.

Example: Is able to explain (verbally or in writing) why certain foods are excluded on the diabetic diet.

Application. At the level of application, one is able to use information, principles, or ideas in concrete situations. Knowledge is understood sufficiently to be able to apply it.

Example: Is able to plan a sodium-restricted menu for the day.

Analysis. This level entails the breakdown of information into its parts to identify the elements, the interaction between elements, and the organizing principles or structure. Relationships may be made among ideas.

Example: Is able to analyze the nutrition labeling on a food product.

Synthesis. Synthesis requires the reassembling of elements or parts to form a new whole. One may assemble a unique verbal or written communication, a plan of operation, or a set of abstract relations to explain data.

Example: Is able to explain the low cholesterol diet accurately to a friend.

Evaluation. At the highest level in the cognitive taxonomy, evaluation is the ability to judge the value of material. Such judgment requires the use of criteria, which may be internal criteria, such as logical accuracy or consistency, or external criteria, such as external standards.

Example: Is able to evaluate a nutrition article from the daily newspaper.

Affective Domain. The affective domain deals with changes in attitudes, values, beliefs, appreciation, and interests. Often, one wants a client or employee not only to comprehend what to do, but also to value it, accept it, and find it important. Attitudes and beliefs about food are widely recognized as important determinants of an individual's food habits. According to Johnson and Johnson, the purpose of nutrition education is "to create informed consumers who value good nutrition and consume nutritious foods throughout their lives."[2] When imparting information fails to bring about behavior change, the common response is to redouble efforts to teach facts and explain why something should be done. Instead, the examination of attitudes and values should be considered.

The affective domain involves a process of internalization. It categorizes the inner growth that occurs as people become aware of, and later adopt, the attitudes and principles that assist in forming the value judgments that guide conduct. For the client learning about prenatal nutrition, the instructor may desire the person not only to be knowledgeable (cognitive domain) about the proper foods to eat during pregnancy, but also to value the knowledge so much (affective domain) that she eats nutritious foods and practices good nutrition. An objective in one domain may have a component in another. Cognitive objectives may have an affective component, and affective objectives may have a cognitive one.

Affective objectives are more nebulous and resist precise definition; therefore, evaluation of their achievement is more difficult. The educational planner may find it a formidable task to describe affective behaviors involving internal feelings and emotions, but they are as important as overt behaviors. Because affective objectives are more difficult to express, most written objectives express cognitive behaviors.

Krathwohl and others published a taxonomy of educational objectives in the affective domain.[22] It includes five categories and a number of subcategories:

1.0 RECEIVING (ATTENDING)
    1.1 Awareness
    1.2 Willingness to receive
    1.3 Controlled or selected attention
2.0 RESPONDING
    2.1 Acquiescence in responding
    2.2 Willingness to respond
    2.3 Satisfaction in response
3.0 VALUING
    3.1 Acceptance of a value
    3.2 Preference for a value
    3.3 Commitment
4.0 ORGANIZATION
    4.1 Conceptualization of a value
    4.2 Organization of a value system
5.0 CHARACTERIZATION BY A VALUE OR VALUE COMPLEX
    5.1 Generalized set
    5.2 Characterization

The ordering of classes describes a process by which a value progresses from a level of mere awareness or perception to levels of greater complexity until it becomes an internal part of one's outlook on life that guides or controls behavior. This internalization may occur in varying degrees, and may involve conformity or nonconformity. At higher levels, behavior may be so ingrained that it is unconscious rather than a conscious response, and responses may be produced consistently in the absence of external authorities, and in spite of barriers. Thus, a client may eventually select a proper diet without thinking about it at the conscious level.

Receiving. At the lowest level of the affective domain, the learner is willing to receive certain phenomena or stimuli. Receiving represents a willingness to attend to what the teacher is presenting. The learner may move from a passive level of awareness or consciousness, to a neutral willingness to tolerate the situation rather than to avoid it, and then to an active level of controlled or selected attention despite distractions.

Example: Is able to listen to instructions on diabetic diets

Responding. The second level, responding, indicates a desire on the part of the learner to become involved in, or committed to, a subject or activity. At the lowest level of responding, the learner may passively acquiesce, or at least comply, in response to the teacher. At a higher level, a willingness to respond or voluntarily make a commitment to his chosen response is evident. Finally, a feeling of satisfaction or pleasure in response involves an internalization on the part of the learner.

Example: Is able to read diet materials with interest and ask questions.

Valuing. At the third level, valuing, the learner believes that the information or behavior has worth. The individual values it based on a personal method of assessment. When the value has been slowly internalized or accepted, the learner displays a behavior consistent with the value. When something is valued, motivation is not based on external authorities or the desire to obey, but on an internal commitment. The learner may demonstrate acceptance of a value, preference for a value, or commitment and conviction.

Example: Is able to select a nutritious meal from the cafeteria line.

Characterization. The highest level, characterization, indicates that the values have been internalized for a sufficient time to control behavior, and the individual acts consistently over time. A generalized set is a predisposition to act or perceive events in a certain way. At the highest level of internalization, beliefs or ideas are integrated with internal consistency.

Example: Is able to select only those foods permitted on the diet at all times.

Behavioral change in the affective domain takes place gradually over a period of time, whereas cognitive change may occur more rapidly. Affective change may take days, weeks, or months at the higher levels.

Psychomotor Domain. The psychomotor domain involves the development of motor or manual skills. Knowledge and attitudes may be necessary to perform these skills. For example, one could not drive a car or operate a meat slicer, tasks requiring manual skills, without some basic knowledge of the equipment. The authors who developed the cognitive and affective domains did not develop a taxonomy for the psychomotor domain, but more than one has been published.[23,24] The performance of motor action proceeds to increasingly complex steps. Simpson's seven levels and subcategories are as follows:[23]

1.00 PERCEPTION
    1.10 Sensory stimulation
        1.11 Auditory
        1.12 Visual
        1.13 Tactile
        1.14 Taste
        1.15 Smell
        1.16 Kinesthetic
    1.20 Cue Selection
    1.30 Translation
2.00 SET
    2.10 Mental set
    2.20 Physical set
    2.30 Emotional set
3.00 GUIDED RESPONSE
    3.10 Imitation
    3.20 Trial and error
4.00 MECHANISM
5.00 COMPLEX OVERT RESPONSE
    5.10 Resolution of uncertainty
    5.20 Automatic performance
6.00 ADAPTATION
7.00 ORIGINATION

Perception. The lowest level of the psychomotor domain is perception. It involves becoming aware of objects by means of the senses— hearing, seeing, touching, tasting, and smelling—and by muscle sensations or activation. The learner must select which cues to respond to in order to perform a task. The individual then must mentally translate the cues received for action.

Example: Is able to recognize a need to learn how to use the meat slicer.

Set. The second level, set, suggests a readiness for performing a task. In addition to being ready mentally, the learner must be ready physically, by correct positioning of the body, and emotionally, by having a favorable attitude or willingness to learn the task.

Example: Is able to demonstrate readiness to learn to use the meat slicer.

Guided Response. The third level is guided response. The teacher or trainer guides the learner during the activity, emphasizing the individual components of a more complex skill. The subcategories include imitation of the teacher and trial and error until the task can be performed accurately. Performance at this level may initially be crude and imperfect.

Example: Is able to practice the steps in using the meat slicer under supervision.

Mechanism. Mechanism, the fourth level, refers to habitual response. At this stage of learning, the learner demonstrates an initial degree of proficiency in performing the task, which results from some practice.

Example: Is able to use the meat slicer properly.

Complex Overt Response. The fifth level of complex overt response suggests that a level of skill has been attained over time in performing the task. Work is performed smoothly and efficiently without error. Two subcategories are resolution of uncertainty, in which a task is performed without hesitation, and automatic performance. Performance is characterized by accuracy, control, and speed.

Example: Is able to demonstrate skill in using the meat slicer.

Adaptation/Origination. Adaptation requires altering motor activity in new but similar situations, such as in adapting slicing procedures to a variety of different foods on the meat slicer. The final level, origination, refers to the creation of new physical acts.

In understanding the psychomotor domain, it may be helpful to recall the process of learning to drive an automobile, responding to the physical and visual stimulation, feeling mentally and emotionally ready to drive, learning parallel parking by trial and error under the guidance of an instructor, developing a degree of skill, and finally starting the car and driving without having to think of the steps. With time, sufficient skill is developed so that the person can adapt quickly in new situations on the road and create new responses automatically.

Using the taxonomies ensures that the objectives of learning are not limited to the lowest levels, that is, to the recall of facts, or to the cognitive domain only. The taxonomies assist the educational planner in thinking of higher levels of knowledge, which may be more appropriate behaviors for the learner. They also serve to remind the planner that there are interrelationships among the three domains. The dietitian should be concerned not only that clients can plan menus using their diets, but also that they think that the diet is important enough to their health to follow it. Employees need not only to know proper sanitation procedures, but also to value them if they are going to practice optimum sanitary procedures regularly.

ADOPTION OF INNOVATIONS

The Cooperative Extension Service of the U.S. Department of Agriculture and other groups have used a model to promote the adoption of innovations.[25] The process by which adults adopt new ideas and practices involves five stages:

1. Awareness. A person becomes aware of a new idea, practice, or procedure. Note that this is the same as level 1.1 in the affective domain.

2. Interest. A person is concerned enough to seek further information about something, is aware of his current behavior, and is willing to discuss it. The individual sees possibilities for the use of something new.
3. Evaluation. A person mentally weighs the advantages and disadvantages of the new idea. The individual asks, "Can I do it?"
4. Trial. A person tries or tests the usefulness of the new idea or practice on a small scale once or twice. It is still a low priority.
5. Adoption (or rejection). A person performs consistently as a habitual procedure indicating that something is accepted, highly valued, and found satisfying.

Nutrition education and employee education are incomplete until stage five is reached. People learn only what they want to learn, and adopt new behaviors to satisfy the basic needs of survival or to achieve some personal goal. Innovations are more readily adopted if they offer sufficient advantage over current practices, if they are compatible with current practices, if they are easy to understand and to use, if they can be divided into smaller units for trial, and if their benefits are clearly and quickly demonstrated. Nutrition education rates poorly on some of these criteria.[26] Research findings suggest that reaching the level of adoption requires considerable communication and a lengthy time span. It may be unrealistic to expect new behaviors to be adopted from short-term educational endeavors. A compromise dietary regimen or the achievement of one or two goals for change may not be what the professional considers best, but limited benefits may be preferable to total abandonment of a dietary regimen.[4]

DETERMINING THE CONTENT

A close examination of the objectives helps to identify the content of the instruction. The objective states what the learner will be able to do when instruction is complete and directs attention to the appropriate content. The preassessment may have eliminated certain objectives as unnecessary, and those that remain should be examined in planning content. Some learners may need to start at the lowest level in the taxonomy, while those who have already mastered the lower level objectives are ready for those at higher levels.

ORGANIZING TRAINING GROUPS

Learning may take place individually or in groups. Groups are advantageous in that they save time and provide opportunities for people to share experiences. Those who are successful in making dietary changes can model behaviors and discuss information with those who have been unsuccessful in coping. The more complex the information to be learned, the greater the need to discuss it in groups.

Even when one individual is involved, the dietitian should consider whether or not others should be present. In nutrition counseling and education, the individual responsible for purchasing the food and preparing the meals should be present. When a child is placed on a modified diet, such as a diabetic diet, usually the mother requires instruction as well, since her cooperation is essential to the child's successful adherence to the diet.

Training sessions for employees may be organized in several ways. Frequently, all new employees are grouped together for initial orientation and training. Although current employees may be grouped by age, educational level, amount of experience, or job title, the best grouping probably occurs when employees with similar learning needs are together. Waitresses may require sessions on sanitary dish and utensil handling, for example, while cooks may need classes on sanitary food handling. The learning needs of employees differ according to their job content and level of current knowledge. The preassessment should show differences in knowledge levels and should assist in making grouping decisions.

Another question is whether supervisors should be grouped in the same classes as their employees. One disadvantage of such a grouping is that the employees may be reluctant to participate by asking questions when the superior is present. The final decision rests on the size of the group. There is more opportunity for individual participation in small groups of 10 to 15 than in groups of 30 to 50 or more.

This chapter has explored the initial steps in planning learning. After preassessment has been completed, performance objectives should be written in the cognitive, affective, and psychomotor domains. Either individual or group instruction may be organized. The content of instruction may be determined from an examination of the objectives. Chapter 10 explores the remaining steps in the framework for education.

REFERENCES

1. Johnson, K.D., and Rinke, W.J.: Nutrition education: A review of results and a report provided by Army dietitians. J. Am. Diet. Assoc., *88*:1582, 1988.
2. Johnson, D.W., and Johnson, R.T.: Nutrition education: A model for effectiveness, A synthesis of research. J. Nutr. Ed., *17*:S1, 1985.
3. Position paper of The American Dietetic Association: Nutrition education for the public. J. Am. Diet. Assoc., *90*:107, 1990.
4. Hochbaum, G.M.: Behavior and education. In Nutrition, Lipids, and Coronary Heart Disease. Edited by R. Levy, B. Rifkind, B. Dennis, and N. Ernst. New York, Raven Press, 1979.
5. Franz, M.J.: Diabetes and nutrition: State of the science and the art. Top. Clin. Nutr., *3*:1, 1988.
6. Shepherd, R., and Stockley, L.: Nutrition knowledge, attitudes, and fat consumption. J. Am. Diet. Assoc., *87*:615, 1987.
7. Fleming, P.L.: Nutrition education and counseling. In Paige, D.M.: Clinical Nutrition. St. Louis, C.V. Mosby Co., 1988.

8. Achterberg, C.: A perspective on nutrition education research and practice. J. Nutr. Ed., *20*:240, 1988.
9. Swenson, L.: Theories of Learning. Belmont, CA, Wadsworth Publ. Co., 1980.
10. Bugelski, B.: The Psychology of Learning Applied to Teaching. 2nd ed. Indianapolis, Bobbs-Merrill, 1971.
11. Knowles, M.S.: The Adult Learner: A Neglected Species. 2nd ed., Houston, Gulf Publ. Co., 1978.
12. Knowles, M.S.: The Modern Practice of Adult Education. New York, Association Press, 1970.
13. Knowles, M.S.: Andragogy in Action. San Francisco, Jossey-Bass, 1984.
14. Tough, A.: The Adult's Learning Projects. Toronto, The Ontario Institute for Studies in Education, 1971.
15. Crockett, S.J., Heller, K.E., and Peterson, J.M.: Assessing beliefs of older rural Americans about nutrition education: Use of the focus group approach. J. Am. Diet. Assoc., *90*:563, 1990.
16. Laird, D.: Approaches to Training and Development. 2nd ed., Reading, MA., Addison-Wesley, 1985.
17. Morrison, J.: Determining training needs. In Training and Development Handbook. 2nd ed., Edited by R. Craig. New York, McGraw-Hill Book Co., 1976.
18. Rose, J.C.: Handbook for Health Care Food Service Management. Rockeville, MD, Aspen Publ., 1984.
19. Kaufman, R.: A needs assessment primer. Training and Development J., *41*:78, 1987.
20. Mager, R.F.: Preparing Instructional Objectives. 2nd ed., Belmont, CA, David S. Lake Publ., 1984.
21. Bloom, B.S., Engelhart, M., Furst, E., Hill, W., and Krathwohl, D.: Taxonomy of Educational Objectives, Handbook I: Cognitive Domain. New York, David McKay, 1956.
22. Krathwohl, D., Bloom, B.S., and Masia, B.: Taxonomy of Educational Objectives, Handbook II: Affective Domain. New York, David McKay, 1964.
23. Simpson, E.: The classification of educational objectives in the psychomotor domain. Illinois Teacher of Home Econ., *10*:110, 1966.
24. Harrow, A.: A Taxonomy of the Psychomotor Domain. New York, David McKay, 1972.
25. Nestor, J., and Glotzer, J.: Teaching Nutrition. Cambridge, MA., Abt Books, 1981.
26. Yarbrough, P.: Communication theory and nutrition education research. J. Nutr. Ed., *13*:S16, 1981.

SUGGESTED ACTIVITIES

1. Make a list of questions you would ask in the preassessment of knowledge of some subject with which you are familiar.

2. Write three performance objectives using active verbs to describe behavior.

3. Write examples of performance objectives containing conditions and a criterion.

4. Write examples of objectives in various levels of the cognitive, affective, and psychomotor domains. Note overlap from one domain to another.

5. Decide which of the following performance objectives are well-written.

A. Presented with a menu, the patient will be able to circle appropriate food selections according to his diet.

B. At the close of the series of classes, the clients will be more positively disposed toward following their diets.

C. After counseling, the patient will know which foods he should eat and which he should not.

D. The patient will be able to explain the diabetic diet to her husband.

6. Examine the following objectives and decide whether each concerns primarily the cognitive, affective, or psychomotor domain.

A. All clerical staff should be able to type 50 words per minute without errors.

B. Given a series of objectives, the student will be able to classify them according to the taxonomies in the chapter.

C. At the end of the session, clients will request more weight control classes.

ANSWERS:
5. A and D
6. A. psychomotor
6. B. cognitive
6. C. affective

10

Implementing and Evaluating Learning

The initial steps in planning learning, discussed in Chapter 9, include a preassessment of the learner's current knowledge and competencies, the development of performance objectives in the cognitive, affective, and psychomotor domains, and the determination of the content to be learned. This chapter discusses the selection and implementation of appropriate learning activities for the cognitive, affective, and psychomotor domains. Learning styles and the sequence of material is also considered. In addition, plans for the evaluation of the results of learning and for documentation are also discussed, as these steps are necessary to complete the educational process.

SELECTING AND IMPLEMENTING LEARNING ACTIVITIES

Various methods and techniques of educational presentation are available to assist adults in reaching the objectives of learning. Techniques are defined as: "the ways in which the educator facilitates learning."[1] They establish a relationship between the teacher and the learner, and between the learner and what he is learning. They include lectures, discussions, simulations, demonstrations, and the like. All are not equally effective in facilitating learning, and each has its advantages and disadvantages, its uses and limitations which are summarized in Table 10-1. In deciding which one will be most effective, the educator may be guided by several factors, including learner preference or style, group size, facilities available, time available, cost, and one's previous experience or the degree of success with the technique.[2] In addition, an examination of the performance objectives may suggest which approach is most appropriate, as methods and techniques may differ for the cognitive, affective, and psychomotor domains. All factors being equal, one should select the technique that requires the most active participation of the learner. As Confucius said:

> I hear and I forget,
> I see and I remember
> I do and I understand.

Lecture. The lecture is the presentation technique most familiar to people. It has been used for years as a method of informing and transfer-

Table 10-1. Strengths and Weaknesses of Teaching Methods.

	Strengths	Weaknesses
Lecture	Easy and efficient Conveys most information Reaches large numbers Minimum threat to learner Maximum control by instructor	Learner is passive Learning by listening Formal atmosphere May be dull, boring Not suited for higher level learning in cognitive domain Not suited for manual learning
Discussion Panel Debate Case study	More interesting, thus motivating Active participation Informal atmosphere Broadens perspectives We remember what we discuss Good for higher level cognitive, affective objectives	Learner may be unprepared Shy people may not discuss May get sidetracked More time consuming More threatening Size of group limited
Projects	More motivating Active participation Good for higher level cognitive objectives	
Laboratory experiments	Learn by experience Hands on method Active participation Good for higher level cognitive objectives	Requires space, time Group size limited
Simulation Scenarios In-basket Role playing Critical incidents	Active participation Requires critical thinking Develops problem solving skills Connects theory and practice More interesting Good for higher level cognitive objectives and affective objectives	Time consuming Group size limited
Demonstration	Realistic Appeals to several senses Can show a large group Good for psychomotor domain	Requires equipment Requires time Learner is passive, unless can practice

ring knowledge—the lowest level in the cognitive domain—from the teacher to the learner, especially in situations where there are large numbers of learners and a great deal of information to be communicated. In spite of the advantages of efficiency, a major drawback is that there is no guarantee that the material is learned and remembered since the learner is a passive participant whose learning depends on listening. This may be the least effective technique. While many educated people may respond positively to lectures because of long experience with this mode, people with less education may learn better with other methods.

Their attention may wane quickly, especially if the lecturer is not an effective speaker or if the lecture is dull, and new information may be rapidly forgotten. Furthermore, lectures do not meet the requirements of adult education, or "andragogy," for self-directed learning and problem solving approaches. (See Chapter 9, "Adults as Learners"). When lectures are employed, ample time should be given for a question-and-answer or discussion period.

Discussion. In discussion techniques, whether on a one-to-one basis or in groups, learners are active participants, and they internalize the knowledge through their responses. Discussion may be guided by the dietitian's raising open-ended questions or key issues, or it may be more group-centered if individuals are fairly well acquainted.[3] Debates and panel discussions, in which several people with specific knowledge informally discuss or debate an assigned topic in front of a larger group, are other approaches. The basis for discussion may be common experiences, problems, topics that were preannounced so that the group has prepared, or case studies of real-life situations, which are developed. For best results, seating should be arranged in a circle so that everyone can see and hear one another, and so that the teacher can participate as a member of the group. There is more opportunity for participation in smaller group sizes of 10 to 15, since increased size means less opportunity for participants to speak and influence others.[3]

While it is more time-consuming than lecture, discussion may be more interesting for learners, and thus more motivating, especially with higher level cognitive objectives and with affective objectives. Discussion and oral summarization facilitate and promote the individual's acquisition and retention of information. When people study alone, or are passive listeners, some cognitive processing may not take place.

Simulation. Simulation of real situations may also be considered, and several means of representation may be utilized, such as scenarios, in-basket exercises, critical incidents, and role-playing. These methods involve learning by "doing" or "experiential learning" rather than learning by "listening." Direct learner involvement is necessary for optimum transfer of learning. Simulation may be based on scenarios or models of real-life problem situations. In-basket exercises test the learner's ability to handle day-to-day challenges. The technique has been used to simulate a supervisor's decision-making ability in handling problems which arrive in the in-basket on the desk each day. Written memos, notes, requests, or reports are given to an individual and require a decision. Critical incidents also require the learner's responses to specific situations. Emergencies or unusual incidents are used, and the learner has to provide a response in handling the situation.

The use of role-playing, in which two or more persons dramatize assigned parts or roles simulating real-life situations, is another possibility. Role playing allows learners to try or practice new behaviors in relatively safe environments, and it can be used to work through real problems.[4] This is followed by discussion of the problem, ideas, feelings, and emotional reactions, as for example, role-playing of an employee disciplinary problem. While time-consuming, simulations may be helpful in providing opportunities for learners to make a connection between theory and practice, to engage in critical thinking, and to develop problem-solving and coping skills. Simulation may be used with both cognitive and affective objectives.[5]

Demonstration. A demonstration may be used to show how something is done, or to explore processes, ideas, or attitudes.[3] Usually, the learner observes as the instructor makes the presentation. The demonstration may be a dramatic learning experience if the learner's attention is held and may be appropriate for any type of learning objective. If skills are demonstrated, the learner will need an opportunity to practice the skill at a later time. Sometimes, duplicate work operations are set up independently of the work site and are used for training.

Audio-Visual Aids. According to an old Chinese proverb, "one picture is worth more than 10,000 words." An effective media presentation can enhance learning by providing variety and improving memory through visual stimulation. One may include the use of audio-visual aids, such as videotape and television, slides, films, flip charts, posters, chalk board, overhead transparencies, food models, actual foods, and audiotapes. A videotape explaining the diabetic exchange lists was found to be both effective and time saving.[6] The appropriateness of such material to the learning situation, and to the individual or group, should be considered. A videotape of one's own setting, for example, would probably foster better learning among employees than one that is purchased. Other teacher-made materials, such as charts, exhibits, and handouts may be effective aids. Such materials are an adjunct to learning and should not be considered the total learning experience. A summary of the advantages and disadvantages of various audiovisual aids is found in Table 10-2.

Other techniques to promote learning by individuals rather than by groups include coaching, programmed instruction, computer-based training which is used by over half of U.S. organizations with 50 or more employees, laboratory experiences, interactive video, apprenticeship, job rotation, job enlargement, and personal reading.[7,8]

Techniques for Different Domains. For learning in the cognitive domain, most of the above techniques may be effective. There are additional factors to consider in fostering learning in the affective and psychomotor domains.

In the affective domain the educator seeks to influence the learner's interests, attitudes, and values. This cannot be accomplished in an hour or a day, but requires ongoing contacts. At the lowest level in the affective domain, receiving and awareness, the professional may gain the learner's attention through the use of audio-visual materials or guided discussion. At higher levels where the adoption of new attitudes

Table 10-2. Advantages and Disadvantages of Audiovisual Aids.

	Advantages	Disadvantages

Chalkboard	Good for large groups
	Gives visual summary of
	  points made
		Can't be seen in large
		  rooms

Overhead
  projector/
  transparencies
	Use for large groups
	Can leave a light on for
	  note taking
		Print size may be too
		  small to be seen

Flipchart	Gives permanent record Use for small groups	Large groups won't see
Slides/filmstrips	Use for large groups Provides visual emphasis	Can't take notes Need ability with projectors May be expensive
Videos/films	Adds motion Shows techniques More true to life	Can't take notes Need ability with projectors May be expensive
Real objects/ food models	Shows actual examples Realistic	

Posters/
  pictures
	Use for small groups	Print size may be too
		  small to be seen

Handouts	Saves note taking
	Audience focuses on
	  listening
	Good for all groups
	Provides an accurate
	  record to take home	

and values is important, the learner must participate more fully. Attitudes are acquired through interpersonal influences, and commitments that are made public are more likely to be adopted than those that are private.[9] Discussion in a group or where experiences are shared, discussion of case studies or critical incidents, and role-playing may be effective, especially if they lead to higher self-awareness and public commitment, and if people perceive that all members of the group support the new attitudes and behaviors. Active oral summarization following discussion is recommended because it leads to more elaborate thinking and integration into the person's conceptual framework.

Effective instructional strategies which influence deeper-level learning of nutrition and the modification of attitudes and dietary behaviors have been recommended. Strategies promoting the active involvement of participants and interpersonal interaction in a group, which are related to the social context, help to achieve deeper-level learning, attitude modification, and behavioral change. The strategies suggested to accomplish this include: (1) cooperative learning, (2) inquiry learning, (3) nutrition experiments and experiences, (4) out-of-class experiences, and

(5) academic controversies.[9] Competitive and individual learning are not as effective.

In cooperative learning, learners work together to achieve goals for learning that are mutually held. They collaborate, effectively share information and analyses, and teach and assist each other. By teaching others, people enhance their own learning.

A second strategy, inquiry learning, requires use of the problem-solving process, which consists of stating a problem, gathering data, analyzing data, selecting possible solutions, testing solutions, and finally selecting the best solution to the problem. Clients can be guided through this process so that they learn to solve their own nutrition problems.

Experiments using laboratory animals for nutrition research and hands-on activities, such as planning nutritious menus and preparing varieties of new foods for a diet, are a third approach. An example of experiences outside of the classroom as a means of instruction is to require learners to shop for and evaluate certain foods.

In using academic controversies, participants take opposing sides of an issue, explore their differences, and try to come to consensus. These five types of experiences promote more elaborate cognitive processing, higher-level reasoning, problem solving, decision making, positive attitudes, and motivation. They can lead to group decisions in which members commit themselves publicly to better food habits.[9]

Modeling is also a method of influencing behavior.[9,10] People learn by imitating others in unfamiliar or new situations. The instructor should behave as the learner is expected to behave, modeling the desirable attitude or behavior. People are more likely to accept new behaviors when they meet and have discussions with people who have successfully adopted them. This technique is appropriate for nutrition education.

Skills in the psychomotor domain are learned with direct experience and practice over time. The professional may begin with a demonstration, but then the learner needs to practice the skill under supervision. Coaching is a term which describes the assistance given to someone learning a new skill, and it can apply to an educational experience as well as a sport. It suggests a one-on-one, continuous, supportive relationship from which an individual learns over time. It is perhaps the best method of on-the-job training of employees. The trainer can give encouragement, confidence, and guidance as the trainee performs the task.[11] Coaching takes into consideration different learning abilities and needs, allows actual practice, and provides people with immediate feedback regarding their performance.

Learning Styles. Each of us has a unique learning style. If you remember your own school experiences, you preferred some teaching methods to others, and retained material presented in a preferred manner for a longer time than material delivered in another way. A unique learning style differentiates individuals in terms of preferences for content, delivery, learning environment, and teaching techniques.

Different styles of learning reflect the fact that learners differ in their preferences for and ability to process various instructional messages. Brilliant individuals who do well learning principles and theories from reading, for example, may be all thumbs in a hands-on experience. Some people prefer to learn in a group, others prefer to learn on their own, and some do well in both situations. While some learn well by listening, those who do not enjoy listening to lectures may like learning in a group discussion. Others are visual learners. These preferences influence learning and have important implications for educators.

Learning styles are defined as "people's characteristic ways of information processing, feeling, and behaving in and toward learning situations."[12] Components of style that influence learning are cognitive, affective, and environmental factors.

Cognitive factors include the person's preferences in thinking and problem solving. Those who think through an experience tend more to abstract dimensions of reality. They reason and analyze what is happening. Schools tend to value the analytical learner. Others who sense and feel tend to prefer to learn through more concrete, actual experiences and are more intuitive. While some learn best by thinking through ideas, others learn best by testing theories or through self-discovery, or by listening and sharing ideas.[13,14]

In addition to perceiving differently, people process information in different ways. Some are reflective, watching what is happening and thinking about it. Others are doers who prefer to jump right in and try things. In a study environment, some require absolute silence, some can block out sound, and others prefer sound and turn on a radio or stereo when learning.

The learner's style preference may vary from situation to situation, affected by the subject matter or skill to be learned. People may learn by thinking and feeling and by reflecting and acting.

Instruction can be improved and learning will be easier and more enjoyable if the teacher identifies and considers the learner's preferred learning style. If learning style inventories are unavailable, the instructor can diagnose learning style by observing how people learn or asking them questions about their preferences, such as "Do you prefer to read, to view, or to listen, or to have actual experience?" "Do you prefer to learn alone or in groups?" Appropriate methods can then be selected.

Teachers need to be able to offer a variety of experiences whereby people learn by listening and sharing ideas, by thinking through ideas reflectively, by hands-on experiences, by solving problems, by experimentation, by trial-and-error, and by self-discovery. Since preferred style varies with the situation, offering a variety of techniques and methods that reflect the variety of ways that individuals acquire knowledge and skills helps the learner.

In addition to learning style, teaching style is a related matter which affects learning significantly. Teaching style refers to the instructor's preferred instructional methods and procedures. Some evidence suggests that teachers tend to select learning activities based on what they themselves prefer when they should be focusing on the learner's preferred style. Teaching behaviors and styles have an effect on learners and on teaching effectiveness.

Task Analysis

In instruction that requires the learner to develop a skill, a task analysis is helpful. Employees need to learn the skills related to their jobs, and clients may need to develop skills in menu planning and food preparation using a new diet. Regardless of the kind of skill involved, the learner needs to be able to perform the skill initially, and then to improve the skill through continued practice. After grasping the basics of tennis, driving a car, or baking a cake, for example, the learner requires repeated experience to develop a skill.

Instruction involving the initial development of a skill requires examination of what the job or task entails, the conditions under which it is performed, and the proper method of performance. The task should be broken down into its elements and key points and put into writing. If available, a job description may be used as a starting point in determining job content, but job descriptions do not give specific enough information for determining the content of training.[15] All of the tasks included in a job should be listed individually. If the job description is unavailable or incomplete, it may be necessary to interview employees or observe their work to determine the job content. Wait staff, for example, complete a number of tasks during the day, such as greeting customers, taking their orders, placing orders in the kitchen, serving the courses of the meal, busing dishes, setting tables, receiving payment for services, and maintaining good public relations. Each is a separate task making up the total job, and each task or set of actions can be defined.

The next step is to complete a written task analysis or series of task analyses for each different task of the job. A task analysis, sometimes referred to as a job breakdown, is a sequential list of the steps involved in performing any task from beginning to end. Usually, the major steps are numbered, and each step describes what to do.[15] Many job-related tasks involve the psychomotor domain; thus actions are listed in the analysis. It is often necessary, however, to have some background knowledge from the cognitive domain in performing the task. Balancing a check book, for example, is both a manual and intellectual skill, as is operating a cash register.

After the sequential steps are listed, each one should be examined to see whether there are explanations from the cognitive domain that need to be added. For example, if step one is to plug in the meat slicer, a key point is to have dry hands to avoid the danger of electrical shock. If a final step in the wait staff's task analysis for busing dirty dishes includes washing hands, an explanation may be added regarding the transfer of microorganisms to clean food and utensils. In food service, sanitation and safety statements are frequently needed. Explanations of how or why a step is necessary or notes on materials or equipment may be considered. There are a number of different ways to complete a task analysis.[11,15-18]

Once written, the task analysis should be used both by the instructor and by the learner. The instructor or trainer may examine the task analysis in order to construct learning objectives, which describe the behavior expected at the end of training. In assessing the learner's need for instruction, the instructor should consider the difference between the skill described in the task analysis and the learner's current skill to define the gap in knowledge or skill that must be addressed. The trainer should demonstrate to the individual what to do, and then allow him or her to perform the task. The learner may use the task analysis as a reference since it describes what to do in sequence. Using the task analysis in coaching or in supervised on-the-job training facilitates the learning of skills.

After mastering the basic skill involved and being able to recognize the correct sequence of procedures, the learner needs repeated practice to improve the skill. With time and practice, improvements in speed and quality of work should develop.

Job Instruction Training

A great deal of employee training takes place not in the classroom, but on the job. New employees require orientation and training with either an experienced worker or a supervisor. Current employees may need retraining periodically, may be assigned new tasks, or receive promotions which require the development of new skills and abilities. During World War II when men left for the military services, there was a great need to train job replacements. A four-step process entitled Job Instruction Training (JIT) was delineated for rapid training of new employees. It was used successfully then, and with refinements, continues to be one means of training. It may be used to teach skills, and is based on performance rather than subject matter. The four steps are (1) preparation, (2) presentation, (3) learner performance, and (4) follow-up. Prior to instruction, a task analysis should be completed, and the work area arranged with the necessary supplies and materials that the employee is expected to maintain.[16]

Part I of JIT prepares the employee psychologically and intellectually for learning. Since a superior may be the trainer, any tension, nervousness, or apprehension in the subordinate employee must be over-

Table 10-3. How to Instruct

Part I: Prepare the learner.

Put the learner at ease.
State the job.
Find out what the individual knows about the job.
Develop interest.
Correct the person's position.

Part II: Present the operation.

Tell, show, and illustrate.
Explain one important step at a time.
Stress key points.
Instruct clearly, completely, and patiently, but no more than the learner can master.
Summarize the operation in a second run-through.

Part III: Try out performance.

Have the learner do the job.
Have the learner explain key points while performing the job again.
Make sure that the learner understands.
Continue until you know that the person knows the job.

Part IV: Follow-up.

Put learner on his own.
Designate where to obtain help.
Encourage questions.
Taper off.
Continue with normal supervision.[8]

come, since it may interfere with learning. A friendly, smiling trainer puts the person at ease by creating an informal atmosphere for learning, where mistakes are expected and tolerated. The trainer states the job to be learned and asks specific questions to determine what the learner already knows about it. When employees become interested in their jobs, their motivation for learning increases. Finally, the trainer should be sure that the employee can physically see what is being demonstrated.

In Part II, the trainer presents and explains the operation as the employee is expected to perform. The trainer shows, tells, and illustrates the operation one step at a time using a prepared task analysis. Key points should be stressed. The instruction should be carried out clearly, completely, and patiently, with the trainer remembering the employee's abilities and attitudes. Since the ability to absorb new information is limited, the trainer needs to determine how much the learner can master at a time. It may be 5 to 10 steps with key points, or it may be more. It may be 15 minutes or 1 hour of instruction. Overloading the learner with information is ineffectual since the information will be forgotten. After this initial instruction, the operation or task should be summarized and performed a second time.

Part III tests how much the learner has retained as he or she tries out the operation using the written task analysis as a reference. The learner does the job while the trainer or coach stands by to assist. Accuracy, not speed, is stressed initially. As the individual completes the task a second time, the trainer should ask the employee to state the key points. To be sure of understanding, the trainer should ask such questions as "What would happen if. . . ?" "What else do you do. . . ?" and "What next. . . ?" Employees may need to repeat the operation 5 times, 10 times, or however many times are needed until they know what to do. The trainer continues coaching and giving positive feedback, encouragement, and reassurance until the employee learns the operation.

Follow-up occurs in Part IV as supervision tapers off. At first, the employee is left alone to complete the task. The individual should always know, however, where to obtain assistance if it is needed. Any additional questions ought to be encouraged since minor points may still arise. Normal supervision continues to ensure that the task is done as instructed, since fellow workers may suggest short cuts which are undesirable.

Mager pointed out that when the learner's experience is followed by positive consequences, the individual will be stimulated to approach the situation, but that when aversive consequences follow, the learner will avoid the situation.[10] A positive consequence may be any pleasant event, praise, a successful experience, an increase in self-esteem, improvement in self-image, or an increase in confidence. Aversive conditions are events or emotions that cause physical or mental discomfort, or that lead to loss of self-respect. They include fear, anxiety, frustration, humiliation, embarrassment, and boredom. In influencing learners in the affective domain, as well as the other domains, the instructor should positively reinforce learner responses.

Sequence of Instruction

Since there is a great deal to learn, instruction requires some type of organized sequence. Sequence of instruction is characterized by the progressive development of knowledge, attitudes, and skills. Learning takes place over time, and the process should be organized into smaller units. Since the ultimate outcome is able performance, it is important to consider how meaningful the sequence is to the learner, not the teacher or trainer, and whether or not it promotes learning. Mager and others provide several recommendations for sequencing. Instruction may be arranged from the general to the specific, from the specific to the general, from the simple to the complex, or according to interest, logic, or frequency of use of the knowledge or skill.[2,17]

In moving from the general to the specific, an overview or large picture should be presented first, and then the details and specifics are presented. For example, an overview of the reasons for the diabetic diet and the general principles of the diet should be presented prior to the details. With a new employee, a general explanation of the job should precede the specifics. Once the learner has digested some information, it is possible to consider a specific to general sequence.

Material may be organized from the simple (terms, facts, procedures) to the complex (concepts, processes, theories, analyses, applications) so that the learner handles increasingly difficult material. If the taxonomies are used in writing objectives for learning, the hierachy of the taxonomies provides a simple to complex sequence.

Another possibility is sequencing according to interest, or from the familiar to the unfamiliar. One may begin instruction with whatever is of most interest or concern to the learner. Initial questions from learners suggest such interest and should be dealt with immediately so that they are free to concentrate on later information. "How long will I have to stay on this diet?" "Can I eat my favorite foods?" Information desired by the learner is a good starting point for discussion. Similarly, if the learner perceives a problem, the dietitian can start with that problem rather than with a preset agenda. As learning proceeds, the individual may develop additional needs for information or goals for learning, which they may then address. Individuals who have assisted in directing their own learning tend to feel more committed to it.

Logic may suggest the sequence. Certain things may need to be said before others. Safety precautions may need to be introduced early, for example, when discussing equipment. Sanitary utensil handling may be important to discuss with wait staff prior to discussing how to set a table.

Frequency of use of the knowledge or skill may also dictate sequence. The skill used most frequently should be taught first, followed by the next most frequently used skill. If training time runs out, at least the learner has learned all except the least frequently used skills. The instructor should teach first what people "need to know" rather than the "nice to know" information.

Finally, the instructor should provide learners with total job practice. While learners may have been practicing individual elements of the job, they also need practice on the total job. This practice may be provided in the actual job situation or through simulation.

EVALUATION OF RESULTS

The step most often overlooked in education is probably that of evaluation. The literature indicates that evaluation of nutrition programs is frequently omitted.[19,20] Evaluation connotes the determination of the value or worth of something. Everyone uses this process daily, both consciously and unconsciously. "Does the food taste good?" "Is she dressed well?" "Was the television show worth watching?" "Did I learn anything?" One's thoughts turn to evaluation automatically. According to Popham, systematic educational evaluation "consists of a formal appraisal of the quality of educational phenomena," such as programs, products, or goals.[21] That it is systematic suggests that advance planning has taken place and that the process will provide data on the merits of the educational endeavor. One must consider not only what to evaluate, but also when to evaluate and how the evaluation will be done.

Although the terms "measurement" and "evaluation" are sometimes interchanged, their meanings should not be confused. Measurement is the process of collecting and quantifying data on the extent, degree, or capacity of achievement. Testing is one kind of measurement, for example. Measurement involves determining the degree to which an individual possesses a certain attribute, as when one receives 85 on a test, but it does not determine worth. Measurement systems require experimental designs, data collection, and statistical analysis of the data.[21] Evaluation is based on the measurement of what people know, think, feel, and do. Evaluation compares the observed value to a standard or criteria of comparison. Evaluation is the process of forming value judgments about the quality of programs, products, goals, and the like from the data. One may evaluate the success of an educational program, for example, by measuring the degree to which goals or objectives were achieved. Evaluation goes beyond measurement to the formation of value judgments about the data. To be effective, evaluation designs should specify not only what will be evaluated, but also when. Sometimes several measurements are needed, as in pretesting and posttesting.

Purpose of Evaluation

There are several purposes of evaluation. Program evaluation may be used for planning, improvement, or justification.[8] Evaluation is a system of quality control to determine whether the process of education is effective, to identify its strengths and weaknesses, and to determine what changes should be made. To determine accountability, one needs to know whether people are learning, whether dietitians are teaching effectively, whether programs yield the desired outcomes, and whether money is well spent. It is important to determine whether the objectives were accomplished, and whether the individual learned what was intended or developed in desired ways.[22] Evaluation helps educators to make better decisions and to improve education. Evaluation will be helpful in making decisions concerning teaching, learning, program effectiveness, and the necessity of making modifications in current efforts or even of terminating them. In times of limited financial resources, accountability requires an examination of cost/benefit ratios. Is the program so useful and valuable that costs are justified? Evaluation provides evidence that what one is doing is worthwhile. Plans for evaluation should be made early when one is in the planning stages of an educational endeavor, and not after it has begun or is completed.

As with other parts of his adult education model, Knowles has suggested that evaluation should be a mutual undertaking between the educator and the learner.[23] He recommends less emphasis on the evaluation of learning, and more on the rediagnosis of learning needs, which will suggest immediate or future steps to be taken jointly by the professional and the learner. This type of feedback from evaluation becomes more constructive and acceptable to adults. Thus, evaluation may be considered something one should do with people, not to people. If problems are apparent, then solutions may be found jointly by the educator and the learner.

Formative and Summative Evaluation

Formative and summative evaluation are two types of evaluation used to improve any of three processes—curriculum construction, teaching, or learning. Formative evaluation refers to that made during the course of education, with the feedback of results modifying the rest of the educational endeavor. Summative evaluation refers to a summary assessment of results at the conclusion of learning.[24]

Formative evaluation is a systematic appraisal that occurs during a course of instruction or learning activity for the purpose of modifying or improving teaching or learning. It can help to diagnose problems in student learning and in teaching effectiveness. It pinpoints parts mastered and parts not mastered and allows for revision of plans, methods, techniques, or materials. Formative evaluation may be performed at frequent intervals. If the learner appears bored, unsure, anxious, quizzical, or lost, or if one is unsure of the person's abilities, it is appropriate to stop teaching and start the evaluation process. Ask the person to repeat what he has learned. In diabetic education, for example, if formative evaluation shows that the individual does not understand the concept of food exchange lists, he will not be able to master more complex behaviors, such as menu planning. Having located the problem that the exchange lists are not comprehended, the dietitian can change approaches to try to overcome the problem. Perhaps the use of an alternative explanation that is clearer or simpler, or the use of concrete illustrations is indicated. Ideas and concepts may need to be reviewed. Sometimes, in group education, a group member is able to provide an explanation that the person understands better than the professional's explanation.

Failure to learn may not always be related to instructional methods or materials per se, but may derive from problems that are physical, emotional, cultural, or environmental in nature. By performing evaluation after smaller units of instruction, one can determine whether the pacing of instruction is appropriate for the patient or employee. Frequent feedback is necessary to facilitate learning. It is especially important when a great deal has to be learned. Mastery of smaller units can be a powerful positive reinforcement for the learner, and verbal reward may increase motivation to continue learning. When mistakes are made, they should be corrected quickly by giving the correct information. Avoid saying: "No, that's wrong." "Can't you ever get things right?" "Won't you ever learn?" Positive, not negative, feedback should be given. Approach the problem by saying, "Let me help you with that."

Summative evaluation has a different purpose and time frame than formative evaluation. Summative evaluation is considered final, and it is used at the end of a term, course, or learning activity. The purpose of summative evaluation may be grading, certification, or evaluation of progress, and the evaluation distinguishes those who excel from those who do not. Judgment is made about the learner, teacher, or curriculum with regard to the effectiveness of learning or instruction. This judgment aspect creates the anxiety and defensiveness often associated with evaluation.

Evaluation should be a continuous process that is preplanned along with educational sessions. Evaluation preassessment determines the individual's abilities before the educational program, and progress should be evaluated continuously during as well as immediately following the educational program. Follow-up evaluation at 3 or 6 months may measure the degree to which one has forgotten knowledge or has fallen back to previous behaviors.

Types of Evaluation

After considering the purpose and timing of evaluation, one should resolve the question of what to evaluate. Four types of evaluation have been suggested. These are (1) participant reactions to programs, (2) measures of change in an organization, (3) measures of behavioral change, and (4) evaluation of learning in the cognitive, affective, and psychomotor domains.[22,25] The evaluation of health education is usually focused on one or more of three types: knowledge, attitudes or beliefs, and/or behavior.[26]

Participant Reaction to Programs. The first type of evaluation deals with participant reactions to educational programs. One needs to decide what should be evaluated. Were participants satisfied with the program, subject matter, content, materials, speakers, room arrangements, and learning activities? When a program, meeting, or class is evaluated, the purpose is to improve decisions concerning its various aspects, to see how the parts fit the whole, or to make program changes.[27] These aspects may include structure, arrangements, administration, physical facilities, and personnel. The quality of such learning elements, such as objectives, techniques, materials, and learning outcomes may be included also. Hedonistic scales have been used to determine a happiness index, or the degree to which participants "liked" various aspects. These judgments are subjective.

Organizational Change. Educators involved with employee training gather a second type of evaluative data to justify the time and expense to the organization. Management may want to know how training will benefit the organization in relation to the cost. Results in terms of the following aspects may be attributed, at least in part, to training: improved morale, improved efficiency or productivity, improved quality of work, less employee turnover, less frequent accidents, better absenteeism and attendance records, dollar savings, number of employee errors, number of grievances, amount of overtime, and the like.

Behavioral Change. A third type of evaluation is the measurement of behavior. Did behavior or habits change based on the learning? In measuring behavior, the focus is on what the person does. In employee training, for example, one may assess changes in job behaviors to see whether transfer of training to the job has occurred. It is necessary to know what the job performance was prior to training and to decide who will observe or assess changed performance—the supervisor, peers, or the individual. The ultimate aim of nutrition education is not merely the improvement in knowledge, but also changes in dietary behaviors and practices as the individual develops better food choices.[28,29] These changes are difficult to confirm and often depend on direct observation, which is time consuming, on self-reports, and on indirect measures, such as weight gain in a person on a weight reduction diet.[26]

Learning. Whether learning has taken place is a separate question, even if the program rated highly on entertainment value. The learning of principles, facts, attitudes, values, and skills should be evaluated on an objective basis, and this task is more complex. If the learning objectives are written in terms of measurable performance, they serve as the source of the evaluation. To what degree were the objectives achieved by the learner? Whether one has succeeded in learning can be determined by developing situations, or test items, based on the objectives of instruction. It is important for the test items to match the objectives in performance and conditions. If they do not match the objectives, it is not possible to assess whether instruction was successful, i.e. whether the learner learned what was intended.

Mager pointed out that several obstacles must be overcome to assess the results of instruction successfully. Some obstacles are caused by the objectives, while others result from attitudes and beliefs on the part of instructors.[30]

One of the problems in evaluation results from inadequately written objectives. If the performance is not stated, if conditions are omitted, and if the criterion is missing, it will be difficult to create a test situation. If these deficiencies are discovered, the first step is to rewrite the objective.

Norm- and Criterion-Referenced Methods. The attitudes and beliefs of the instructor also influence the evaluation of learning. Some attitudes may result from one's own experiences in school. One may believe that the test should not be too easy, but the degree of difficulty of a test is not important. The question is whether or not the learner can perform what is stated in the objectives. Perhaps the instructor believes that some of the questions have to be difficult so that a spread of scores is produced, to separate the brightest from the rest, the "A's" from the "B's" and "C's." Tests are purposely developed so that not everyone is successful, and variation in individual scores is expected. Students are graded in a norm-referenced manner by comparison with others on the same measuring device or with the norm of the group. A norm-referenced instrument indicates whether the individual's performance falls in the 50th percentile or the 90th in relation to the group norm.[21,30]

Another approach to evaluation is the criterion-referenced method. Instead of comparing learners with each other, the instructor compares each individual with an objective standard of what the learner is expected to be able to know or to be able to perform after instruction is complete. A criterion-referenced measurement ascertains the person's status in respect to a defined objective or standard, and test items correspond to the objectives. If the learner can perform what is called for in the objective, the learner has been successful. If not, criterion-referenced testing, which tends to be more diagnostic, will indicate what is lacking, and more learning can be planned.[21] No doubt everyone has had the experience of being told to learn one thing and then being tested on another. Instruction should benefit the learners, not the teacher. What is important should be made known to the learners so that their time and effort are not wasted. Well-written performance objectives accomplish this. They should be the basis for assessing the results of instruction. If everyone does well on the evaluation, the instruction has been successful.[30]

Mager suggested a series of steps to select appropriate test items:[30]

1. match the performance and conditions of the test item to those of the objective
2. check whether the performance is a main intent or an indicator
3. if the performance is an indicator, note the main intent. Note whether the performance is covert or overt
4. test for the indicator in objectives containing one

The first step is to see whether the performance specified in the test item is the same as that specified in the objective. If they do not match, the test item must be revised, since it will not indicate whether the objective has been accomplished. If the objective states that the performance is "to plan menus," or "to operate the dish machine," the test should involve planning menus or operating the dish machine. It would be inappropriate to ask the learner to discuss the principles of writing menus or to label the parts of the dish machine on a diagram.

In addition to matching performance, the test should use the same specific circumstances or conditions that are specified in the objective.

Example: (Given the disassembled parts of the meat slicer), is able to reassemble the parts in correct sequence.

The conditions are "given the disassembled parts of the meat slicer." The instructor should provide a disassembled machine and ask the learner to reassemble it. An inappropriate test would be to ask the learner to list the steps in reassembling the meat slicer, or to discuss the safety precautions to be taken.

If the learner must perform under a range of conditions, it may be necessary to test performance using the entire range. If a client eats at home and in restaurants, the dietitian must determine whether the individual is capable of following the dietary regimen in both environments. If students are learning to take a diet history, they should be taught to handle the range of conditions, including people of different ages, socioeconomic, and ethnic groups. Not every condition will be taught and tested, but the common conditions that the learner will encounter should be included in the objectives and in testing.

The main intent of an objective may be stated clearly or it may be implied. The main intent is the performance, while an indicator is an activity through which the main intent is inferred.

Example: (Given a copy of a sodium-restricted diet,) is able to plan a menu for a complete day.

The main intent is to discriminate between foods permitted and omitted on the diet, and the indicator is the ability to plan menus. One infers that the learner knows what is permitted and what is not if accurate sodium-restricted menus are planned. One should test for the indicator in objectives which contain one.

Some performances are overt while others are covert. Overt actions are visible or audible, such as writing, verbally describing, and assembling. If the performance is overt, determine whether the test item matches the objective.

Example: Is able to reassemble the parts of the meat slicer.

The employee should be provided with the parts of the meat slicer and asked to reassemble them. Performance tests are appropriate when skills are taught. If the employee is being taught to use equipment, the evaluation should be to have him demonstrate its operation. If a student is learning interviewing skills, an interview session is indicated as the evaluation. Covert actions are not visible, but are internal or mental activities, such as solving problems or identifying. If the performance is covert, an indicator should have been added to the objective as explained in Chapter 9, and the indicator should be tested.

Example: Is able to identify the parts of the meat slicer (on a diagram or verbally).

For this example the learner should be provided with the indicator, a diagram of a meat slicer, and asked to identify the parts.

The discussion to this point has used examples of objectives in the cognitive and psychomotor domains. Affective objectives describe values, interests, and attitudes. While the cognitive and psychomotor domains are concerned with what an individual can do, the affective domain deals with what he is willing to do. These changes are covert or internal, and may develop more slowly over a period of time. Evaluation of their achievement is more difficult and needs to take different forms. In measuring attitudes, the person needs the opportunity to express agreement rather than deciding on "right" or "wrong" answers. To assess whether the learner has been influenced by education, the professional may conduct a discussion and listen to what the learner says or observe what he does, since both saying and doing are overt behaviors. To evaluate change in the learner's behavior, the evaluator attempts to secure data that permit an inference to be made regarding the learner's future disposition in similar situations. In the affective domain, this is a more difficult task.

It is conceivable that the learner may display a desirable overt behavior only in the presence of the instructor. The attitude toward following a diabetic diet or an employee work procedure may differ depending on the dietitian's presence or absence. Since time is required for change in the affective domain, evaluation may have to be repeated at designated intervals. To determine realistically how the person is disposed to act, the measurement approach needs to evaluate volitional rather than coerced responses.

Other outcomes of nutrition education may be measures of nutritional status, such as weight lost; change in clinical or biochemical indices, such as serum cholesterol level in cardiovascular disease, hemoglobin level in pregnancy, and glycosylated hemoglobin level in diabetes; or reduction in risk factors for disease and improved health, both long-term goals. Care must be taken in interpreting some of these results since they may reflect other variables besides education. For example, stress can affect one's blood sugar even when the diabetic diet is followed.[31]

Data Collection Techniques

There are a number of techniques for collecting evaluation data. They include paper-and-pencil tests, questionnaires, interviews, visual observation, job sample or performance tests, simulation, rating forms or checklists, individual and group performance measures, individual and group behavior measures, and self-reports.[22,25] As measurement devices that will be analyzed statistically, they require the use of specific experimental designs. Regardless of the particular instrument or technique used, it should be pretested with a smaller group prior to actual use. Since comparisons are desired, it is usually necessary to collect preliminary data on current performance or behaviors.

Tests, especially written tests, are probably the most common devices for measuring learning. Tests sample what you know. Schools depend heavily on them, and as a result, they are familiar to everyone. Multiple-choice, true-false, short answer, completion, matching, and essay questions are used to measure learning in the cognitive domain.[24] These tests have been used when several people are expected to learn the same content or material. Sometimes, both a pretest and a posttest are used to measure learning. This method assists in controlling variables, but one should be careful not to attribute all of the change noted on the posttest to the learning experiences, since other factors may have been involved.[21] In a child's school experiences, the teacher assigned grades based on tests. With adults, the educator should avoid evoking childhood memories associated with the authoritarian teacher, the dependent child, or the assigned degree of success and failure based on right or wrong answers. In one-on-one situations, the educator may ask the learner to state verbally what he has learned as though he were telling it to a spouse or friend.

Questionnaires may be preplanned and are often used to assess attitudes and values, which do not involve correct answers. Questions may be open-ended, multiple choice, ranking, checklist, or alternate response, such as yes/no or agree/disagree.

Interviews conducted on a one-to-one basis are another form of evaluation. They are the oral equivalent to written questionnaires used to measure cognitive and affective objectives. Prior to the interview, the evaluator should draw up a list of questions that will indicate whether learning has taken place. After instruction, evaluation may consist of asking the client or employee to repeat important facts. An advantage of an interview is that the evaluator can put the person at ease and immediately correct any errors. Another advantage is that the interviewer can probe for additional information. Although this method is time consuming, it is appropriate for the illiterate or less educated.

In many cases, visual observation is an appropriate method of evaluating learning. The behaviors to be observed should be defined, and an observation checklist may be helpful. When employees are under direct supervision, systematic ongoing observation over a period of time is a basis for evaluating learning. The professional can observe whether the employee is operating equipment correctly or following established procedures properly. If the employee has been taught sanitary procedures, for example, the professional can see whether or not they are incorporated into the employee's work. One should evaluate the performance, using what was taught as a standard. If discrepancies are found, further learning may be indicated.

Where direct observation is not possible or would be too time consuming, a simulated situation or performance test can be observed. Performance tests are appropriate in the cognitive and psychomotor domains. One could ask wait staff to set a table, a cook to demonstrate the meat slicer, or a client to indicate what to select from a restaurant menu. The patient could be given a list of foods, some of which are permitted on the diet and some of which are not, and asked to differentiate them. Audiotape or videotape may be used to record the simulation, so that the instructor and learner may discuss the results together and plan further learning to correct any deficiencies. The learner should give permission in advance if taping is to be used. The observer needs to delineate which behaviors are being observed and what is to be acceptable behavior.

Rating scales or checklists have been used to evaluate learner performance and teacher effectiveness. Categories or attributes, such as knowledge level or dependability are listed, and these should be defined in detail to avoid ambiguity. Emphasis should be placed on attributes that can be confirmed objectively rather than judged subjectively. A five- or seven-point scale is used, allowing a midpoint, and the ratings should be defined, e.g., from "excellent" to "poor" or from "extremely acceptable" to "very unacceptable." The list should include as a possible response, "No opportunity to observe."

Rating scales are subject to a number of errors. Two evaluators may judge the same individual differently. To avoid error, definition of the terms and training of evaluators are essential. The ratings may suffer from personal biases. In addition, some raters have the tendency to be too lenient. Error may result if the rater is a perfectionist. Some evaluators tend to rate most people as average, believing that few people rank at the highest levels. Another possible error is the "halo" error, in which an evaluator is so positively or negatively impressed with one aspect of an individual that he judges all other qualities according to this one impressive aspect.

In employee training programs, individual and group performance measures, such as work quality and quantity, and number of errors, may be assessed. Individual and group behavioral measures, such as amount of absenteeism, number of grievances, and other types of non-performance problems that affect work performance, may be noted.

Self-reports are another approach to evaluation. In the affective domain, written questions or statements are presented, and the individual supplies responses. Responses may be distorted if the learner can ascertain the socially acceptable answer. Role-playing, simulation, and attitudinal scales have also been utilized. Self-reports, such as a three-day food record have been used to measure behavioral change, and in the Multiple Risk Factor Intervention Trial (MRFIT), a food score was developed, permitting participants to score their own food choices.[32]

All methods of evaluation have advantages and limitations, which need to be considered. In assessing adult learning, the evaluator should be careful to protect the individual's self-concept and to treat errors as indicators for additional instruction.

Reliability/Validity

The concepts of reliability and validity are important to the measurement of learning. Validity indicates whether a test measures what it is intended to measure. There are different types of validity, such as content, construct, concurrent, and predictive validity, all of which help to "defend" the validity of the instrument. Content validity, which is the simplest and probably the most important for criterion-referenced testing, refers to whether the test items correspond to the content of instruction or to the knowledge and skills taught. Reliability refers to the consistency with which a test or device measures something in the same way in each situation. For example, if a test is given twice to the same students to sample the same abilities, the students should place in the same relative position to others each time if the test is reliable. Methods for determining the reliability and validity of tests may be found in the educational literature.[21] In all cases, one must keep in mind that the test or measuring device should assess whether the learner has attained the requisite knowledge, skill, or competence needed. If the learner has not attained the intended knowledge or skill, additional learning may be indicated.

Once the data from evaluation have been collected, they should be compiled and analyzed. The statistical analysis of data that is required is a lengthy subject of its own beyond the scope of this book. Future plans or programs may be modified based on the results of the evaluation. Results should be communicated through evaluation reports to such others as participants, to management staff, decision makers, and future learners.

LESSON PLANS

A lesson plan is a written summary of information about a unit of instruction. It is prepared and used by the instructor and may be submitted to an administrator. Various formats for lesson plans are available, but the content is essentially the same.

A lesson plan is a blueprint that describes all aspects of instruction. It includes the plans for preassessment; the performance objectives; the content outline, how the content will be sequenced; a description of the activities learners will engage in to reach the objectives; instructional procedures, materials, teaching aids, media, and equipment to be used; the amount of time allotted; facilities to be used; and the method of evaluating whether the learner reached the objectives.[17] Once written, a lesson plan is a flexible guide to instruction that can be used with many different individuals or groups. A series of lesson plans may be grouped into a larger unit of instruction. Sample lesson plans are found in Tables 10-4 and 10-5.

Table 10-4. Sample Lesson Plan on Sanitary Dish Handling.

I.   Target Audience: New wait staff
II.   Objective: When setting tables, wait staff will be able to handle dishes and utensils in a sanitary manner.
III. Time Allotted: 15 minutes
IV.   Preassessment: Question new employees to determine what they already know about sanitary dish and utensil handling.
V.   Content and Sequence:
      1. Handling of flatware by the handles.
      2. Handling of cups by the base or handle and glassware by the base.
      3. Handling plates and bowls on the edge without touching the food.
      4. Use of a tray.
      5. The hands and skin as major sources of disease causing bacteria and their transmission to food and utensils.
      6. Proper bussing of dishes to avoid contamination of the hands.
      7. Hand washing.
VI.   Learning Activities:
      Demonstration and discussion of proper handling of dishes and utensils when setting tables, serving food, and bussing tables.
      Discussion of hand washing.
      Actual practice by new wait staff.
VII. Materials: Dishes, utensils, tray, handout of important points to remember.
VIII. Evaluation: Whether or not dishes and utensils were handled properly during the actual practice; continued observation of the employee's performance on the job.

DOCUMENTATION

Dietitians are accountable for the nutritional care they provide in all settings, including private practice. Accepted standards of practice and accreditation agencies mandate that dietetic services be documented and communicated to other health professionals providing care. Patient records also provide evidence in malpractice suits and are important to the denial of liability.[33] Documentation has been described as "the method by which others are made aware of specific approaches to client problems and outcomes," and it provides a "developmental history" of nutrition services to clients.[20] What takes place between the dietitian and the client should be recorded, including such data as nutritional assessment, nutrition care plans with timetables, goals, means of achieving goals and their outcomes, nutrition counseling and education provided, patient's or client's reactions, progress notes, actual outcomes, as well as where efforts ought to be directed in the future. The information communicated demonstrates what the nutrition professional contributes to health care delivery and that their service provides the patient or client with a specific benefit that will offset the cost of the service.

The usual place for documentation is in the medical or client's record. Frequently, the dietitian makes notes on the patient's medical record using the SOAP procedure. The acronym SOAP stands for Subjective data, Objective data, Assessment, and Plan. Subjective data includes the client's perception and thoughts about the nutrition problem and his or her food intake. Objective data are the results of laboratory tests, such as serum albumin, or physical findings, such as weight and height.

Assessment is the dietitian's analysis of the person's problem based on the subjective and objective data. The Plan tells what the dietitian recommends or intends to do to solve a particular problem, such as plans for patient counseling, education, or other follow-up practices.[34]

Documentation of employee education and training programs is also essential. Records should be kept of all information included in employee orientation. The use of an orientation checklist is helpful in ensuring that everything the employee needs to know has been communicated to him. Records should be kept on file showing the date and content of ongoing training sessions such as inservice programs, and off-the-job experiences such as continuing education.

This chapter has examined the selection and implementation of learning activities in the cognitive, affective, and psychomotor domains. The use of a task analysis and job instruction training have been explained. The final step in planning learning is evaluation, in which data are collected and analyzed to determine the success of educational endeavors.

The educator seeks to influence behavior by imparting information to learners. The nutrition educator seeks to change people's eating practices, and the employee trainer seeks to change the employee's job performance. Techniques and strategies that influence the acquisition of knowledge, the development of appropriate attitudes, and behavioral change were discussed. The relationship of knowledge and attitudes

Table 10-5. Sample Lesson Plan on Calcium in Pregnancy.

I. Target Audience: Pregnant women
II. Objective: To be able to identify foods and quantities of foods which will meet the daily calcium RDA for pregnancy and plan menus using these foods.
III. Time Allotted: 30 minutes
IV. Preassessment: Question audience about what foods contain calcium and how much of these foods should be eaten daily during pregnancy. Determine any previous pregnancies and what was eaten.
V. Content and Sequence:
   1. Total daily calcium needs (RDA) with the important functions of calcium during pregnancy.
   2. Dairy foods as a source of calcium with quantities of calcium in each.
   3. Other foods as good sources of calcium with quantities of calcium in each.
   4. Calcium sources for lactose intolerant individuals.
   5. Have audience suggest a breakfast, lunch, dinner and snacks meeting the RDA for calcium.
   6. Questions from the audience.
   7. Have each individual plan her own menu for tomorrow.
VI. Learning Activities: Group discussion of food sources of calcium. Show actual foods and food models for portion sizes. Group planning of a day's menu followed by each individual planning something appropriate for herself for the next day's menu.
VII. Materials: Actual food samples, food models, paper and pencils for menu planning, chalkboard or flipchart for writing menus, handout with good sources of calcium and the amount of calcium in each including the RDA for pregnancy and a sample menu.
VIII. Evaluation: The menu planned by each individual. Discussion with individuals during their follow-up prenatal visits.

to behaviors is complex, however, since behavior is subject to many motivations all operating at the same time. The fact that clients and employees are informed does not mean that they will always act intelligently. Motives may be conflicting, and information may be disregarded or altered to serve one's own purposes.[9] If time is limited, for example, little thought may be given to food choices. Instructional techniques that promote interpersonal interaction and reflect the social context are important influences in nutrition education.

REFERENCES

1. Hutchinson, D.: The process of planning programs of continuing education for health manpower. In Fostering the Growing Need to Learn. Rockville, MD, Division of Regional Medical Programs, 1973.
2. Tracey, W.R.: Designing Training and Development Systems. Revised edition. New York, American Management Associations, 1984.
3. Spitz, H.: Choosing Techniques for Teaching and Learning. Washington, D.C., National Education Assoc., 1970.
4. Pfeiffer, J.W., and Ballew, A.C.: Using Role Plays in Human Resource Development. San Diego, University Associates, Inc., 1988.
5. Craig, R.L. (ed): Training and Development Handbook. 2nd ed., New York, McGraw-Hill Book Co., 1976.
6. Bethea, C.D., Stallings, S.F., Wolman, P.G., and Ingram, R.C.: Comparison of conventional and videotaped diabetic exchange lists instruction. J. Am. Diet. Assoc., *89*:405, 1989.
7. Holste, P.: High tech—hot talk. Computer-based training. Special report. Training Magazine, 1988.
8. Knox, A.B.: Helping Adults Learn. A Guide to Planning, Implementing, and Conducting Programs. San Francisco, Jossey-Bass, 1986.
9. Johnson, D.W., and Johnson, R.T.: Nutrition education: A model for effectiveness, A synthesis of research. J. Nutr. Ed. *17*:S1, 1985.
10. Mager, R.F.: Developing Attitudes Toward Learning. Palo Alto, CA, Fearon Publishers, 1968.
11. Rose, J.C.: Handbook for Health Care Food Service Management. Rockville, MD, Aspen Publications, 1984.
12. Smith, R.M.: Learning How to Learn. Chicago, Follett, 1982.
13. McCarthy, B.: The 4 Mat System: Teaching to Learning Styles with Right/Left Mode Techniques. 2nd ed., Oakbrook, IL, Excel, Inc., 1981.
14. Herrmann, N.: Brain dominance technology. In Training and Development Handbook. 3rd ed., Edited by R.L. Craig., New York, McGraw-Hill Book Co., 1987.
15. Wexley, K., and Latham, G.: Identifying training needs. In The Training and Development Sourcebook. Edited by L. Baird, C.E. Schneier, and D. Laird. Amherst, MA, Human Resource Development Press, 1983.
16. McCord, A.B.: Job training. In Training and Development Handbook. 3rd ed., Edited by R.L. Craig. New York, McGraw-Hill Book Co., 1987.
17. Mager, R.F., and Beach, K.M.: Developing Vocational Instruction. Belmont, CA, Fearon Publishers, 1967.
18. Laird, D., and House, R.: Training Today's Employees. Boston, CBI Publishing Co., 1983.
19. Hornik, R.C.: Development Communication: Information, Agriculture, and Nutrition in the Third World. New York, Longman Inc., 1988.
20. Wills, B.B.: Documentation: The missing link in evaluation. J. Am. Diet. Assoc. *85*:225, 1985.

21. Popham, W.J.: Educational Evaluation. 2nd ed., Englewood Cliffs, NJ, Prentice-Hall, 1988.
22. Phillips, J.J.: Handbook of Training Evaluation and Measurement Methods. Houston, Gulf Publishing Co., 1983.
23. Knowles, M.S.: The Adult Learner: A Neglected Species. 2nd ed., Houston, Gulf Publishing, 1978.
24. Bloom, B.S., Hastings, J.T., and Madaus, G.F.: Handbook on Formative and Summative Evaluation of Student Learning. New York, McGraw-Hill Book Co., 1971.
25. Kirkpatrick, D.L.: Evaluation. In Training and Development Handbook. 3rd ed., Edited by R.L. Craig. New York, McGraw-Hill Book Co., 1987.
26. Dignan, M.B.: Measurement and Evaluation of Health Education. Springfield, Charles C Thomas, 1986.
27. Edwards, P.K., Mullis, R.M., and Clarke, B.: A comprehensive model for evaluating innovative nutrition education programs. J. Nutr. Ed., *18*:10, 1986.
28. Lewis, M., Brun, J., Talmage, H., and Rasher, S.: Teenagers and food choices. The impact of nutrition education. J. Nutr. Ed., *20*:336, 1988.
29. Franz, M.J.: Diabetes and nutrition: State of the science and the art. Top. Clin. Nutr., *3*:1, 1988.
30. Mager, R.F.: Measuring Instructional Intent or Got a Match? Belmont, CA, Lear Siegler Inc., 1973.
31. Fruin, M.F., and Davison, M.L.: Some considerations in the measurement of change. J. Am. Diet. Assoc., *73*:15, 1978.
32. Remmell, P.S., Gorder, D.D., Hall, Y., and Tillotson, J.L.: Assessing dietary adherence in the Multiple Risk Factor Intervention Trial (MRFIT). J. Am. Diet. Assoc., *76*:351, 1980.
33. Cross, A.J.: Legal requirement of private practice medical records. J. Am. Diet. Assoc., *88*:1272, 1988.
34. Mason, M., Wenberg, B.G., and Welsch, P.K.: The Dynamics of Clinical Dietetics. 2nd ed., New York, John Wiley and Sons, 1982.

SUGGESTED ACTIVITIES

1. Complete a task analysis for using a procedure or a piece of equipment, listing the sequential steps and key points.

2. Using the Job Instruction Training sequence and a task analysis, teach someone to use an unfamiliar piece of equipment.

3. Plan learning using one of the techniques in the chapter (other than lecture,) such as discussion, simulation, or a demonstration. Carry out the plan.

4. Develop one or two performance objectives on a topic of interest for a target audience defined by age, sex, socioeconomic status, and educational level. The audience may be pregnant women, mothers, school children, adolescents, adult men or women, elderly, employees, executives, sports figures, or a person with a chronic disease. Plan the preassessment, content, techniques for presentation, teaching aids and handouts, and evaluation methods. Carry out the educational plan.

5. Develop one or two visual aids to use in teaching.

6. Give a pretest of knowledge on a subject. Instruct the learner on the subject. Follow up with a posttest.

7. List three ways in which one might evaluate whether an employee learned from a training program. List three ways in which one might evaluate whether a patient comprehended instruction regarding a diabetic diet.

8. Identify which of the following is a norm-referenced test and which is a criterion-referenced test?

A. Learners are given a national test of knowledge and individual scores are reported and compared.

B. Learners are given a test prepared by the teacher based on the learning objectives.

ANSWERS:

8 A. norm-referenced

8 B. criterion-referenced.

11

Motivation

A major theme of this book has been the need for dietitians to motivate clients and staff. Motivation is important in setting goals, planning behavior modification strategies, designing and executing educational curriculum or training seminars, counseling others individually or in groups, and defusing hostility or working through conflict situations. Dietitians who understand motivational concepts and have the skills to adapt them to particular situations significantly increase their chances for being professionally successful.

Motivation can be defined as something that causes a person to act or the process of stimulating a person to action. It is concerned with the question of why human behavior occurs. The word itself is frequently used to describe those processes that (1) arouse and instigate behavior; (2) give direction and purpose to behavior; (3) continue to allow behavior to persist; and (4) lead to choosing or preferring a particular behavior.[1-2] It is concerned not only with what people can do, but also with what they will do.

Individuals can be motivated in many ways. Some can motivate themselves, while others must be goaded, threatened, or challenged to act. Those in the first category are referred to as "motivation seekers" and are motivated primarily by the nature of the task or job they perform. Most people, however, need to be stimulated to act, particularly when a change in life-style, diet, or health practices is necessary.[3]

Motivation is complex, and there are a number of factors or variables, both intrinsic and extrinsic, that influence the process at any one moment in time. Today's motivational influences may differ from tomorrow's, and short-term goals may take precedence over the long-term ones. Having knowledge of how one should work to get the most accomplished, of what one should eat to become or remain healthy, or of what one should do to cope with a current physiological condition such as diabetes may easily be overpowered by other motivational factors. The problem is that being motivated to work, to become or remain healthy, or to learn what one needs for appropriate cardiovascular or diabetes care involves long-term goals, and eating something such as chocolate cake, or coming in late for work "just this once," meets a short-term goal of pleasure. Some people may delay the long-term for the immediate pleasure. Although there is a great deal of knowledge concerning motivation that is helpful, there are no miracle methods or universal answers to difficult motivational problems.[2]

Motivation can arise from factors that are either intrinsic or extrinsic, and these factors can affect the individual either positively or negatively. Intrinsic motivation arises from within individuals, owing to their needs, desires, drives, or goals. Individuals who desire to be promoted, for example, have internal goals that motivate their performance. A man who has recently suffered a heart attack may be intrinsically motivated to change his dietary practices. External or extrinsic factors may supplement intrinsic motivation positively, or they may serve as barriers having a negative impact on motivation. Examples of positive external factors enhancing motivation include support from others, praise, or material rewards. An individual's motivation toward achieving dietary goals, however, may be hampered by social occasions or by family or friends who are not supportive and offer improper foods.

Dietitians are involved daily in motivating employees and clients, and they need to understand this complicated concept and its multiple processes. The administrative dietitian influences the motivation of employees, who must learn the procedures necessary to work effectively, do their jobs conscientiously without close supervision, and grow to improve in the work environment. The clinical dietitian must motivate not only staff, but also clients, who may need to learn about such things as the effects of diet on prenatal care, or the problems of sodium, cholesterol, or sugar in the diet. After they have been motivated to learn and to appreciate their problem or situation cognitively, motivation becomes a factor in obtaining their participation in dietary counseling and compliance with a dietary regimen.

This chapter discusses motivation in the three contexts previously mentioned: as an aid to client compliance, as an aid to teaching, and as an aid to managing staff. Although these three areas are treated separately in the chapter, the same motivational principles and theories apply to all of them.

MOTIVATION OF CLIENTS AND PATIENTS

The aim of nutrition counseling and education is to change food and eating behaviors so that the individuals select healthier diets. Food selection is a part of a complex behavioral system, which is shaped by a vast array of variables. The food selection of children is determined primarily by parents and by the cultural and ethnic practices of their group. Early experiences and continuing interactions with food determine the food preferences, habits, and attitudes exhibited by adults. In addition to the profound role of family and culture in making dietary choices, influences include price of food, prestige value of food, religion, geography, peer and social influences, advertising, facilities, food preparation and storage, skills of the consumer in food preparation, time factors and convenience, and personal preferences and tolerances. All of these factors make food consumption a highly individual matter and resistant to change.[4]

In spite of problems associated with changing food behaviors, some people do change. People today are consuming less red meat and eggs than previously, for example. A summary of some of the motivational forces that influence the eating practices of clients is presented in Figure 11-1. Practitioners and other health educators should consider these factors with their clients and possibly add others, from their own experience. More detailed discussion of some of the variables are found in previous chapters.

Knowledge of which foods to consume is a first step in influencing healthful food behaviors, but it is probably overrated. When people do not follow their diets, some health educators tend to devote more and more time to teaching, redoubling their efforts and assuming that the problem is a deficit in knowledge, rather than exploring other motivational factors that may be more important. The relationship between what people know and what people do or how they behave has been described as a "highly tenuous one," with only a weak relationship, if any, between nutritional knowledge and dietary practices.[5] Knowledge does not instigate change, but functions as an instrument if and when people want to make changes.[6] Better educated people may rely more on facts and knowledge as motivators for changing behavior than those who are less educated.[5]

Other motivational factors, both intrinsic and extrinsic, may encourage changes in food behaviors. People's interest in health, and their beliefs regarding nutrition as a factor in health promotion and disease prevention, may affect food choices. For example, a health belief that food was "good for them" correlated strongly with dietary practices among older women, but less so for those among younger women.[4] Positive cognitions such as "Nutrition is important" and "This dietary change is worth the effort" are helpful. Since food's flavor, convenience, and cost are prime motivators of food choices, Hochbaum has suggested that a nutritious diet should offer these advantages, and that these aspects should be stressed more than potential health benefits.[6] Dietians, therefore, need to overcome the public's perception that nutritious diets are costly, insipid, and inconvenient to purchase and prepare. They must promote the perception that dietary changes are pleasurable and possible. Previous chapters have emphasized the importance of having clients set one or two short-term goals for change and have suggested the use of self-monitoring of food intake and written contracts.

Motivation provided by intrinsic factors may be supplemented by extrinsic factors. Praise and material rewards are positive consequences for proper food behaviors, and they may serve to enhance motivation. The support of significant others—family, friends, and the health counselor—is helpful. People who model proper skills can influence others

VARIABLES MOTIVATING CHANGE IN FOOD CHOICES AND HEALTH BEHAVIOR

Fig. 11-1. Variables motivating change in food choices and health behavior. A given behavior, such as healthful food choices, is affected by more factors that an individual's knowledge of what to do. Level of motivation is influenced by a number of interacting variables, which may differ on a daily basis.

to follow. Needless to say, healthful foods should be made readily available while improper foods should not. Alternative activities, such as physical activity, may also serve to promote change.

In spite of positive motivational and life-style factors, barriers to motivation may arise. Clients should be told to expect problems. The health educator should examine these problems with clients and attempt to reduce or eliminate them. Social occasions, holidays, eating in restaurants, weekend activities, food shopping, and travel require preplanning. A particular time of day, a particular day of the week, or just a lack of time may be barriers to healthful food choices. Problems may also arise from a person's workplace and job associates, and from not having the right foods available. Negative cognitions such as "It's not worth it" and "I'd rather die young and happy than follow this diet" interfere with motivation. Some people discover cues to improper eating in their physical environment, such as in certain rooms of the house. The characteristics of the regimen, such as complexity and cost, are other factors.

Food choices are also influenced by several affective factors involving attitudes, beliefs, and values. Attitudes are thought to be predispositions to action.[7] Such emotional states as boredom, anxiety, and depression may lead to eating the wrong food, but so may happiness and elation. Fear of illness or death can be a motivating factor, as can stress and the individual's physical condition. Whether people are tired or rested, whether their medical problem is new or not, the severity of their illness, and its perceived threat to health may each influence motivation.

Motivation to make and maintain dietary changes is complex, for behavior is influenced by many motivational factors operating simultaneously. The interrelationships among knowledge, attitudes, and behavior are described as "more intricate than many of the studies of nutrition education acknowledge."[7] While knowledge of proper food choices is an essential first step in changing food behavior, knowledge may be easily overpowered by something that seems more important at the moment. Following a proper diet to promote health and prevent disease is a long-term goal with rewards situated in the future, which may do little to enhance motivation. More immediate rewards may take precedence, such as eating a luscious piece of chocolate cake right now for the pleasure of it.

Nothing is known about the relative importance of each of the variables involved in motivation, the possible interaction of the factors, or the strength of their effect on food selection. Motivational variables directing today's food choices probably differ from tomorrow's and next week's choices, owing to the changes in environmental dynamics. Behavioral change requires a major personal commitment, the setting of goals for change, support from others in one's efforts to modify long-standing practices, and reduction or elimination of barriers in the social, cultural, physical, and psychological environments of the individual.

Although studies have focused on knowledge and attitude changes affecting eating practices, few studies have dealt with the complexity of all of the behaviors involved in food selection.[6]

MOTIVATION IN TEACHING

Teaching is a job responsibility of most dietitians, and nutrition education of the public is viewed as an obligation of all practitioners. The clinical dietitian may teach an individual or a group such subjects as proper nutrition practices for senior citizens, recommended prenatal nutrition, preparing nutritious meals on a limited budget, losing weight, and so forth. The administrative dietitian's teaching responsibilities include providing orientation for new employees, training staff in new practices and procedures, and coaching subordinates on a one-on-one basis. One of the keys to successful teaching is learner motivation.

Motivation is complicated and multifaceted. There is no single element that controls success. The best lesson plans, optimal materials, a well-informed and highly motivated dietitian-teacher, and an interesting and current curriculum cannot continuously guarantee that individuals will want to learn.[2]

Teachers do not motivate learners directly. They can make learning attractive and stimulating, however, provide opportunities and incentives, encourage the development of competence, and match the learner's interest with learning activities. Because there is no direct line of control between teacher behavior and students' motivation, the intervening variables of the learners' perceptions, values, personalities and judgments ultimately account for their degree of motivation.

This section is intended to enhance the dietitian's teaching and to facilitate learning by focusing on the practical use of knowledge about motivation. Though it is incomplete, the extant knowledge on motivation is considerable and can be applied logically and effectively through careful planning.

Time-Continuum Model of Motivation. Learning situations can be divided according to a three-period time continuum, consisting of a beginning, middle, and end, with motivation being facilitated during each of the stages through a motivational method.[1] Wlodkowski discusses the critical periods and the factors that can be applied to motivational strategies within each period (Fig. 11-2).[1]

The first critical period ("beginning") occurs when the learner enters the learning process. Two general motivational factors during this stage are (1) the learner's attitude toward the learning environment, teacher, subject matter, and self, and (2) the learner's needs at the time of learning. Needs are experienced by individuals as forces moving them in the direction of a goal. The second period ("during") occurs when the person is involved in the body or main content of the learning process. The general motivational factors during this stage are (1) the

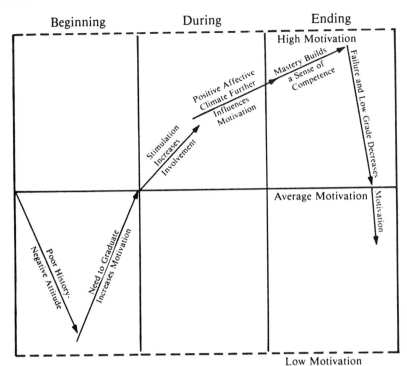

Fig. 11-2. Model indicating the relationships and influences on motivation during three time periods. (From Wlodkowski, R.J.: Motivation and Teaching. Washington, DC, National Education Assoc., 1984).

stimulation process, which affects individuals as they become involved in the learning experience, and (2) the simultaneous affective or emotional experience of the learner. The third period ("ending") occurs when the person finishes or completes the learning process. The motivational factors during this stage are (1) the sense of competence developed from the person's learning experience and (2) the quality of the reinforcement that results from the learning experience.

To facilitate motivation, to prevent problems with motivation, and to diagnose potential for motivation in learning situations, the dietitian needs to understand and evaluate the six factors described in the preceding paragraph as they occur during the critical time periods of a learning event. The following example is intended to illustrate how the multiple motivational factors interact on a dynamic basis to help or hinder motivation along a time continuum (see Fig. 11-2).

A woman receiving public assistance may have had little success in working with health professionals and as a result may feel defensive and have a poor "attitude" toward the subject matter. This same individual, however, may "need" the information the dietitian has to share to feed her family well on a limited budget; thus, she may feel some sense of determination to complete the program. At this beginning stage, the dietitian has a client who is not enthusiastic but is willing to "give it a try." If the professional provides material and experiences that are interesting and appropriate, the client may find the class "stimulating" and sincerely try to do well. If she enjoys the other participants in the program, and if they work well together in solving mutual problems, she may become even more motivated by the "affective" climate. At the end of the program, if the client feels that she has mastered the content and has a sense of confidence and "competence," she will feel encouraged or "reinforced," and will probably continue with this new interest in the future.

One might infer from Figure 11-2 that the three phases of motivational impact are independent of one another. Wlodkowski points out, however, that the motivational influence constantly interacts with the learner. At the end stage, for example, the competence and reinforcement value interact with the previous factors to affect the learner's motivation at the moment. This interaction results in new attitudes and needs.

Any single motivational factor can have an overwhelming influence on a particular learning situation. The negative influence of one factor may be so powerful that it prevents involvement in learning. Alternatively, the positive influence of a factor may be so strong that it produces a desire to learn that supersedes the possible negative influence of the other factors. For example, a storeroom employee with a negative attitude may refuse to try to learn even though he needs the skills presented in the training for future advancement. The negative attitude may prevail even though he has peers in the course whom he enjoys, has the ability to master the material that is presented in a stimulating way, and knows that he will receive a wage increase upon successful completion. Another employee, whose desire for future advancement is strong, may learn in spite of course material that he believes is useless, instructors whom he experiences as boring, and a sense of isolation between himself and his peers. In most instances, however, influence of the motivational factors is more equally distributed.

Because dietitians generally do not know which of the six factors is going to be the most critical for individuals, they should plan strategies for each factor, providing continuous and interactive motivational dynamics (Fig. 11-3). Six basic questions useful in planning a learning experience are:

1. What can the instructor do to encourage a positive attitude toward the learning situation?
2. What can be done to satisfy an individual's needs through the learning activities?
3. Are there ways to stimulate the individuals continuously while they are learning?
4. What might increase the positive affective or emotional climate for this particular learning activity?

5. How can this learning activity be structured to increase the person's feelings of competence?
6. What reinforcement will this activity provide?

MOTIVATION OF EMPLOYEES

This section explores the concept of motivation as it relates to employees and examines theories of motivation and their behavioral implications for dietitians. Although the concept of motivation was defined earlier in this chapter, the reader should keep in mind that motivational forces are usually multiple rather than singular, that they differ in strength, and that more than one may be present at a given time.

Maslow and Herzberg. Two theorists who have made major contributions to the study of motivation are Abraham Maslow and Frederick Herzberg. Maslow correlated human motivation with individual desires.

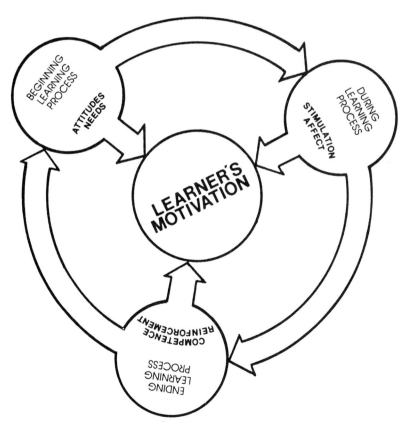

Fig. 11-3. Organizational aid to be applied to groups of individuals. When the dietitian attends to the six factors, he can, in any learning situation, design motivation strategies for his clients and staff throughout the learning process. (From Wlodkowski, R.J.: Motivation and Teaching. Washington, DC, National Education Association, 1984).

In his "hierarchy of needs" theory and "need-priority" model, he lists five universal needs to explain human motivation: physiological needs; the need for safety and security; social needs; the need for esteem; and the need for self-realization (Fig. 11-4). For each need to become active as a motivating factor, the desire immediately preceding the need must be fulfilled. In simplified terms, Maslow would say that the way to stimulate motivation in individuals is to determine which of their wants is most unsatisfied and then to structure their work so that in the accomplishment of the work goal, they satisfy their personal goals as well.[8] Wlodkowski has described Maslow's theory as being the most holistic and dynamic approach offering an interrelated set of guidelines to enhance learner motivation.[1]

The most basic human requirements are physiological. Sickness and hunger tend to take precedence over all other human needs. Only after they are satisfied does one experience the desire to satisfy the other needs. Indigent persons who are able to take care of only their physiological necessities may work regardless of the working conditions for their own and their families' sustenance and shelter. Once they have enough money to satisfy these basic essentials, however, working

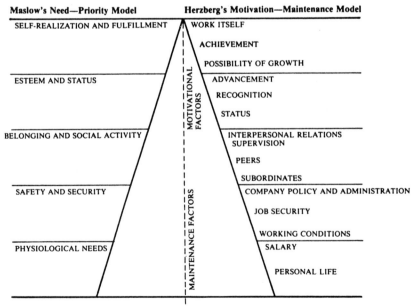

Fig. 11-4. A comparison of Maslow's need-priority model with Herzberg's motivation-maintenance model. (Adapted from Herzberg, F.: Work and the Nature of Man. Cleveland, OH, World Publishing Co., 1966, and from Maslow, A.H.: Motivation and Personality. New York, Harper and Bros., 1954.)

merely for nourishment and shelter is no longer adequate. At that point, the motivation to work arises from a drive to maintain safety and security. In most organizations today, these needs are satisfied through work contracts, unions, governmental regulations, and various insurance plans. With the fulfillment of biological and security needs, the individual's urge for social affiliation and activity becomes the dominant unsatisfied needs, and they should therefore be considered in designing work goals to motivate the employee. Social needs can be experienced as a desire to become a member of, and participate in, a recognized group: family, church, community, work, neighborhood business, union, and so forth. Should this need become satiated, the employees' motivation is stimulated by their desire for esteem and status, which is commonly experienced as the need to attain recognition for accomplishments.

Although each of the five areas of needs becomes dominant at some time, the strongest motivator at a given moment is the one immediately above the last need satisfied. Once the requirement for esteem is no longer lacking, for example, the desire for self-realization will become dominant. Self-realization is the highest human urge and most self-centered. This drive for self-realization and the opportunity to grow as a person can be fulfilled only when most other needs are met. This need is commonly experienced as an urge for personal and professional growth through the work experience.

It is difficult for dietitians to apply Maslow's theory with any degree of certainty, although social scientists still recognize his hierarchy of needs as fundamental to designing an effective structure to facilitate motivation.[9] Unless, however, one has few others reporting to her, the task of getting to know subordinates well enough to infer their current need level accurately is not likely to be accomplished; furthermore, need intensity at each level can vary from day to day, and sometimes from hour to hour. One may be operating at the need level for increased esteem, suddenly have an accident, and become overwhelmingly concerned with the physiological needs of being able to feed the family if one is incapacitated and unable to work. In spite of the limited applications of Maslow's theory, however, it does provide insight into the process of motivation and can often be useful in designing jobs, selecting staff, and developing strategies to maintain enthusiasm and interest among employees.

Frederick Herzberg, a contemporary of Maslow's, is credited with the "two-factor theory of motivation" or the "motivation-maintenance model," which complements Maslow's theory and provides additional perspectives.[10] Herzberg reviewed previous theories and studies and attempted to ascertain the essence of motivation by asking employees what they liked about their jobs and what they disliked about their jobs. After examining the data, he determined that the answers to the first question ("What do you like about your job?") were "motivation factors," while the answers to the second question ("What do you dislike about your job?") were what he termed "maintenance factors" (see Fig. 11-4). The five motivators he compiled in response to the first question were the work itself—being personally involved in the work, with a sense of responsibility and control; achievement—feeling personal accomplishment for having done a job well; growth—experiencing the opportunity for challenge in the job and the chance to learn skills and knowledge; advancement—knowing that the experience and growth will lead to increased responsibility and control; and recognition—being recognized for doing a job well, resulting in increased self-esteem.

Herzberg called the answers to the second question maintenance factors because he found that they maintained but did not improve current levels of production. Maintenance factors were physical conditions—e.g., lighting in the office and food in the cafeteria; security—a feeling of certainty about the future and of contentment; economic factors—salary and fringe benefits; and social factors—relationships with fellow workers and the boss.

Herzberg found that when the maintenance factors were poor, productivity decreased. Inadequate maintenance factors, then, hindered production while adequate maintenance factors only maintained the current level. Thus, maintenance factors merely "satisfy" workers; they do not motivate them. Although Herzberg's theory first gained prominence in the 1960s, it remains the basis for current research in the area of motivation.[11] As indicated in Figure 11-4, Herzberg's motivational factors are similar to those at the top of Maslow's "need priority" model, and his maintenance factors are toward the bottom of Maslow's model.

Motivation Through Enhancement of Self-Esteem. Key issues of the 1990s will be the attraction and retention of skilled workers. Shortages of human talent, rather than surpluses, will characterize United States business during this decade. As a result of the baby boom, those born between 1945 and 1964, and the following baby bust, there will be fewer entrants to the job market in the 1990s; it seems there are not enough workers in the small cohort of people born in the 1964-1975 period to fill the bottom level of the typical corporate pyramid. The majority of the work force today is composed of baby boomers and their children or younger brothers and sisters. Both groups tend to define success in terms of power, prestige, and money, and this definition is generally supported by senior management as well. Managers face a challenge in responding creatively to these new demographics, and a major concern of the contemporary manager is to understand the new workforce and how to adapt its needs to those of the organization.[12-13]

Another employment issue results from the fact that the number of highly qualified people in the workforce is growing at a much faster rate than is the number of senior-level jobs. Consequently, supervisors must understand how to spot the plateau problem and deal with it effectively before the employees have no alternative but to quit the organization. The worker who has hit a career plateau suffers from losses in productivity and/or self-esteem. When employees' careers have plateaued and the company does not want to lose them, they can redefine success so that the sense of having plateaued does not arise.[14-16] Success can be redefined, for example, through various forms of public recognition, such as company awards, plaques, and so forth.

A third reality of the 1990s, particularly in the health professions, is that organizations will have to continue to maintain as lean and as motivated a staff as possible to compete and to comply with governmental regulations. In the process of becoming "lean" by eliminating and combining as many positions as possible, those staff members who have survived may feel insecure, defensive, hostile, and fearful of losing their jobs, and may object to having had their former positions changed or enlarged without any monetary compensation. They may be unwilling to extend themselves because of the inference that the organization does not care about them. The manager or supervisor who is attempting to "motivate" staff under these conditions has a considerable challenge. While monetary increases are being kept to a minimum, the manager is expected to obtain more work from fewer people, who are already feeling unappreciated and overworked. Given this depressing but not unrealistic scenario, the manager needs to know and to exercise every motivational option available.

Many members of the current work force differ from their predecessors. Recent surveys indicate that baby boomers' values are distinctly different from those of their parents.[17-19] These younger employees generally are more affluent and educated, and are less willing to rely on authority figures. They have different perceptions of themselves and are generally unwilling to tolerate a disrespectful supervisory style. What today's workers indicate they want most are a heightened sense of self-esteem, realization, recognition, autonomy, responsibility, and managers who recognize their capacity for these achievements.[20-23] Although some employees can always be motivated by the hope of merit salary increases, contemporary administrative dietitians will benefit most from enhancing their staff's self-esteem and confidence as the prime method of increasing motivation to perform competently.[24-26]

A great deal is known about the relationship between motivation and increased self-esteem or recognition. For more than half a century, social scientists have been aware of the phenomenon of the "self-fulfilling prophecy," which suggests that people perform and develop according to others' expectations of them. In one study, students and instructors were selected randomly, and some instructors were told that they had been selected to have all the brighter students in their classes. These instructors had students who performed statistically and significantly better than those in classes where instructors had no previous expectations.[27] Individuals who are told that they are incompetent and will be unable to achieve a specific goal or task perform poorly as compared with those who are told that they are competent and will be able to achieve the task, even though neither group has had previous experience with the task. An individual's self-perceived ability, based on previous performance, is positively related to later performance. Success begets success, and failure begets failure.[20]

Unfortunately, an appreciation of the implications of this phenomenon for business and industry has only recently become apparent. Whenever supervisors acknowledge success in subordinates, they add to the likelihood that subsequent tasks will be performed successfully. For this reason, supervisors need to select carefully the right worker for the task, to provide adequate training to ensure employee success, and to assign work tasks that are manageable and accomplishable.

Dietitians can enhance the self-esteem of employees by providing opportunities for their achievement, growth, recognition, responsibility, and control, which increase their motivation to improve or to continue to do well. Several specific suggestions are described in the following paragraphs. They include involving employees in decision making, showing them respect, building their confidence, providing them with achievement experiences, increasing their personal and professional growth, and sharing time with them.

Dietitians must seek opportunities to observe and acknowledge their staff performing tasks properly. Employees are motivated when their esteem is enhanced through recognition of their work. Once employees know what is expected of them, positive strokes for good performance yield more positive performance.[28] The manner in which the work is recognized is a major factor in motivating employees. Simply saying "good job," for example, may be better than no comment at all, but it is not nearly as effective as a specific comment, such as, "the kitchen has never looked so organized. You did a splendid job of rearranging the storage cabinets." Needless to say, frequent reinforcement must be honest and must not sound patronizing.

Staff members can be motivated when they sense personal growth through their work. Learning new skills and exercising judgments can be motivating. When dietitians believe staff members are competent enough to succeed at special assignments—those that are perceived as "job enrichment" and that offer opportunities to develop skills—and they allow the employees adequate time to perform the new task successfully, they are, in fact, motivating them. Notice the qualifying comments in the preceding statement. A staff member should be selected only when the chances of success are high. Asking employees to perform tasks for which they are not prepared may decrease motivation. Adequate resources and time are critical to success.

Somewhat similar to the motivational effect of assigning special projects to staff is delegating responsibilities that had formerly been the supervisor's. When such assignments are made, it is important that they be given to employees who will not resent the added responsibility, but will see it as it is intended—a form of recognition.

Taking the time to interact with employees on a person-to-person basis and listening to their comments about their work can be motivating when the employee perceives such interaction as a sign of respect and caring. The dietitian may be busy and prefer to go on working without acknowledging the employee; however, as being listened to is motivating, being ignored is non-motivating and demoralizing.

When employees make suggestions that the dietitian intends to consider, writing them down in the presence of the employee acknowledges that intention and decreases the possibility of the comments being forgotten. As with the other motivational strategies, however, the motivational potential of this technique will be short-lived if the employee interprets it as manipulation. When dietitians write down a suggestion, the expectation is that within a reasonable time, they will act on it. Accumulating and ignoring a drawer full of such suggestions will eventually discourage motivation in employees.

Acknowledging the feelings of employees who are obviously unhappy or excited is a way of showing caring and respect, as is recognizing important events in employee's lives. Attending funerals or sending flowers and greeting cards for specific occasions can be motivating if the employee perceives such acts as genuine signs of respect and recognition. Engaging in small talk with subordinates, visiting with them for a few minutes, and asking about their families or commenting on new clothes all tend to go beyond the content of the message and express caring and acceptance of the employee.

Documenting some exceptional success provides the employee with a sense of recognition among the entire staff. For example, sending copies to the organization's director of a letter sent from a grateful client who comments on the work of an employee, and pinning a copy on the bulletin board, can provide recognition and build esteem.

If there is occasion to support the actions of subordinates and defend them to others in the organization, the dietitian should do so. All organizations have informal communication grapevines, and employees will eventually hear that their supervisor extended herself on their behalf. Such actions have the potential to motivate many others as well, who, seeing themselves as members of the department's team, may vicariously feel defended as well.

The rationale for involving staff in decision making is discussed in detail in Chapter 7. When staff are consulted by their supervisor and involved in a decision, they not only tend to gain confidence from the experience, but also are motivated through the supervisor's appreciation of their worth.

Maintaining a motivated staff must be viewed as an ongoing process, and one that can be reinforced frequently through the quality of dietitians' and employees' interaction. The dietitians' admitting when they are wrong, for example, and saying to subordinates, "You are right," are actions that acknowledge respect for the subordinate. When problems arise in an employee's performance, the manner in which the assistance is offered or the employee is questioned is significant. Showing constructive concern in explaining the error adds to the employee's self-esteem; belittling, humiliating, or embarrassing an employee, especially in front of peers, diminishes it. Physical contact with subordinates can indicate caring and enhance self-esteem. Shaking hands with employees or patting them on the back for a job well done are examples of human respect, caring, and affection, not sexual harassment. Many of the foregoing suggestions may seem obvious and simple, but it is their frequent absence that erodes the self-esteem of employees and inhibits their motivation to improve.

High turnover rates, mediocre performance, and chronic absenteeism are symptoms of the erosion of self-esteem and the inability of supervisors to develop it in staff. Several supervisors, with whom one of the authors (R.J.C.) was working as a managerial consultant, were asked whether they would be willing to make a special effort to give recognition, or a word of praise, to one of their workers for something he did well. Although they all claimed to be willing to do this, a subsequent meeting of the group found that none carried out the assignment. The reasons given included, "You just don't praise men," "Workers will think you are setting them up for something," and "It's a sign of weakness to praise people for what they do." One group member acknowledged that he simply did not know how to give praise.

Smiling and looking pleasant can also be a factor in maintaining a supportive relationship with staff. Employees cannot read the dietitian's mind, so if she looks angry and upset, the natural tendency is for employees to infer that they, the employees, have somehow caused the unpleasant expression. Supervisors need to monitor their nonverbal behavior so that it does not suggest negative messages unintentionally. When the supervisor is genuinely upset and subordinates are not at fault, they should be reassured that they are not the reason for her negative demeanor.

Providing employees with new equipment or other resource materials is another way to show confidence in their abilities, and it reinforces the impression that the dietitian wants them to succeed. Dietitians should try to learn from the employees themselves what they believe they need to work more efficiently. Whenever possible, employees should be provided with the resources requested.

A way to acknowledge excellence in subordinates is to ask them to share their knowledge by teaching others. Giving the employee an assignment to train a new staff member, for example, is a form of recognition and a sign of confidence. Deferring to subordinates at meetings by asking them to explain procedures and solve problems accomplishes this as well.

Keeping and being on time for appointments with subordinates, notifying them well in advance if an appointment cannot be kept, and generally respecting the employee's time are signs of respect. Giving employees sufficient time to understand a particular procedure or set of directions, rather than leaving them feeling confused and insignificant, also adds to their perceptions of the supervisor's regard for them.

Motivation Through Setting Goals. Too often, subordinates believe that they are pleasing their supervisors only to learn that what they were doing was not what was desired or expected. When giving instructions, the dietitian should select language that is specific in meaning. Telling an employee to "work hard," to "be sincere," to "be confident," to "be conscientious," to "show cooperation," or to "maintain an open-minded point of view" are examples of vague instructions that could confuse employees and cause them to fail. Telling an employee to "type a letter," "interview a patient," "conduct a performance appraisal," "investigate an accident," "ask questions," or "come to work on time" are examples of specific instructions that encourage success by allowing the employees to know exactly what is being asked of them.[20]

One of the most damaging on-the-job sources of stress is the absence or delay of feedback on one's performance.[20,29] Setting goals with subordinates as well as following up with subsequent periodic reviews provides feedback and promotes improved performance. Telling an employee, "Do your best," is useless. To the employee, who is faced with numerous alternatives for ways to spend his "working" time, this instruction can mean dozens of things. Setting goals complements the theories of Maslow and Herzberg. An effective way to assist others who wish to increase their esteem, growth, development, realization, and achievement is to teach them to be proactive in planning specific ways to accomplish more or to improve quality by setting goals.

The effect of setting goals on individual performance has been demonstrated. Theory and experiments support the proposition that supervisors should play an active role in setting goals with subordinates. Goals should be specific, clearly stated, and measurable. When they fulfill these conditions, they provide a criterion for feedback, accountability, and evaluation. An individual can be highly motivated by knowing the objective and working on a plan with the administrative dietitian to accomplish it. The three identifiable elements in goal setting are (1) an action verb, (2) a measurable result, and (3) the cost and/or date by which the objective will be accomplished. It is essential for both the employee and dietitian to agree on their mutual expectations, to clarify the difference, for example, between "I want you to get your work done soon," and "I want to see an increase of 10% by June 16th." Perhaps the single most significant advance in the field of management has been the growth of participative management. A major advantage of goal setting, a form of participative management, is that it directs work activities toward organizational goals and forces planning.[30]

Individuals who have specific and challenging goals tend to perform best. Goals seen as "sure things" may discourage motivation as much as those that are believed to be impossible. The best goals—the ones that inspire quality performance—are those that are perceived as difficult and challenging but attainable. A major proposition, supported experimentally, is that employees who set or accept harder goals perform at levels superior to those who set or accept easier goals.[31-32]

Regardless of whether the goal is actually set by the dietitian or the employee, the two parties need to agree. When staff members feel that they are actively participating in setting their own goals, even if the goals are originally proposed by the supervisor, they are more solidly motivated to perform with distinction than if they feel that they are merely being told what to do.[33] For the process to work, however, employees must trust their supervisors. When employees feel used, or when they feel that the goals are a means of exploiting them, they tend to resist the goals.

Motivation Through Reinforcement. Reinforcement, knowing how to encourage desirable behavior and to discourage undesirable behavior, is related to motivation. One way to increase the likelihood that a performance or behavior will recur is to follow the performance with a positive event. A positively reinforced response has a greater probability of recurring simply because it pays off. Most of the suggestions in the previous sections on motivation through enhancement of self-esteem and recognition are examples of positive reinforcement.

Another type of reinforcement is the removal of something negative after the performance. In this case, the persons are likely to repeat the behavior because something they dislike is taken away as a consequence of the behavior. This removal or elimination of adverse conditions is referred to as negative reinforcement. A hospital dish washer, for example, who is constantly being checked by the dietitian and who has been able to decrease dish breakage by 30% from the previous month, will be motivated to continue improving if the dietitian checks this dish washer less often during the following week. The dietitian, then, can encourage the desired action by removing an unfavorable condition, the frequent inspections.

Two strategies that may discourage a given behavior are punishment and extinction. Reprimanding an employee for being late is an example of formal punishment. Although punishment is often used to eliminate undesirable behavior, its value is questionable because of its negative side effects. Punishment can make an employee hostile and prone to retaliation. If the punishment is perceived as unwarranted by the employees, they may resume the undesirable behavior as soon as punishment stops. The way to overcome the employee's feelings of resentment when punished are to provide frequent constructive feedback each time an infraction occurs. In that way, when formal punitive action is taken, it is perceived by the employee as warranted and rational.

The other basic technique for decreasing the likelihood of a behavior is extinction. With extinction, the undesirable performance is neither punished nor rewarded; it is simply ignored. Ignored behaviors tend to diminish, and ultimately to become extinguished, as a result of a consistent lack of reinforcement. For example, a dietitian who never acknowledges an employee's suggestions is actually encouraging the employee to stop sending them. Although its use may be unintentional, extinction is an effective technique for terminating behavior. A manager should be aware of the potentially negative consequences of ignoring desired behavior. Motivated performances can be unintentionally extinguished by managers through carelessness.

Summary of Recommendations. Managers should give recognition to the employees in the presence of their peers. Recognition provides positive feedback and builds a worker's confidence and self-esteem. Organizations can benefit from involving their employees in the decision-making process. The more employees are involved, the higher the level of their performance and satisfaction. Employees who participate in making decisions feel a sense of ownership and commitment.

Administrators at all levels lessen stress and increase efficiency and motivation when they provide employees with clearly defined goals and objectives. The more employees understand what they are expected to do, the more highly motivated they become. Supervisors should give respect and dignity to their staff. The more they respect the rights and privileges of employees, the better the employees feel about themselves and the more they produce. Managers must become familiar with reinforcement techniques, training themselves to recognize and comment on good work in order to reinforce it. Ignoring good work may lead to extinction of desired behavior. Top management needs to instill in lower-level management an appreciation of the human resources of the organization, supporting the development of increased self-esteem, recognition, and growth among all staff.

This chapter has emphasized the complexity of motivation and has discussed its behavior implications for dietitians. Dietitians are involved daily with motivation of both staff and clients. Understanding motivational concepts and being able to employ the strategies and techniques associated with them can add immeasurably to the professional's effectiveness.

REFERENCES

1. Wlodkowski, R.J.: Motivation and Teaching. Washington, DC, National Education Assoc., 1984.
2. Wlodkowski, R.J.: Motivation and Teaching. Washington, DC, National Education Assoc., 1986.
3. Peckos, P.S.: Stimulating the patient in self-motivation. J Am. Diet. Assoc., *61*:423, 1972.

4. Krondl, M., and Lau, D.: Social determinants in human food selection. In The Psychobiology of Human Food Selection. Edited by L.M. Baker. Westport, CT, AVI Publishing Co., 1982.

5. Hochbaum, G.M.: Behavior and education. In Nutrition, Lipids, and Coronary Heart Disease. Edited by R. Levy et al. New York, Raven Press, 1979.

6. Hochbaum, G.M.: Strategies and their rationale for changing people's eating habits. J. Nutr. Ed., *13*:S59, 1981.

7. Johnson, D.W., and Johnson, R.T.: Nutrition education's theoretical foundation. J. Nutr. Ed. *17*:S8, 1985.

8. Maslow, A.H.: Motivation and Personality. New York, Harper and Bros., 1954.

9. Clark, K.: Simply motivate. Industrial Society. *22*:26, 1989.

10. Herzberg, F.: Work and the Nature of Man. Cleveland, World Publishing Co., 1966.

11. Herzberg, F.: Innovation: Where is the relish. J. Creative Behavior, *21*:179, 1987.

12. Wendling, W.: Responses to a changing work force. Personnel Administrator, *33*:50, 1988.

13. Sandroff, R.: What managers need to know about the hiring crisis of the '90's. Working Woman, *14*:92, 1989.

14. Little, K.: The baby boom generation: confronting reduced opportunities. Employment Relations Today, *16*:57, 1989.

15. Modic, S.: Motivating without promotions. Industry Week, *238*:24, 1989.

16. Karp, H.: Supervising the plateaued worker. Supervisory Mgmt., *34*:35, 1989.

17. Mills, D., and Cannon, M.: Managing baby boomers. Management Review, *78*:38, 1989.

18. Blanchard, M.: Motivating people to top performance. Executive Excellence, *6*:11, 1989.

19. Welter, T.: New-collar workers. Industry Week, *237*:36, 1988.

20. Rosenbaum, B.L.: How To Motivate Today's Workers. New York, McGraw-Hill Book Co., 1982.

21. Wiegand, R.: The care and nurture of the company yuppie. Business Horizons, *31*:62, 1988.

22. Ahmadian, A.: Motivation: in search of a better way. J. of Human Behavior and Learning, *4*:17, 1987.

23. Kiechel, W.: The workaholic generation. Fortune, *119*:50, 1989.

24. Knippen, J., and Green, T.B.: Building self-confidence. Supervisory Mgmt., *34*:22, 1989.

25. Penzer, E.: How to motivate a small staff. Incentive, *163*:186, 1989.

26. Pierce, J.L., et al.: Organization-based self-esteem: construct definition, measurement, and validation. Academy Mgmt. J., *32*:622, 1989.

27. Rosenthal, R., and Jacobson, L.: Pygmalion in the Classroom. New York, Rinehart and Winston, 1968.

28. Richardson, H.L.: Communicate through listening. Transportation and Distribution, *30*:32, 1989.

29. Larson, J.R., Jr.: The dynamic interplay between employees' feedback-seeking strategies and supervisors' delivery of performance feedback. Academy Mgmt. Review, *14*:408, 1989.

30. Boissoneau, R.: New Approaches to managing people at work. Health Care Supervisor, *7*:67, 1989.

31. Chruden, H.J., and Sherman, A.W., Jr.: Managing Human Resources, 8th ed. Cincinnati, South-Western Publishing Co., 1988.

32. Quick, T.L.: The best-kept secret for increasing productivity. Sales Marketing Mgmt., *141*:34, 1989.

33. Mia, L.: The impact of participation in budgeting and job difficulty on managerial performance and work motivation: a research note. Accounting, Organizations Society, *14*:347, 1989.

SUGGESTED ACTIVITIES

1. List the factors that motivate you to go to work or to continue with your present job. Explain your reactions in terms of the Maslow and Herzberg models.

2. Interview someone who is on a diet, and determine the positive and negative influences for motivation that have resulted from adherence to it. Discuss your interview and data using the variables motivating change in food choices and health behavior model presented in the chapter (see Fig. 11-1).

3. Examine the forces that motivate you to learn something new. Are they related to your desire to remain physically well, secure, well-liked and respected, or are they related to your desire to prepare yourself for taking on additional responsibility, having more control, and achieving realization and actualization?

4. Indicate why the following statements would have a negative impact on an employee's motivation and how they might be amended so that they maintain the employee's self-esteem.
   A. That job has been done incorrectly! What do I have to do to get you to understand?
   B. I'm tired of listening to you complain. Just keep still and do your job.
   C. You will probably make a mess of this, but there isn't anyone else to do it.
   D. If you would listen, you would understand.
   E. You can't be serious about that suggestion.

5. For each of the following examples, list the reinforcement technique used and the feelings it might produce in the employee.
   A. Employee: Mrs. Jones, since you told us to be on the lookout for problems with equipment, we have discovered two more.
   Dietitian: Yes, but I'm looking for Helen now. Have you seen her?
   B. Employee: Mrs. Jones, I've finished all the work in the kitchen and have begun to rearrange the cabinets.
   Dietitian: You mean it took you all this time just to do that?
   C. Dietitian: Mary, I am putting you on suspension for 3 days.
   D. Dietitian: Mary, I want you to know that I appreciate how effectively you work with others. Several people have told me how thorough you are in using the new procedures.

Answers:
   5A. Extinction. The employee would probably feel ignored and rejected.
   5B. Punishment. The employee would probably feel angry and defensive.

5C. Punishment. The employee's feelings would be affected by whether she felt that the punishment was warranted. If she felt it was unwarranted, she would feel angry.

5D. Positive reinforcement. The employee would probably feel appreciated and respected.

Appendices

APPENDIX A

DIET HISTORY FORM

NAME: _____ Age _____ Current diet _____
Ht. _____ Wt. _____ Usual wt. _____ Desirable wt. _____

First Meal (food, amount)   Food Frequency
                                            (amount per day/week)
                                          Milk, cheese, dairy ____
                                          Coffee, tea ____
                                          Alcohol ____
                                          Other beverages, pop ____
Second Meal (food, amount)   Fruit, juice ____
                                          Vegetables ____
                                          Breads/cereals ____
                                          Meat, poultry, fish ____
                                          Eggs ____
                                          Fats and oils ____
Third Meal (food, amount)   Sweets, desserts ____
                                          Snack foods ____
                                          Vitamin supplements ____

Snacks (food, amount)

Food preparation methods:

Time and place of meals and snacks:

Number of family members:

Who purchases foods and cooks the meals?

What are the identified antecedents (cues to eating)?

What are the eating behaviors to be changed?

What are the eating consequences (reinforcement)?

APPENDIX B

Counseling Guidelines—Initial Session

Step	Topic	Questions to Ask	Questions to Avoid
1.	*Candidly review the problems of dietary change.*		
	1. Review overall rationale and objectives for recommended diet.		
	2. Acknowledge difficult nature of dietary change.	What are your thoughts and feelings about this diet?	Do you have any opinion about this diet?
	3. Listen to patient's concerns about the recommended diet.		
2.	*Build some commitment to solve problems.*		
	1. Indicate your willingness to work with patient.		
	2. Clarify to patient that he must assume primary responsibility for making dietary changes.		
	3. Propose program of frequent meetings over next 3 months, close self-observation of diet, phone contact.		
	4. Emphasize slow but steady approach to change.		
	5. Obtain patient's verbal commitment to meet any of your proposals.	What aspects of this program are you willing to try now?	Do you want to try anything now?

Counseling Guidelines—Initial Session (Continued)

Step	Topic	Questions to Ask	Questions to Avoid
3.	*Plan some specific changes in diet during coming month.*		
	1. Emphasize good points of 3-day record.*		
	2. Look on record for ideas on dietary changes.		
	3. Probe patient for more ideas.		
	4. Pinpoint *one* aspect of diet pattern to change.	What do you see that could be changed or improved?	Do you see anything to change?
	5. Acknowledge patient's desire for radical and fast changes in diet, but re-emphasize that the most successful approach is slow and steady.		
	6. Help patient set realistic dietary change goals (e.g., one meatless evening meal per week, substitution of a salad bowl for usual main entree at one lunch per week).	What is a realistic goal for you?	Is this a realistic goal?
4.	*Plan how to make a change successful.*		
	1. Identify problems that are likely to interfere with achieving goal. Consider problems in the following areas:	What problems are likely to interfere with your plans?	Are any problems going to interfere with your plans?
	a. Physical environment (e.g., what foods are available in house, snacking in front of T.V. in evening, absence of reminders on refrigerator or dining table)	What can you change in your home, office, or car that will help you achieve your goal?	Do you need any reminders?
	b. Social environment (e.g., influential people, such as spouse, children, business associates, whose approval and support—criticism—can affect achievement of dietary change goal)	Who can help, what can they do, and what can I do to help during the next few weeks?	Do you need any help?

*Prior to initial counseling session, patient should be given materials and instructions for completing a 3-day food diary.

Counseling Guidelines—Initial Session (Continued)

Step	Topic	Questions to Ask	Questions to Avoid
c.	Cognitive or private environment (e.g., what patient says to himself when confronted with personal thoughts such as the following) —what others will say about his planned behavior —thoughts of failure or disappointment when he is not perfect in his behavior	What encouraging things can you say to yourself when confronted with these inevitable thoughts? Other's approval Potential failure	Will you give yourself encouragement?
5.	*Plan how to keep track of progress.* Devise an unobtrusive and convenient way for patient to keep a record of the desired or target behavior (e.g., count egg cartons, measure side of vegetable oil container, attach pencil *and* paper to refrigerator, table, wallet, etc.)	How are you going to keep track of (target behavior)?	Can you keep track of (target behavior)?
6.	*Plan counseling continuity and support.*	When is it convenient for me to call and discuss your progress? When can we schedule our next appointment?	Do you want me to contact you sometime?
7.	*Make certain that spouse, if present, is involved in answering questions, providing ideas, and discussing potential problems and solutions.*		

From Wilbur, C.S.: Nutrition Counseling Skills. Audio Cassette Series 5. Chicago, The American Dietetic Association, 1980.

APPENDIX C

Counseling Guidelines—Follow-Up Sessions

Step	Topic	Questions to Ask	Questions to Avoid
1. *Review patient's progress.* Emphasize the positive and check commitment.*		What thoughts do you have about this approach to lowering your cholesterol?	Do you have any thoughts about this approach to counseling?
2. *Discuss the problems that interfered with achieving the goal and how patient attempted to solve them.*		What problems did you face?	Did you have any problems?
3. *Plan next specific change in diet for coming month.* a. Look at old food record for ideas. b. Probe patient for ideas. c. Pinpoint one aspect of diet pattern to change. d. Reacknowledge patient's probable desire to make fast, radical changes, but re-emphasize the importance of slow but steady approach. e. Set a realistic behavior change goal. f. *Include plans for patient to continue with the changes he accomplished last month.*		What do you see that could be changed or improved?	Do you see anything to change?
4. *Plan how to make change successful.* 1. Identify problems that are likely to interfere with achieving goal. Consider problems in the following areas a through c.		What problems are likely to interfere with your plans?	Are any problems going to interfere with your plans?

*Be prepared to handle *either* the patient's success *or* failure in achieving previous goal.

Counseling Guidelines—Follow-Up Sessions (Continued)

Step	Topic	Questions to Ask	Questions to Avoid
	a. *Physical environment* (e.g., what foods are available in house, snacking in front of T.V. in evening, absence of reminders on refrigerator or dining table)	What can you change in your home, office, or car that will help you achieve your goal?	Do you need any reminders?
	b. *Social environment* (e.g., influential people, such as spouse, children, business associates, whose approval and support—or criticism—can affect achievement of dietary change goal)	Who can help, what can they do, and what can I do to help during the next few weeks?	Do you need any help?
	c. *Cognitive or private environment* (e.g., what patient says to himself when confronted with personal thoughts such as the following:	What encouraging things can you say to yourself when confronted with these inevitable thoughts?	Will you give yourself encouragement?
	—What others will say about his planned behavior		
	—Thoughts of failure or disappointment when he is not perfect in his behavior	Other's approval	
	—Negative feelings (hunger, irritability) that will accompany behavior change	Negative reactions to change	
	—Feeling goal not as important as once thought (usually 4-5 days after counseling session)	Devaluation of goal over time	
5.	*Plan how to keep track of progress.*		
	Devise an unobtrusive and convenient way for patient to keep a record of the desired or target behavior (e.g., count egg cartons, measure side of vegetable oil container, attach pencil *and* paper to refrigerator, table, wallet, etc.)	How are you going to keep track of (target behavior)?	Can you keep track of (target behavior)?

Counseling Guidelines—Follow-Up Sessions (Continued)

Step	Topic	Questions to Ask	Questions to Avoid
6.	*Plan counseling continuity and support.*	When is it convenient for me to call and discuss your progress? When can we schedule our next appointment?	Do you want me to contact you sometime?
7.	*Make certain that spouse, if present, is involved in answering questions, providing ideas, discussing potential problems and solutions.*		

From Wilbur, C.S.: Nutrition Counseling Skills. Audio Cassette Series 5. Chicago, The American Dietetic Association, 1980.

APPENDIX D

Interview Evaluation Form

Parts of the Interview	Quality	Suggestions for Improvement
Preplanning		
Interview guide		
Physical environment		
Patient context		
Psychologic privacy		
Opening		
Greeting		
Statement of purpose		
Development of rapport		
Physical comfort		
Nonverbal signals		
Interviewer		
Respondent		
Body of Interview		
Sequence of topics		
Maintenance of rapport		
Nonverbal signals		
Interviewer		
Respondent		
Questions Open-ended		
Closed		
Primary		
Secondary		
Leading		
Neutral		
Probes		
Clarification		
Paraphrase		
Repetition		
Summary		

Interview Evaluation Form (Continued)

Parts of the Interview	Quality	Suggestions for Improvement
Use of silence		
Responses Understanding		
Confrontational		
Evaluative		
Hostile		
Reassuring		
Pace of interview		
Vocabulary level		
Talking vs. Listening (%)		
Closing Appreciation		
Questions requested		
Future contacts		
Nonverbal signals		
Interviewer		
Respondent		

Note: A numerical scale such as very good (3), adequate (2), and needs improvement (1) may be used. A tally system may be used to count the different kinds of questions asked.

APPENDIX E

Paraphrase Exercise

Directions: Statements reflect an individual's feelings about a diet. Select the response that best communicates to the client your understanding and acceptance. Evaluate the alternative responses and identify them as evaluative, advice giving, reassurance, or confrontation.

1. Joan: "I'm trying to stay on my low calorie diet, but I feel deprived when I can't eat the high calorie foods I enjoy.
    A. "Enjoy the foods that are on your diet instead of thinking about the foods that aren't."
    B. "You'll be sorry if you don't stay on your diet."
    C. "You feel like you're missing something special when you can't eat your favorite high calorie foods."
    D. "You seem to have a lot of difficulty following your diet."

2. Bob: "I get upset and feel as if I need to eat something when I'm at a party and I don't know anyone."
    A. "It sounds like you feel nervous at social gatherings and then you need to eat something."
    B. "You are using eating as a crutch to hide your nervousness."
    C. "Try to find someone to talk to instead of eating."
    D. "You probably eat every time you get nervous."

3. Sue: "Whenever I see candy lying around the house, I want to go off my diet."
    A. "You feel tempted to go off your diet when you see candy."
    B. "When you see candy lying around, exercise your will power and go into a different room."
    C. "Think about how fat you'll get if you let yourself eat candy."
    D. "You can't be serious about losing weight if you're tempted to eat candy every time you see it."

4. Steve: "When others eat pizza, the smell makes me want some too."
    A. "Think of how sorry you'll be if you eat any pizza."
    B. "Just tell yourself that it doesn't taste as good as it smells."
    C. "I hear you saying that you feel deprived when others eat pizza and you can't have any."
    D. "Don't worry. The diet will get easier as you go along."

5. Harry: "I'm happy to say that I've been able to lose weight and keep it off by following my diet."
    A. "You'd better not go off your diet or you'll gain back the weight you lost."
    B. "There's no reason to follow your diet as closely now that you've lost the extra weight."

C. "You sound pleased and proud because you've lost weight and you haven't gained it back."

D. "You've probably been able to keep the weight off because you feel so good about yourself now."

6. Betty: "I'm depressed because my friend has lost weight and I haven't, even though we're both dieting."

A. "Some people just have an easier time losing weight than other people. Keep trying."

B. "You sound upset because you haven't lost weight by dieting and your friend has."

C. "If you give up on your diet now, you'll never lose weight."

D. "Just stick to your diet and be more patient. It takes time."

7. Joe: "My wife could really help me follow my low salt diet if she would cook without salt."

A. "You feel that it would be easier to follow your diet if your wife was more helpful and cooked differently."

B. "You should also avoid foods with salt outside of the house."

C. "By asking her for help, you're not accepting responsibility for what you eat."

D. "You don't need her help to stay on your diet. You can do it yourself."

8. Cris: "I have a difficult time resisting sweets when my friends offer them to me."

A. "Just tell yourself you don't want any sweets."

B. "Think about how bad sweets are for you."

C. "It is hard for you not to accept sweets when your friends offer you some. You feel tempted to take some."

D. "You have a tough time resisting sweets because you have a sweet tooth."

Modified from: Evaluation Handbook for Health Education Programs in Nutrition. Prepared for The Center for Health Promotion and Education, Centers for Disease Control. Culver City, CA, IOX Assessment Assoc., 1983.

Answers:

1. A. advice
   B. evaluative
   C. understanding
   D. confrontation

2. A. understanding
   B. evaluative
   C. advice
   D. confrontation

3. A. understanding
   B. advice
   C. advice
   D. confrontation

4. A. evaluative
   B. advice
   C. understanding
   D. reassurance

5. A. advice
   B. advice
   C. understanding
   D. evaluative

6. A. reassurance
   B. understanding
   C. advice
   D. reassurance

7. A. understanding
   B. advice
   C. evaluative
   D. advice

8. A. advice
   B. advice
   C. understanding
   D. evaluative

APPENDIX F

Role Plays

Directions. The interviewer should be given the information at the beginning of the case. For practicing interviewing skills, the purpose of the interviewer is to establish and maintain a supportive environment and to ask questions to gather information on the case. The person playing the role of the client/employee as well as the audience should be given the whole case.

Alternatively, triads can be formed with one person the interviewer, one the client/employee, and the third an observer. Roles may be rotated in the second and third rounds.

The audience, while observing the role play, should answer the following questions to be discussed at the conclusion of the role plays:

1. How could the supportive environment be improved?
2. Was accurate information obtained?
3. What would you have done differently? Why?
4. What kinds of questions (open, closed, etc.) and probes were used? What else would you ask?
5. Did the interviewer give any information?
6. What did you notice about the nonverbal behavior of the participants?
7. What proportion of time did each talk?

The same cases may be used to practice counseling skills. For counseling, the audience and the client/employee should be given all of the information. The purpose is to establish and maintain a supportive environment, discuss and define the problems, set priorities for solving the problems, set goals for change using the goal setting process in Chapter 4, and plan for follow-up.

Case 1. Sarah Smith, a 19-year-old pregnant woman, is referred by her obstetrician for nutrition counseling. She appears to be 5 or 6 months pregnant. Known to Sarah Smith and to be revealed if the proper questions are asked by the interviewer/counselor:

She has a 14-months-old child.
She lives with her mother who does the cooking.
She cannot tolerate milk.
The physician prescribed a vitamin-mineral supplement but she does not always remember to take it.
She has gained 20 pounds in the past 6 months.
Her only food intake in the morning is a glass of coke.
Candy and snack foods are her favorites.
She is receiving Aid to Dependent Children (ADC).

Case 2. Mrs. Carla Johnson and her 4-year-old son John are referred for nutrition counseling because Mrs. Johnson is worried about John's failure to eat proper meals. John is 40 inches tall, weighs 50 pounds, and is overweight. Known to Mrs. Johnson and to be revealed if the proper questions are asked by the interviewer/counselor:

> John is the youngest of 3 children. The siblings are ages 8 and 10 and of normal weight.
> John's father is obese, but his mother is of normal weight.
> Mr. Johnson is a bus driver who works days. Mrs. Johnson works part time 3 to 4 evenings a week.
> At meal times, John picks at his food and seems to have a poor appetite.
> John likes sweets and snack foods. His brother and sister give him snacks between meals.
> In the evening, John and his father spend time together watching television. They both enjoy snacks.

Case 3. Susan Smith is a 45-year-old obese woman with mild hypertension who is referred by her physician for weight reduction. She is 5 feet 5 inches tall and weighs 200 pounds.

Known to Susan Smith and to be revealed if the proper questions are asked by the interviewer/counselor:

> Mrs. Smith has dieted many times in the past on her own. She has lost weight initially, but has always regained it.
> She was an obese child.
> She has a 16-year-old daughter who is 20 pounds overweight and an 18-year-old son who is of normal weight. Her husband's weight is within normal limits.
> Mrs. Smith is a homemaker who enjoys watching soap operas on television.

Case 4. John Archer was hired 6 months ago as an assistant in the food storeroom. Other employees complain about his work, that he does not deliver the food they need on time, and that he has an unpleasant personality and is difficult to deal with. As John's supervisor, you call him in to talk. Known to John Archer and to be revealed if the proper questions are asked by the interviewer/counselor:

> John is unaware that other employees are complaining about him and his work.
> John thinks he is doing a satisfactory job.
> John dislikes his job.
> John very much wanted the assistant cook position which was open at the same time he was hired, but someone else was promoted to that job and he was hired for the storeroom position instead.

Case 5. According to the time records, Julie Jones has been late to work at least twice a week for the past 3 weeks. As her supervisor, you call her in to talk. Known to Julie Jones and to be revealed if the proper questions are asked by the interviewer/counselor:

She moved further away from work recently and now has to commute 45 minutes.

She and an employee in another department ride together, sharing the driving.

The other employee has a new baby. Sometimes her babysitter is late arriving so she leaves home later than usual.

It is summer and the highway is under repair.

Case 6. As you walk into the salad area of the kitchen at the end of the day, you notice that it was not cleaned adequately before the end of the work shift and that food which should have been refrigerated is left out. Since Margaret was the last of four employees to leave, you call Margaret in to talk the next day. Known to Margaret and to be revealed if the proper questions are asked by the interviewer/counselor:

Dorothy, a new employee hired 2 weeks ago, is a slow worker who is not carrying her share of the work load.

The produce delivery was late, throwing all of the work off schedule.

There was a catered party requiring 100 extra salads in addition to the regular production.

Margaret had a doctor's appointment after work so left immediately at the end of her work shift.

APPENDIX G

Sample Evaluation Forms
Presentation Evaluation Form

PRESENTER _____ TOPIC _____ DATE _____

	YES	NO	
INTRODUCTION Clearly states topic			
Gains attention of audience			
DISCUSSION Makes points clearly			
Organized in a logical sequence			
Shows evidence of knowledge of subject			
Uses facts, statistics, quotes			
CONCLUSION Cues audience that conclusion is coming			
Briefly summarizes main points			
Asks audience to take action			
PRESENTATION Uses notes or outline			
Does not read from notes			
Varies eye contact around the room			
Uses gestures			
Speaks clearly at a slow rate, varying pitch			
Avoids nervous habits			
Does not pace			
Avoids verbal habits (OK, umm)			

Workshop Evaluation Form

WORKSHOP NAME AND NUMBER ....

DATE ....

WORKSHOP LEADER ....

Use the following letters for your responses to the questions below and place a check by the appropriate letter for each question.

a. Strongly agree   b. Agree   c. Disagree
d. Strongly disagree   e. Not relevant

1. The workshop fulfilled my expectations and need for information of this topic.
a.   b.   c.   d.   e.

2. The workshop was well presented.
a.   b.   c.   d.   e.

3. The information presented will be useful to me in my job.
a.   b.   c.   d.   e.

4. The workshop's supplementary handout material and visual aids were useful.
a.   b.   c.   d.   e.

5. Miscellaneous Comments

Signature (optional) _____

SPEECH EVALUATION FORM

NAME: ROUND:

SUBJECT: DATE:

CONTENT: DELIVERY:
Introduction   Mental alertness
    Get attention?__   Aware of meaning as ut-
        tered?
    Orientation sufficient?__   Keen sense of communi-
        cation?
Development
    Organization: Body
      Soundly planned?__   Eye contact adequate?__
      Transitions clear?__   Posture acceptable?__
      Summaries sufficient?__   Movement meaningful?__
      Easily followed?__   Gestures effective?__
    Supporting Material: Voice
      Clear?__   Distinct?__
      Interesting?__   Sufficient variety?__
      Believable?__   Rate?__ Pitch?__
      Impressive?__   Volume?__
    Pronunciation satisfac-
    tory?__

Conclusion   SUBJECT & PURPOSE:
    Provide a note of finality?__   Subject worthwhile?__
    Put speech in focus?__   Purpose clear?__

LANGUAGE: SYMBOLS:
    Avoid expressions peculiar to
      writing?__   X - No
    Convey ideas clearly?__   √ - Yes
    Grammar correct?__
    Increase interest & impact?__

COMMENTS:

SUGGESTIONS:

INDEX

Page numbers in italics indicate illustrations; page numbers followed by "t" indicate tables.